GREGG

Transcription Simplified

LOUIS A. LESLIE

CHARLES E. ZOUBEK

shorthand written by Charles Rader

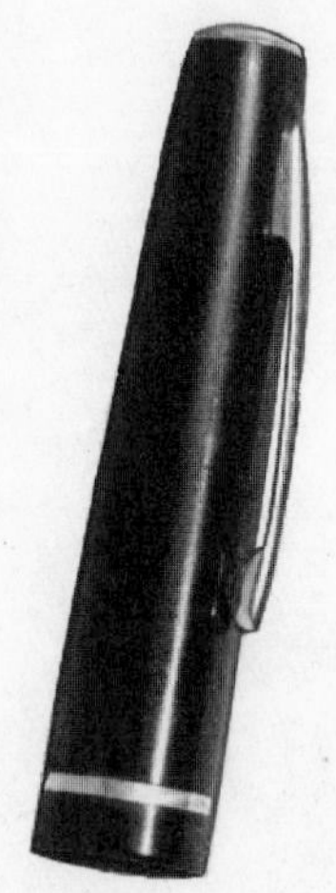

GREGG PUBLISHING DIVISION

McGRAW-HILL BOOK COMPANY, INC.

New York Chicago Dallas Corte Madera, Calif.
Toronto London

GREGG

Transcription Simplified

Second Edition

GREGG TRANSCRIPTION SIMPLIFIED, SECOND EDITION

Library of Congress Catalog No. 56-7562

37274

8 9 0 RRD-56 9 8 7 6 5 4 3 2

PUBLISHED BY GREGG PUBLISHING DIVISION
McGraw-Hill Book Company, Inc.
Printed in the United States of America

Acknowledgments

The authors wish to acknowledge the valuable help that they received from shorthand teachers all over the country. Special acknowledgment is due to Mr. Charles Rader for the beautiful shorthand; to Mrs. Madeline S. Strony for her guidance and encouragement; and to Mr. Robert Sutter, designer, who is responsible for the physical attractiveness of the book.

The photographs in the book were taken in the showrooms of the Herman Miller Furniture Company.

PREFACE

Gregg Transcription Simplified, Second Edition, performs a vital function in the shorthand student's stenographic training. It teaches him to apply his skills in shorthand, typewriting, and English, to produce mailable letters – letters that are accurately transcribed, accurately typed, correctly spelled and punctuated, and attractively placed on the letterhead.

Gregg Transcription Simplified, Second Edition, is designed to meet the following objectives:

1. To review and strengthen the student's knowledge of Gregg Shorthand.

2. To develop further his ability to construct new outlines from dictation.

3. To develop further his ability to spell and punctuate.

4. To enable him to handle the problems of office-style dictation.

5. To train him to place letters attractively on the page.

6. To enable him to turn out mailable letters, not only accurately but also rapidly, by teaching him efficient transcription techniques.

Transcription Features. In *Gregg Transcription Simplified,* Second Edition, the transcription features of the First Edition have been retained or modified to make them more effective. In addition, many new features have been added.

1. *Marginal Reminders.* In the First Edition, the explanation of all the marginal reminders appeared in the back of the book. In the Second Edition, a complete review of the transcription pointers that have been presented previously is given in Chapters 1 and 2. The new marginal reminders are presented in Chapters 3 and 4.

For emphasis, all marginal reminders appear in color.

2. *Chapter Openings.* Each of the 16 chapters opens with a discussion of a problem of transcription, illustrated by photographs taken especially for this book. These discussions, written in story form, show what the student should do *before* he takes a businessman's dictation; what he should do *while* he is taking dictation; and what he should do *after* he has taken dictation. What the student learns from these discussions prepares him to approach his first job as a stenographer with confidence and poise.

3. *Word Studies.* Two types of word studies are provided, to continue the growth of the student's English vocabulary:

a. Transcription Word Studies, in which words selected from the Reading and Writing Practice exercises are briefly defined.

b. Shorthand Language Studies,

in which the student is given the meaning of common word beginnings and endings, together with a list of shorthand words that illustrate that meaning.

4. *Shorthand Spelling Drills.* Analogy is of very real assistance both in learning to spell and in learning to write shorthand. The illustrations given in the shorthand spelling drills not only enable the student to master the spelling of large families of words but also make a contribution to his ability to construct new outlines.

5. *Office-Style Dictation.* Twelve problems of office-style dictation are presented to the student. Each office-style problem is explained and illustrated. A shorthand letter, in which the student is shown how he would treat the problem in his dictation, follows each explanation.

6. *Accuracy Practice.* The accuracy practice exercises are designed to make the student aware of the important part that proportion plays in accurate transcription. The student who practices these drills thoughtfully will not only be able to read his notes more rapidly, but he will also save himself many embarrassing mistranscriptions.

7. *Transcription Quiz.* The transcription quizzes, with which the student is familiar through his work with the *Gregg Shorthand Manual Simplified,* Second Edition, and *Gregg Dictation Simplified,* Second Edition, are continued. Additional problems, however, are added, including the correction of inconsistencies, inaccuracies in figures, and similar problems.

8. *Placement by Judgment.* Through an ingenious device, the student is taught how to place letters attractively on a letterhead in the way an experienced stenographer places them – by judgment rather than by reference to a placement scale.

9. *Phrasing on the Job.* In Chapter 15, the student is told how he can make the taking of dictation on the job easier by devising special phrases or shortcuts for frequently recurring expressions that are peculiar to the industry or line of business in which his employer is engaged.

10. *Model Letters.* The student is supplied with four letter models that show him the commonest letter setups used in business today.

11. *Names and Addresses.* In the back of the book is a list of names and addresses that are correlated with the letters in *Transcription Dictation,* which is the source book for the teacher. *Transcription Dictation* contains the letters that are to be dictated to the student and transcribed.

Review Drills. In *Gregg Transcription Simplified,* Second Edition, a constant review of the major elements of Gregg Shorthand is provided in the following ways:

1. *Theory Brushup Drills.* The Theory Brushup Drills deal with word beginnings and endings, word families, phrases, and the major word-building principles in Gregg

Shorthand.

2. *Brief-Form and Derivative Drills.* The Brief-Form and Derivative Drills help to fix the brief forms and their derivatives firmly in the student's mind.

3. *Recall Drills in Appendix.* The Recall Drills in the Appendix contain all the word beginnings and endings, brief forms, and special phrases in Gregg Shorthand. These drills can be used for a few minutes in class each day or as needed for remedial purposes.

4. *Reading and Writing Practice.* The finest and most effective review of the entire system is provided in the shorthand letters in the Reading and Writing Practice exercises. The more reading and copying of good printed shorthand that the student does, the more facility will he develop in the construction of new outlines from dictation and the faster will he write.

Connected Practice Material. Substantially 80 per cent of the letters in *Gregg Transcription Simplified,* Second Edition, are new. Many of the letters retained from the First Edition have been revised so that they read even more smoothly or so that they illustrate more effectively some point of shorthand theory, spelling, or punctuation.

To add interest to the student's shorthand study, each of the 16 chapters in the text is devoted to a specific industry or line of business.

Transcription Dictation. In the transcription phase of the student's stenographic training, it is vital that the student take from dictation and transcribe large quantities of new-matter dictation, graded in difficulty and problems of transcription. *Transcription Dictation* is designed to supply this material.

Transcription Dictation supplies more than 500 letters, correlated lesson by lesson with *Gregg Transcription Simplified,* Second Edition. The first three letters in each lesson are answers to the first three letters in the text; the remaining letters are related to the same industry or line of business.

In addition, a shorthand preview and a discussion of the transcription problems that the letter presents are given with each letter.

Teachers will find *Transcription Dictation* a splendid aid in developing students' transcription ability.

The authors of *Gregg Transcription Simplified,* Second Edition, are grateful to the teachers who have used the First Edition and who have made many valuable suggestions that have guided the authors in the preparation of this Second Edition. The authors are confident that *Gregg Transcription Simplified,* Second Edition, will enable teachers of Gregg Shorthand to do an even more effective job of the teaching of transcription.

Louis A. Leslie
Charles E. Zoubek

Contents

Part I

Predictation

Preparation

Your secretarial desk

Mary Brown has earned for herself the enviable reputation of being a rapid transcriber. When her employer, Mr. Baker, dictates a letter that he wants mailed immediately, he knows that the letter will shortly be on his desk ready for his signature. Mary's ability to transcribe rapidly is due largely to the fine shorthand she writes; her speed as a typist; and her command of grammar, spelling, and punctuation. It is also due in part to the way she organizes the materials with which she works. Everything she needs in order to transcribe a letter is at hand, so that she can find and reach it without a wasted motion.

Take her stationery, for example. She keeps this in the upper left-hand drawer of her desk in the following order:

1. Large and small envelopes
2. Letterhead paper
3. Carbon paper
4. File-copy paper
5. Thin onionskin for additional carbons
6. Second sheets for two-page letters
7. Plain manuscript paper

You can quickly see the advantage of Mary's system. Most of her letters call for a letterhead, a carbon sheet, and a file copy. Consequently, she has these sheets placed in the order in which she uses them.

The less frequently used types of paper are toward the back of the drawer.

Then Mary's middle drawer contains such items as clips, rubber bands, pencils, scissors, and other supplies that she needs in her transcribing work.

Mary also has the top of her desk efficiently organized. There she has:

1. A copyholder, conveniently placed so that she can read her notes without eyestrain and so that it will not interfere with the operation of the typewriter.

2. An "in" box, in which she places all work that is to be done.

3. An "out" box, in which she places all completed letters.

4. A set of reference books.

5. Two erasers—a sand eraser for originals and a soft eraser for carbons.

Of course, you may not have the same type of secretarial desk as Mary's; but whatever the type of desk you find in your office, you will be wise to organize it efficiently.

Marginal reminders, 1

One of your main objectives as you work with *Gregg Transcription Simplified,* Second Edition, is to learn to turn out mailable letters that a businessman will be proud to sign. It is at this stage that your ability to spell and punctuate correctly will be put to test. No doubt your spelling and punctuation have already improved considerably as a result of your attention to these factors in your shorthand work up to this point. In *Gregg Transcription Simplified,* Second Edition, you will continue to give attention to these two important factors of transcription while you are at the same time developing your shorthand speed and building your vocabulary.

In *Gregg Transcription Simplified,* Second Edition, you will again find each punctuation mark encircled in red, with a brief "marginal reminder" at the left of the page explaining the reason for the use of the punctuation. In those marginal reminders you will also find a number of words that were selected from the Reading and Writing Practice for special spelling drill.

In *Gregg Transcription Simplified,* Second Edition, you will be introduced to a number of new uses of the comma and semicolon; you will also study the use of the colon. In addition, you will take up several points of typing style that will be helpful to you when you transcribe.

Before taking up these new marginal reminders, however, you will review those with which you should already be familiar

Practice Suggestions: To be sure that you derive the greatest benefit from these marginal reminders, follow these practice suggestions as you work with each Reading and Writing Practice.

1. Read carefully the explanations and illustrative examples of the marginal reminders that follow these explanations.
2. Each time you meet an encircled punctuation mark as you read the Reading and Writing Practice, glance in the left margin of the page to be sure that you know the reason why that punctuation mark was used.
3. As you copy the Reading and Writing Practice, insert each punctuation mark in your shorthand notes and encircle it.
4. Spell all words in the marginal reminders once, preferably aloud.

In Chapter I you will review the following common uses of the comma:

, parenthetical

A writer will sometimes insert in a sentence a word or an expression that could be omitted without changing the meaning of the sentence. These added words or expressions are parenthetical and are set off from the rest of the sentence by commas.

I shall, of course, be glad to help you.
You may write me personally, Mr. Brown.

, apposition

Sometimes a writer mentions a person or a thing and then, in order to make his meaning clear, says the same thing in different words. This added explanation is known as an expression "in apposition." An expression in apposition is set off by two commas, except when it occurs at the end of the sentence, in which case only one comma is necessary.

Our representative, Mr. Barnes, will call.
On Friday, May 30, the street will be closed.
Leave the papers with my secretary, Miss Jones.

, series

When three or more similar expressions (words, phrases, or clauses) occur in a series with a conjunction before the last expression, a comma should be placed before the conjunction as well as between the items.

He will need letterheads, carbon paper, and envelopes.
The customer made payments on June 1, on June 15, and on June 30.

, conjunction

A comma is used to separate two independent clauses that are joined by a conjunction.

The book will be shipped on June 15, but we will not bill you until July 15.
Shall I call you at home, or do you prefer to call me?

, *when* clause
, *as* clause
, *if* clause
, introductory

A comma is used to separate a dependent, or subordinate, clause from a following main clause. Each subordinate clause beginning with *when*, *as*, or *if* has been marked as such in the marginal reminders. All other dependent clauses have been grouped under the general marginal reminder ", introductory."

> When he arrives, I will see him.
> As you know, our funds are very low.
> If you are late, please report to the office.
> Once you get here, we can discuss our plans.

When the main clause comes first, however, no comma is used between the main clause and the dependent clause.

> I will see him when he arrives.
> Please report to the office if you are late.

A comma is also required after such introductory words and phrases as *frankly, consequently, on the contrary, for instance*.

> Frankly, I am unhappy about the situation.
> On the contrary, he is the one who is wrong.

These introductory words and phrases are also indicated in the marginal reminders as ", introductory."

Lesson 1

1. Theory Brushup. The theory brushups that you will find in the first four chapters are designed to give you a thorough recall of all the major principles of Gregg Shorthand. Cover up the key to the lists and read each line as rapidly as you can. When you come to an outline that you cannot read, spell it. If the spelling does not give you the meaning immediately, refer to the key. At this stage, you will probably not have to refer to the key very often.

Can you read through the list in one minute or less?

Phrases: Omission of Words

1

Word Beginning: Inter-, etc.

2

Word Ending: -pose

3

Word Family: -er

4

Blend: Nt, Nd

5

1. **One of the, one of them, some of the, some of them, one of our, none of the, up to date, at a time.**

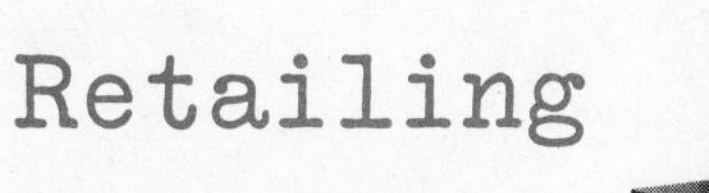

2. Interest, interested, uninteresting; introduce, introduction, introduced; enterprise, entering, entered.
3. Compose, position, disposition, imposition, propositions, composed, disposal, proposes, composes.
4. Render, former, customer, timer, adjuster, offer, finer.
5. Recent, excellent, consent, center; friend, trend, bend, brand.

Reading and Writing Practice

2. Transcription Word Study. A command of words is one of the stenographer's greatest assets. To help your vocabulary and understanding of words grow, you will find a Transcription Word Study in each lesson. Each Study contains brief definitions of a number of words or expressions selected from the Reading and Writing Practice. Read these definitions before you start your work on the Reading and Writing Practice; it will make your task easier.

mailing list A file of customers' names and addresses, usually kept on stencils, to which advertising material is mailed from time to time.

exclusively Alone, excluding all others.

account book A book in which payments are recorded.

business connection Job, position, business relationship.

3. *preparing catalogue*

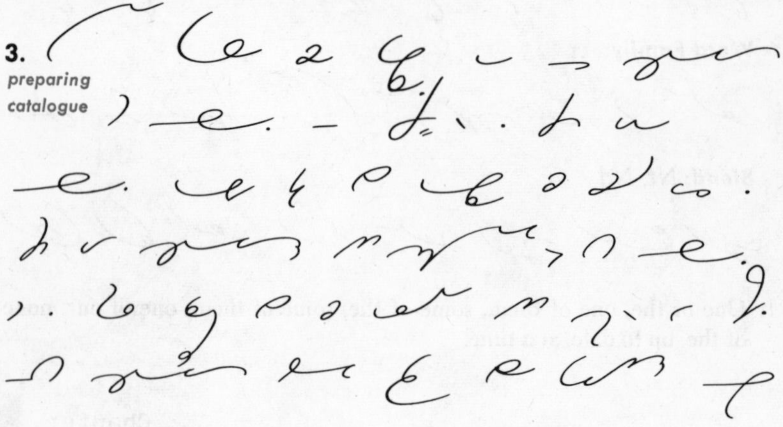

purchased
definite
residents

enclosing
convenience

(131)

4.

, conjunction
whether

, if clause
Personnel

Director
, apposition

Tuesday
, series

substantial
everyone

(121)

5.

, conjunction
probably

, introductory
already

, introductory
whether

exclusively
, parenthetical

, if clause
discuss
convenience

(144)

6.

, as clause
customer

, if clause
adjust

, when clause

settle
, if clause

(129)

7.

thousands
earliest

, if clause

(99)

Lesson 2

8. Theory Brushup

Phrases: Ago

1

Word Beginning: For-

2

Word Ending: -ult

3

Word Family: -cate

4

Omission of Vowels: Ow

5

1. Months ago, years ago, days ago, weeks ago, hours ago.
2. Former, formal, inform, informed, information, fortunate, effort.
3. Consult, result, insult, consulted, resulted, insulted, insults, consultation.
4. Reciprocate, indicate, confiscate, certificate, advocate, complicate, educate.
5. Down, town, brown, frown, ground, count, account, discount.

Reading and Writing Practice

9. Transcription Word Study

take legal action To sue.

reciprocate To return a kindness or favor.

financial statement Report of results of business operations during a given period and the condition of a business on a specific date.

10.

against
balance
bearing

aware
legal
unpleasant

(117)

11.

, apposition
formerly
appreciate

JUDD-KANE, INC.

CABLE ADDRESS: JUDKANDEN

1410 GLENARM STREET • DENVER 2, COLORADO • TABOR 5-7500

September 19, 19--

Mr. Edward H. Green
Standard Products Company
316 Broadway
Milwaukee 6, Wisconsin

Dear Mr. Green:

Thank you for the contract with the Wilson Company that you sent me.

I notice that this contract does not have a date for billing purposes. As you know, a space for this date is provided at the top of each contract. I have noticed the same omission on one or two other occasions, and it occurs to me that you may be under the impression that the date is to be filled in by us. Such is not the case.

The Wilson contract represents a fine piece of business. Congratulations.

Cordially yours,

John M. Brown, President

JMB:EA

Short Letter
Blocked Style
Standard Punctuation

promptly

, series

, *if* clause

reciprocate

, *if* clause

, parenthetical

(93)

12.

, *as* clause

requesting

financial

, introductory

, *as* clause

customary

, *when* clause

future

accurate

, *if* clause

, parenthetical

(153)

13.

, introductory
preferred

wear
, conjunction

, introductory
, as clause
guarantee

furthermore
, parenthetical
, if clause

(145)

8½ x 11 double space – write shorthand between typed lines

✓14.

fulfills
, introductory

immediate
, conjunction

(114)

✓15.
, conjunction
reason
opportune

, if clause
machinery

(97)

Lesson 3

3 Times

16. Theory Brushup.

Phrases: Understand, Understood

1

Word Beginning: Ex-

2

Word Ending: -ort

3

Word Family: -ually

4

Blend: Men, Min, Mem, etc.

5

1. We understand, I understand, they understand, I do not understand; I understood, he understood, it is understood.
2. Expanded, extended, expire, explain, unexplained, inexpensive, express, extreme.
3. Sport, export, report, import, exported, imported, exportation, deportation, assort.
4. Mutually, actually, gradually, annually, perpetually.
5. Examination, month, mend, remain, maintain, minute.

Reading and Writing Practice

17. Transcription Word Study

reactions Responses.

mutually profitable Profitable to both sides.

optical Relating to vision or the eyes.

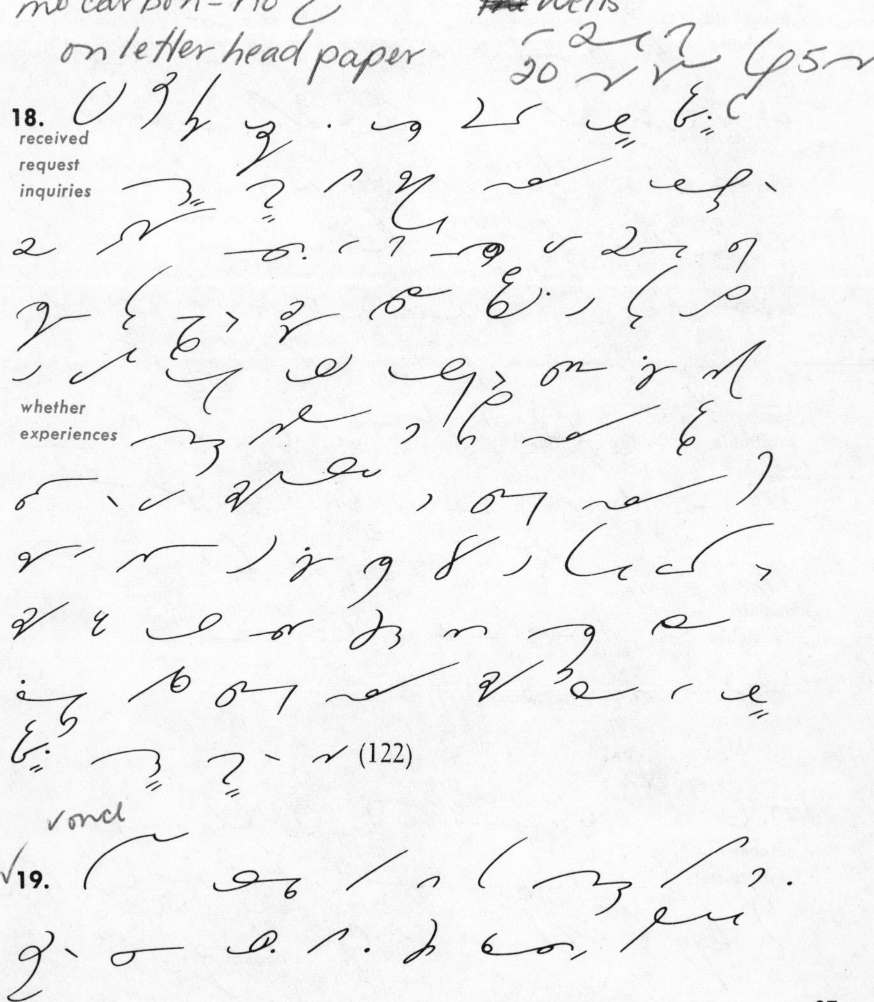

reactions
directors

, if clause

household
, if clause

, if clause

believe
acquainted

, series
profitable

dealers'
, as clause

(159)

√**20.**

account
, introductory

, parenthetical

purchases

, conjunction

(137)

21.

, introductory

operate

, introductory

infrequently

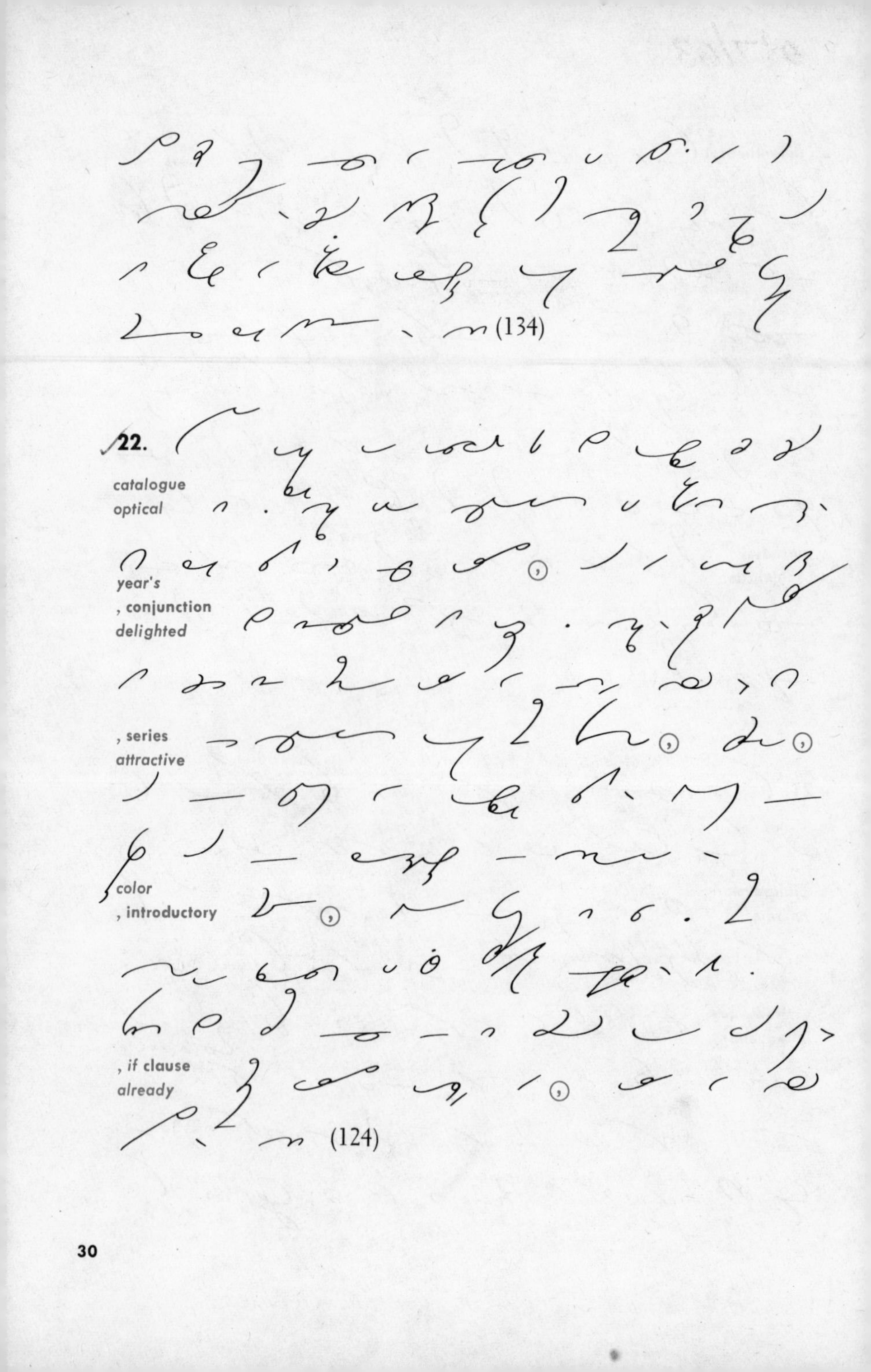

(134)

22.

catalogue
optical

year's
, conjunction
delighted

, series
attractive

, color
, introductory

, if clause
already

(124)

Lesson 4

23. Theory Brushup

Phrases: *Been*

1

Word Beginning: Con-, Com-

2

Word Ending: -ful

3

Word Family: -cally

4

Blend: *Rd*

5

1. You have been, I have been, who have been, I have not been, you have not been, could have been, should have been, would have been, it has been.
2. Convenient, contract, convey, control, contemplate; complete, complain.
3. Successful, thoughtful, grateful, harmful, cheerful, helpful, helpfully, helpfulness.
4. Automatically, chemically, practically, physically, artistically, radically.
5. Record, guard, toward, accordance, hardly, hardness, cards.

Reading and Writing Practice

24. Transcription Word Study

prominent Outstanding; notable.

automatically Mechanically; without conscious effort.

invariably Always; uniformly.

3 times

25.

pleasant
ones
overdue

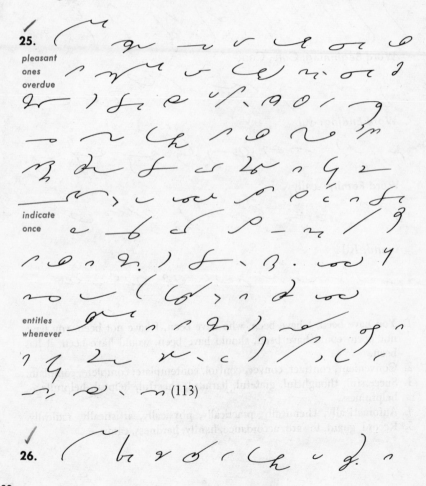

indicate
once

entitles
whenever

(113)

26.

, conjunction
confident
successful

deserving
organization
prominent

, if clause
immediately

150

(150)

27.

promptly
, parenthetical

152^{50}

mattress
, series
, apposition

10

, conjunction
received
won't

152 50 60 (121)

28.
, introductory
recently

merchandise
, if clause

floor
, conjunction

, introductory
automatically

(136)

29.

everywhere
discussing

invariably
, introductory

, conjunction
, *if* clause
succeeding

, apposition
, introductory

, when clause

(148)

once and punctuate

Short Letters

When Mary Brown is ready to transcribe a letter, she does not figure out exactly how many words there are in the letter, consult a letter-placement scale, and finally set her margin stops and start typing.

Instead, she glances at her notes and decides that her left-hand margin stop should be set "about here," and the right-hand margin stop "about there." She then types the date two spaces below the bottom of the letterhead, hits the carriage return a few times, and is ready to type the inside address. All of this takes only a few seconds.

As you gain experience as a transcriber, you, too, will be able to place letters attractively after only a brief glance at your shorthand notes.

The following suggestions will help you learn how to place letters by judgment.

Most one-page letters can roughly be placed in three classifications:

1. Short letters, containing up to approximately 100 words.
2. Average letters, containing 100 to 200 words.
3. Long letters, containing more than 200 words.

This lesson deals with the judgment placement of a short letter.

Refer to letter No. 25 on page 37. This is a short letter—as it was written by Mary Brown in her shorthand notebook. Her transcript was made on a machine that had pica (large) type.

You will notice that Mary required two-thirds of a column. Whenever a letter takes approximately two-thirds of a column in her notebook, she starts the inside address about an inch below the date line and sets her margin stops for about 2-inch margins at the left and the right.

If she is transcribing on a machine with elite (small) type, she starts the inside address about 1½ inches from the date line. Her margins are again about 2 inches on each side.

As the first step in learning how to place by judgment, copy letter No. 25 in shorthand, and see how much space in a column of your shorthand notebook you require. If your notes are large, you will require more space than Mary did; if they are small, you will require less space. Then, if possible, transcribe the letter from your notes, setting it up by judgment. See how close you can come to making your transcript look like Mary's.

In class, try to determine whether each letter that you take from dictation is a short, average, or long letter.

MATTHEWS, INC.

SMITH TOWER, 806 SECOND AVENUE
SEATTLE 4, WASHINGTON

December 6, 195-

Mrs. E. R. Caster
33 East 78 Street
New York 15, New Yo

Dear Mrs. Caster:

Most of the le
tomers are not plea
ask them for paymen
is why it gives me
this letter to you
payment on the furn
months ago.

Our records in
ments were made on
we have to write yo
record of which you

Your fine reco
credit whenever you
store. All you hav
closed card.

AB:BCA

2/7/63

Lesson 5

30. Theory Brushup

Phrases: Modified Words

1

Word Beginning: Pro-, Per-

2

Word Ending: -lity, -lty

3

Word Family: -tain

4

Omission of Vowel: Short I and E

5

1. Your order, your orders, thank you for your order, as soon as, as soon as possible, to us, to me, to do, to do so.
2. Profit, provide, approach, promise, permit, perhaps, permanent, perform.
3. Personality, individuality, reality, facilities, penalty, faculty.
4. Contain, maintain, retain, sustain, pertain, container, maintained.
5. Various, tedious, seriousness, harmoniously, curious, furious, courteous.

Reading and Writing Practice

31. Transcription Word Study

atmosphere Air.

invalid A weak or sickly person.

imprinted Stamped on or printed on.

strict confidence Not to be told or transmitted to anyone else.

32.

pleasure
various

handling
strict

beginning
profitable

(101)

33.

air-conditioning
installed

experience
, introductory

, parenthetical

, introductory
penny

amazement
losing

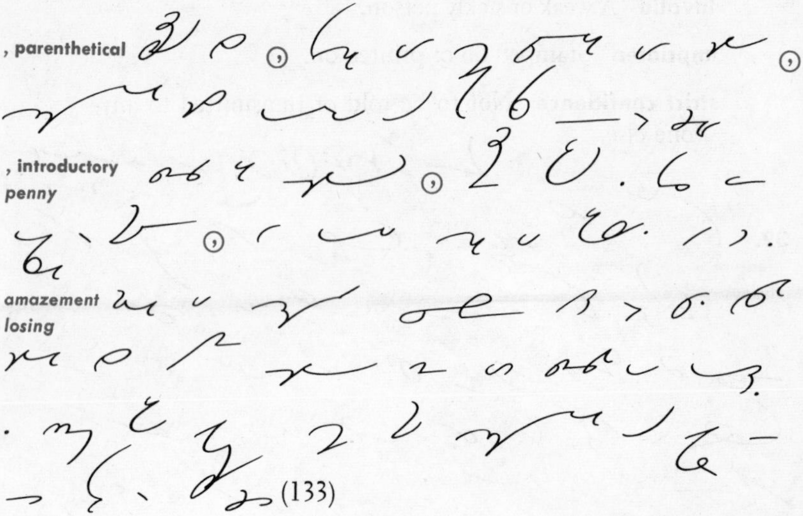

(133)

34.
recently
Philadelphia
, conjunction

invalid
, as clause

, if clause

references
, if clause

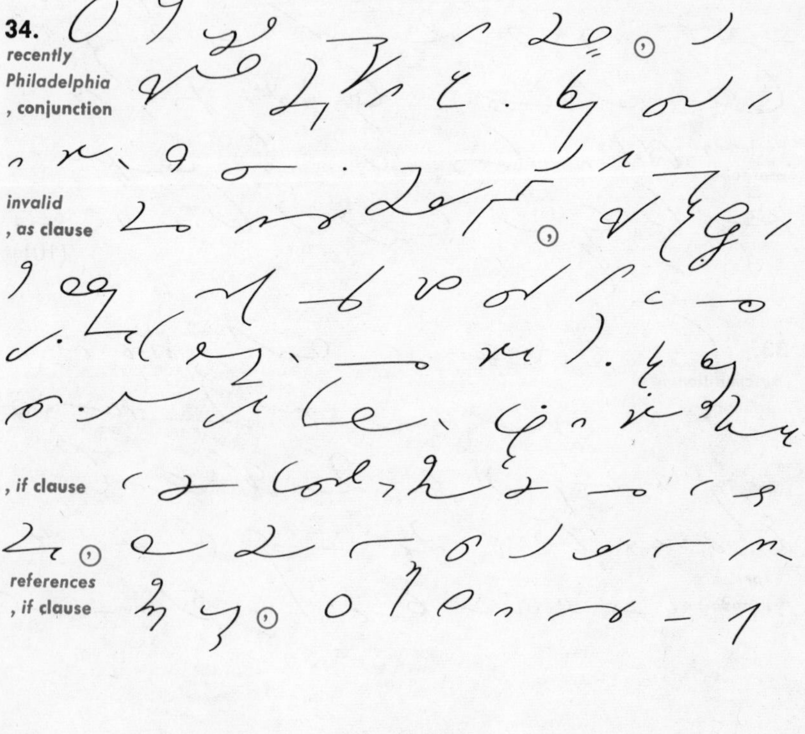

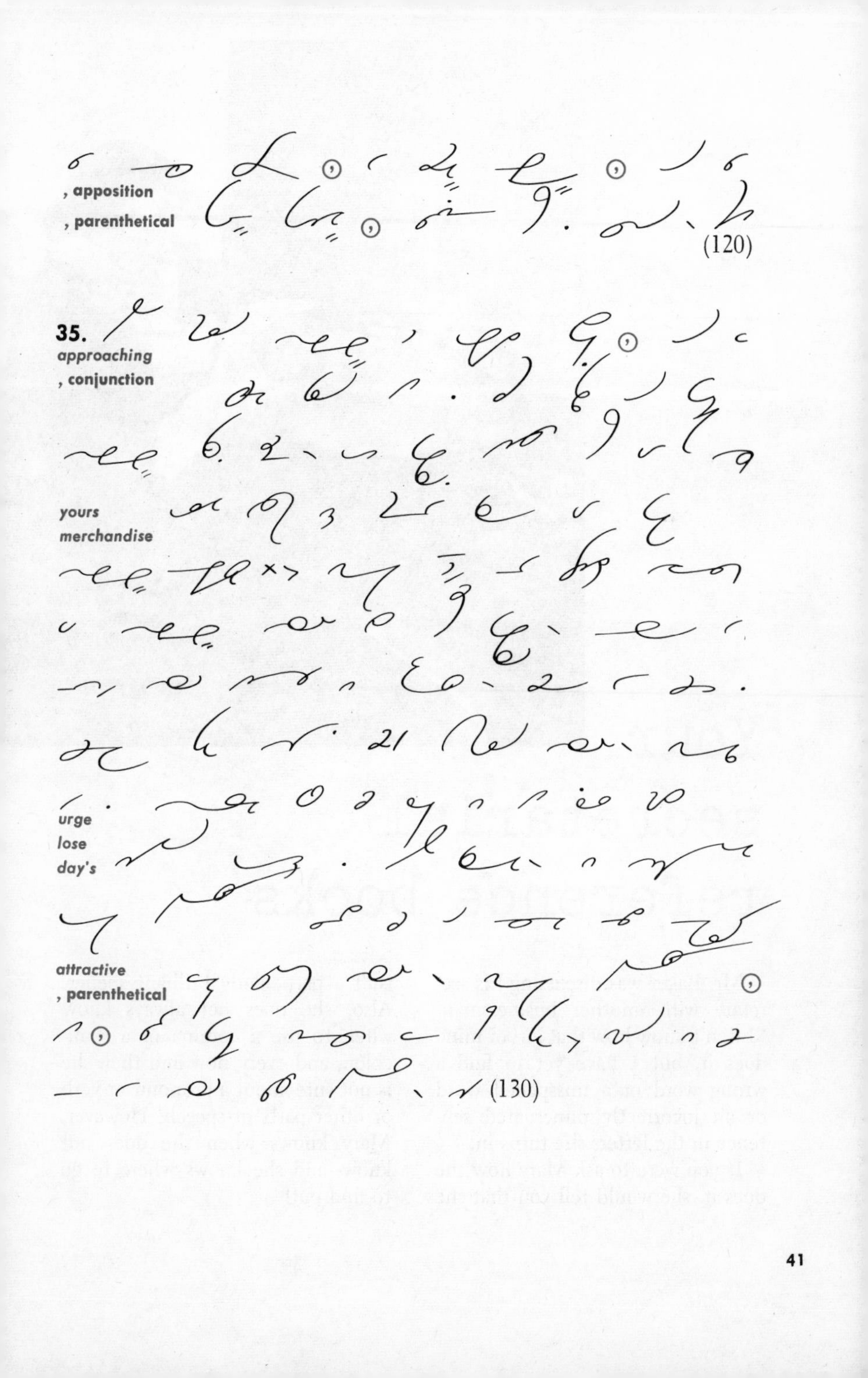

, apposition
, parenthetical

(120)

35.
approaching
, conjunction

yours
merchandise

urge
lose
day's

attractive
, parenthetical

(130)

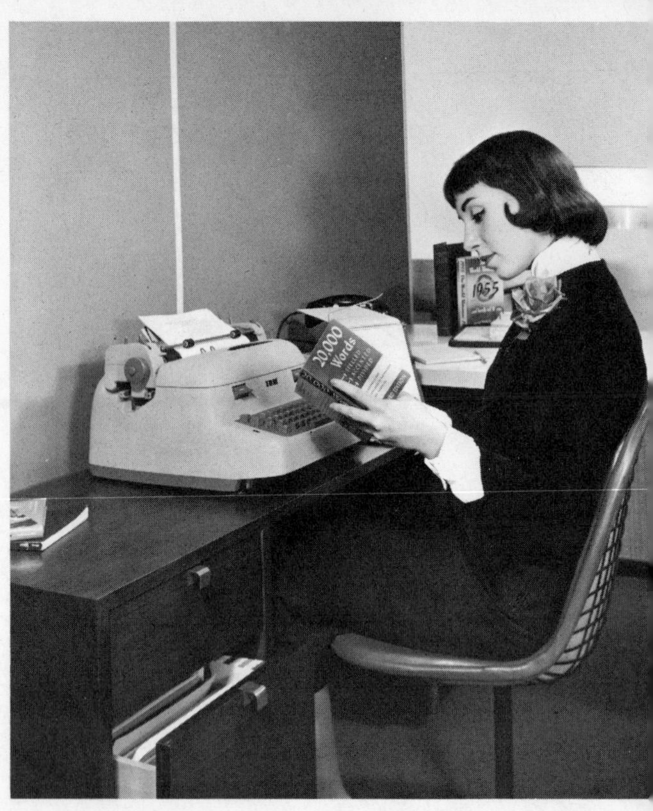

Your secretarial reference books

Mr. Baker was discussing his secretary with another businessman. "I don't know how that girl of mine does it, but I have yet to find a wrong word or a misspelled word or an incorrectly punctuated sentence in the letters she turns in."

If you were to ask Mary how she does it, she would tell you that she isn't a particularly brilliant speller. Also, she does not always know when to use a comma or a semicolon, and every now and then she is not sure about a pronoun or verb or other parts of speech. However, Mary knows when she does not know—and she knows where to go to find out!

On Mary's desk are the following reference books which she uses when necessary:

1. *20,000 Words.* This is the reference book that she uses most frequently. She refers to it when she is in doubt about the way a word is spelled or hyphenated. It is a handy size, and the fact that it contains only spellings and syllabications enables her to find the spelling or hyphenation of any word in a matter of seconds.

Some stenographers keep *20,000 Words* with the reference books at the back of their desks. Mary, however, keeps hers next to the typewriter, where she can pick it up without any wasted motion.

2. A Dictionary. Mary uses the dictionary when she comes across a word with which she is unfamiliar or has some doubt about its exact meaning or derivation. She does not, however, use it as a spelling or hyphenation reference unless she is looking for some rather unusual word that is not likely to be given in *20,000 Words.*

3. *Reference Manual for Stenographers and Typists.* Mary, of course, mastered all the simple uses of the various punctuation marks and ordinary business usages in her schoolwork, but occasionally she is not sure whether to use a semicolon or a colon or a dash. Sometimes she wonders how to address a minister or an army general. Then again she may not be sure whether to type a number in words or in figures.

She quickly resolves her doubts by referring to her *Reference Manual for Stenographers and Typists.* No stenographer or secretary should be without one.

4. *The World Almanac.* Mary wouldn't be without a copy of the *World Almanac,* because it contains information on just about everything.

These reference books are of value to every stenographer or secretary. The stenographer or secretary may, however, find other reference books helpful, depending on the type of work in which her firm is engaged. For example, a stenographer for a travel company may find a railroad guide, an airplane guide, and a hotel directory helpful.

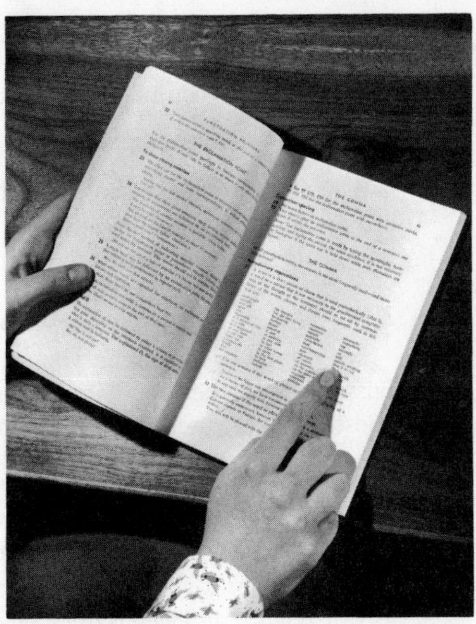

Marginal reminders, 2

In this chapter you will review two of the most frequent uses of the semicolon. You will also review the apostrophe, hyphenated words, and several points of typing style.

; because of comma

As you already have learned, a comma is used to separate two independent clauses that are joined by a conjunction. When a comma occurs within one of or both the independent clauses, a semicolon is used to separate the two clauses.

> So far, I have not heard from you; and I should not be human if I were not worried.
>
> I have not heard from you; and I should not be human, Mr. Smith, if I were not a little worried.

; no conjunction

A semicolon is used to separate two independent, but closely related, clauses when no conjunction is used to connect the clauses.

> I am planning to go home; he is planning to remain.

The above sentence could be written as two sentences, with a period after *home*. However, because the two thoughts are closely related, the use of the semicolon seems more appropriate.

apostrophe

No doubt by this time you know where to use the apostrophe in possessives. To be sure that you continue to be "apostrophe conscious," apostrophes are used many times in your Reading and Writing Practice.

hyphenated before noun
no noun, no hyphen
no hyphen after *ly*

You can quickly decide whether to use a hyphen in expressions such as *worth while* and *well trained* by observing these rules:

1. If a noun follows the expression, use a hyphen.
2. If *no* noun follows the expression, no hyphen is used.

He made a worth-while contribution to the book. (Noun follows the expression.)
His contribution was very much worth while. (No noun follows the expression.)

No hyphen is used, however, in a compound modifier where the first expression ends in *ly*. For example, no hyphen would be used in the expression *widely read magazine*. To be sure that you are not tempted to put a hyphen in such expressions, they are occasionally called to your attention in the Reading and Writing exercises by the marginal reminder "no hyphen after *ly*."

dates

The correct form for transcribing dates is *January 15*, with no *th* after the figures when the month precedes the day. The reminder in the margin reads:

Transcribe:
January 15

amounts

The correct form for transcribing even amounts of dollars is $120, with no decimal point and no ciphers. The reminder in the margin reads:

Transcribe:
$120

street address

In transcribing a street address, the form recommended for use in your transcripts is *115 West 82 Street*—without a *d* after the street number.

More and more authorities are recommending the omission of *th*, *st*, and *d* from numbered street addresses because the omission adds to the readability of the address.

The marginal reminder for the foregoing address would be:

Transcribe:
82 Street

. courteous request

Very often one businessman may wish to persuade another to take some definite action. He could make his request for action with a direct statement, such as:

> I want to hear from you by return mail.

A direct statement of this type, however, might antagonize the reader. Many businessmen, therefore, prefer to make such a request in the form of a question.

> May I hear from you by return mail.

Where a request for definite action is put in the form of a question, a period is used at the end of the sentence.

This is the way you can decide whether to use a question mark or a period:

1. If the question calls for an answer in the form of action, use a period.
2. If the question calls for an answer in the form of words, use a question mark.

Lesson 6

36. Theory Brushup

Phrases: Few

1

Word Beginning: Sub-

2

Word Ending: -ward

3

Word Family: -ization

4

Th

5

1. For a few months, for a few days, in a few days, in a few minutes, in a few moments, few times.
2. Submit, substantial, subdivide, substitute, subnormal, subway, substandard.
3. Upward, outward, inward, onward, forward, forwarded, reward, rewarded, backward.
4. Authorization, realization, utilization, naturalization, civilization.
5. Moth, cloth, growth, oath, booth, tooth, truth, smooth.

Chapter 2 Household supplies

Reading and Writing Practice

37. Transcription Word Study

authorization Permission.

proceed To go ahead. (Be careful not to confuse *pro-ceed* with *precede,* which means "to come before.")

estimate (*noun*) A statement of the amount for which certain work will be done by one who undertakes to do it.

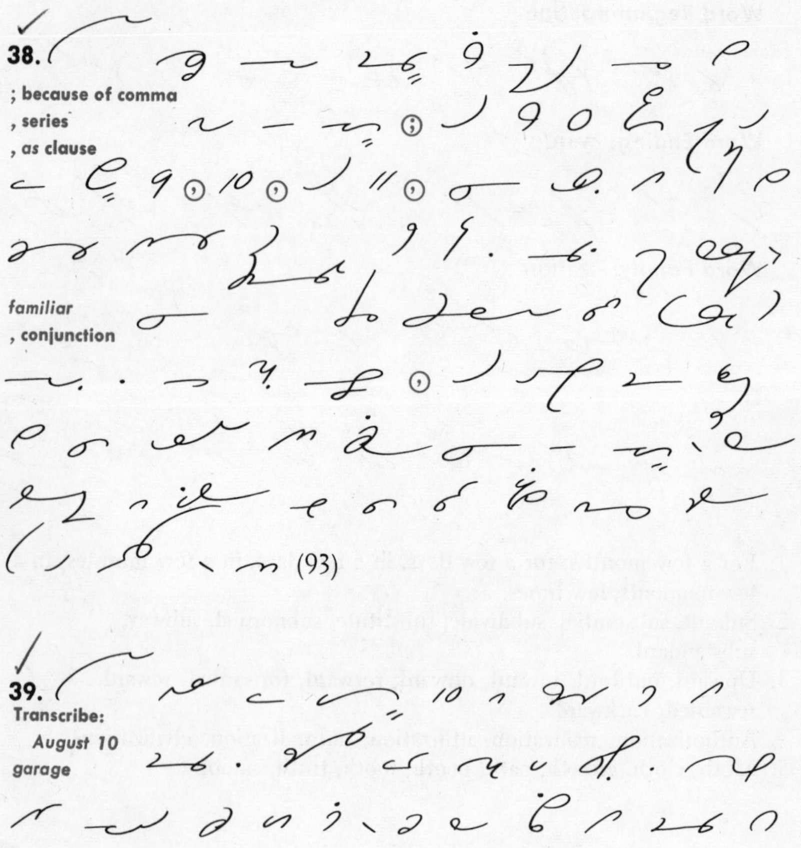

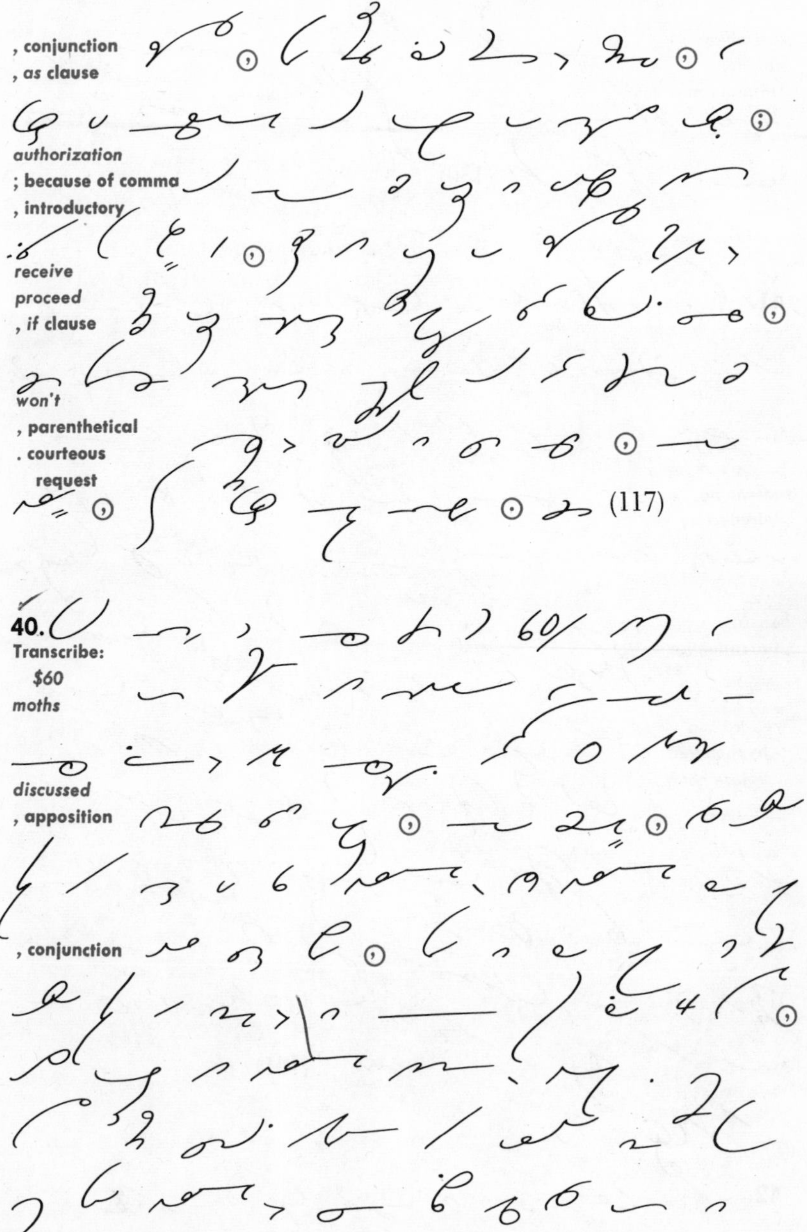
, conjunction
, as clause
authorization
; because of comma
, introductory
receive
proceed
, if clause
won't
, parenthetical
. courteous request
(117)
40.
Transcribe:
$60
moths
discussed
, apposition
, conjunction

controlling
situation
, introductory

(130)

41.

reasonable
, introductory

benefit
, parenthetical

well-trained
hyphenated
before noun

(141)

42.

one-year hyphenated before noun

naturally

, introductory

laundry ironer

; no conjunction

Transcribe: $180

180 (137)

43.

, *if* clause

; no conjunction

attractive

, introductory

(57)

Lesson 7

44. Theory Brushup

Phrases: Want

1

Word Beginning: Short-, Ship-

2

Word Ending: -ure

3

Word Family: -tifying

4

Ther

5

1. We want, I want, you want, he wants, if you want, do you want, they want, who wants, she wants.
2. Shortly, shorter, shortsighted, shortstop, shorten, shortened; shipshape, shipwreck.
3. Temperature, feature, secured, natural, naturally, procures.
4. Testifying, notifying, certifying, rectifying, ratifying, gratifying.
5. Rather, either, bother, farther, weather, gather, together, neither, other.

Reading and Writing Practice

45. Transcription Word Study

installation The setting up or placing in a position for use.

survey An inspection to provide exact information.

route (pronounced *rōōt*) The course that is to be traveled or followed.

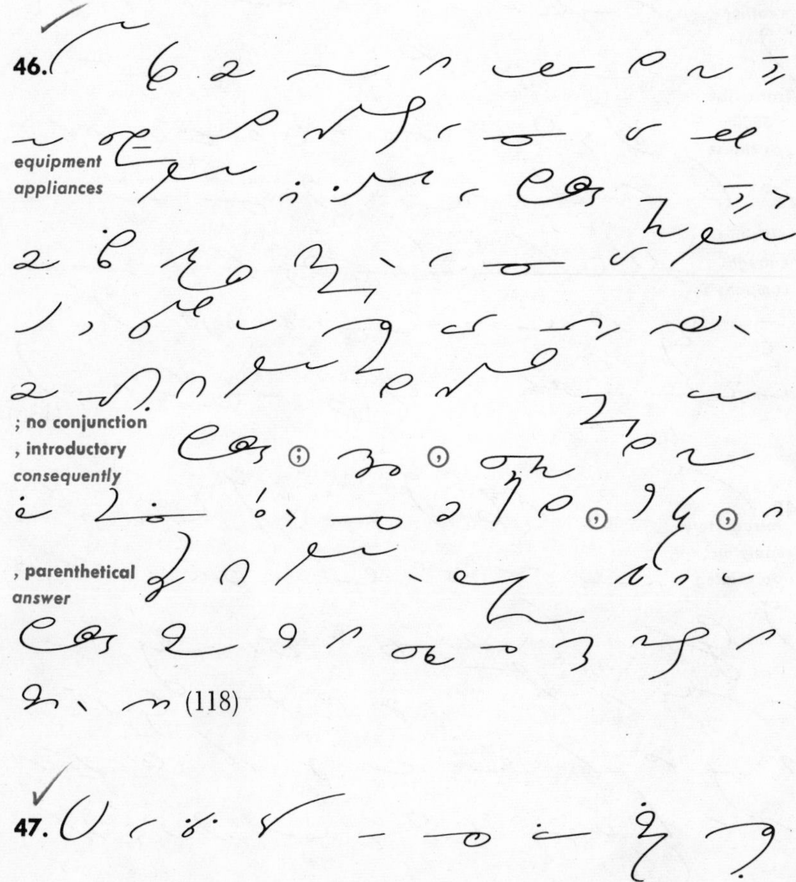

past
; because of comma
, parenthetical

result
, introductory

installation
weather

Transcribe:
$800
, as clause

, if clause
enough
company's

(136)

48.
, introductory
supplying
appreciated

, *if clause*
delivery
route

enclosed
. courteous
request

(116)

49.

system
, conjunction

well written
no noun,
no hyphen

principles
, introductory

50

, conjunction
Transcribe:
15 Street

416 15

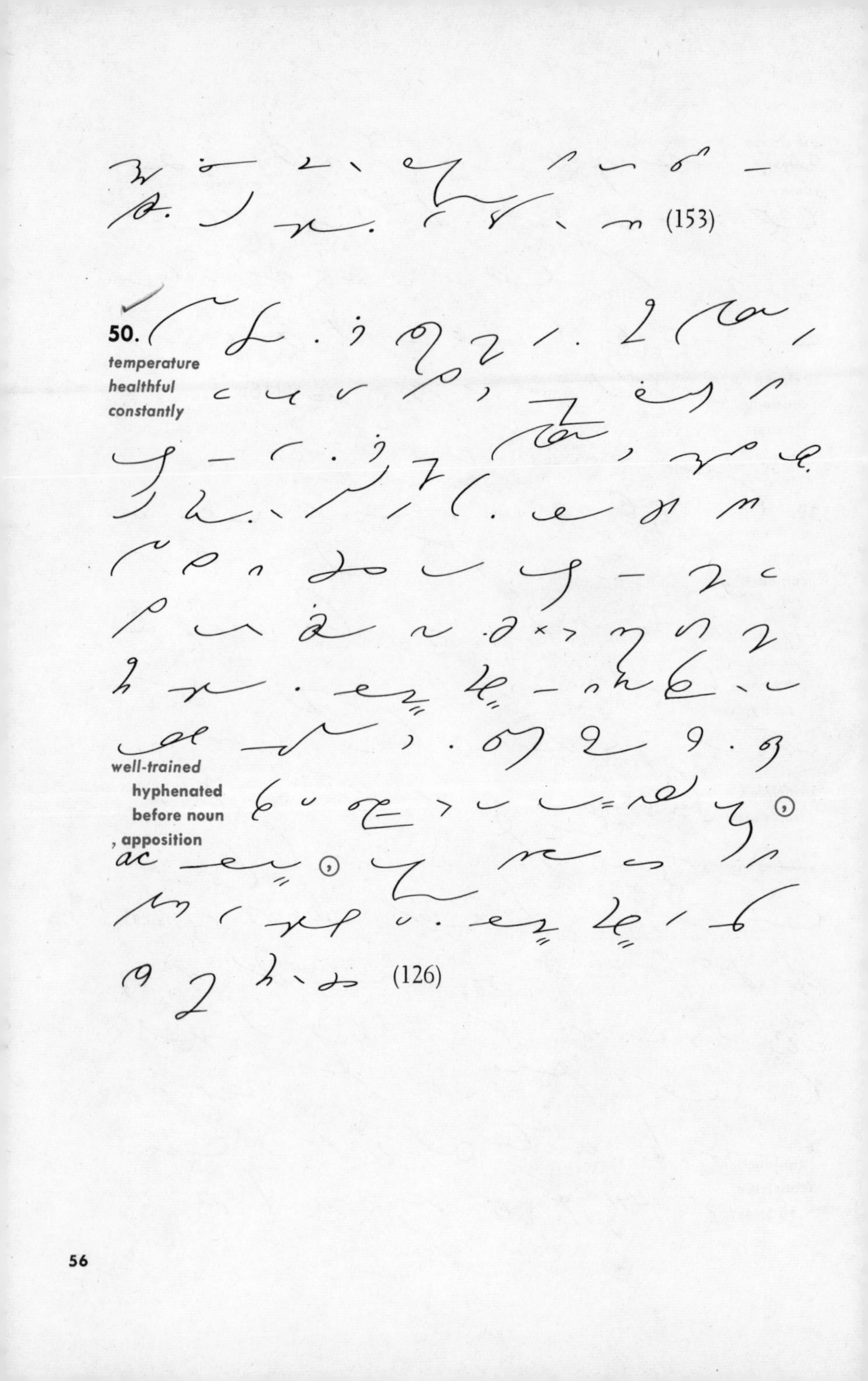

(153)

50.

temperature
healthful
constantly

well-trained
hyphenated
before noun
, apposition
ac

(126)

Lesson 8

51. Theory Brushup

Phrases: *Let Us*

1

Word Beginning: *Dis-, Des-*

2

Word Ending: *-ings*

3

Word Family: *-rate*

4

Blend: *Ld*

5

1. Let us, let us know, let us see, let us say, let us have, let us make.
2. Discuss, discussion, display, distress, dislike; describe, description.
3. Furnishings, savings, greetings, meetings, earnings, hearings, sayings, buildings.
4. Operate, operated, narrate, accurately, decorator, generate, overrate.
5. Hold, sold, older, folded, golden, mildly.

Reading and Writing Practice

52. Transcription Word Study

economical Thrifty.

unmindful Forgetful.

innovations New and novel things.

53.

, series
fourth

up-to-the-minute
hyphenated
before noun

best-known
hyphenated
before noun

, if clause
installing

, apposition
discuss

(138)

54. Transcribe:
May 15
guarantee

economical
Transcribe:
$8

adjustments
, if clause

, if clause
, parenthetical
, introductory

, if clause
; no conjunction

(168)

55.

reference
installation
, as clause

annoy
; because of comma
, parenthetical

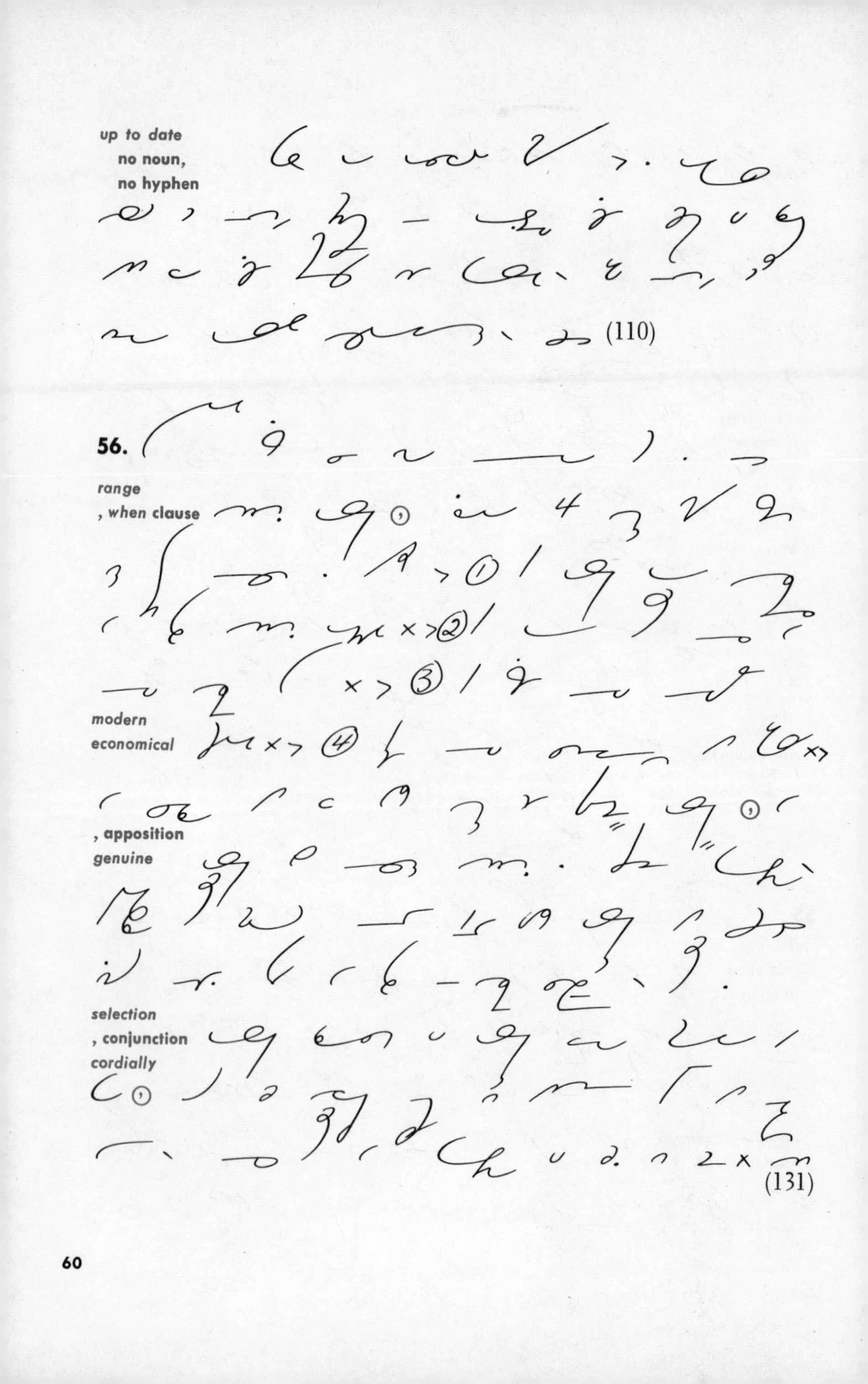

up to date
no noun, no hyphen

(110)

56.

range
, when clause

modern
economical

, appposition
genuine

selection
, conjunction
cordially

(131)

57.

grateful
freezer

1940

highly prized
no hyphen
after ly

research
engineering

innovations
, conjunction

, as clause

(128)

58.
, as clause
pictures
cabinets

descriptions
, introductory

(57)

Lesson 9

59. Theory Brushup

Phrases: Hope

1

Word Beginning: Al-

2

Word Ending: -ment

3

Word Family: Rec-

4

Blend: Tem, Dem

5

1. I hope you will, I hope you can, I hope it will, I hope to be; we hope you will, we hope you can, we hope it will be, we hope to have.
2. Already, almost, also, although, alternate, alternative, almanac, alteration.
3. Payment, agreement, complimentary, experimentation, departmental.
4. Recall, recollect, reconsider, recommit, recommend.
5. Temper, temperature, temperament, estimate, damage, seldom.

Reading and Writing Practice

60. Transcription Word Study

prune To cut off dead or useless branches of a tree or shrub.

spray To apply chemicals to the leaves of trees and shrubs to kill insects and bugs.

entrusting Delivering to the care of.

61.

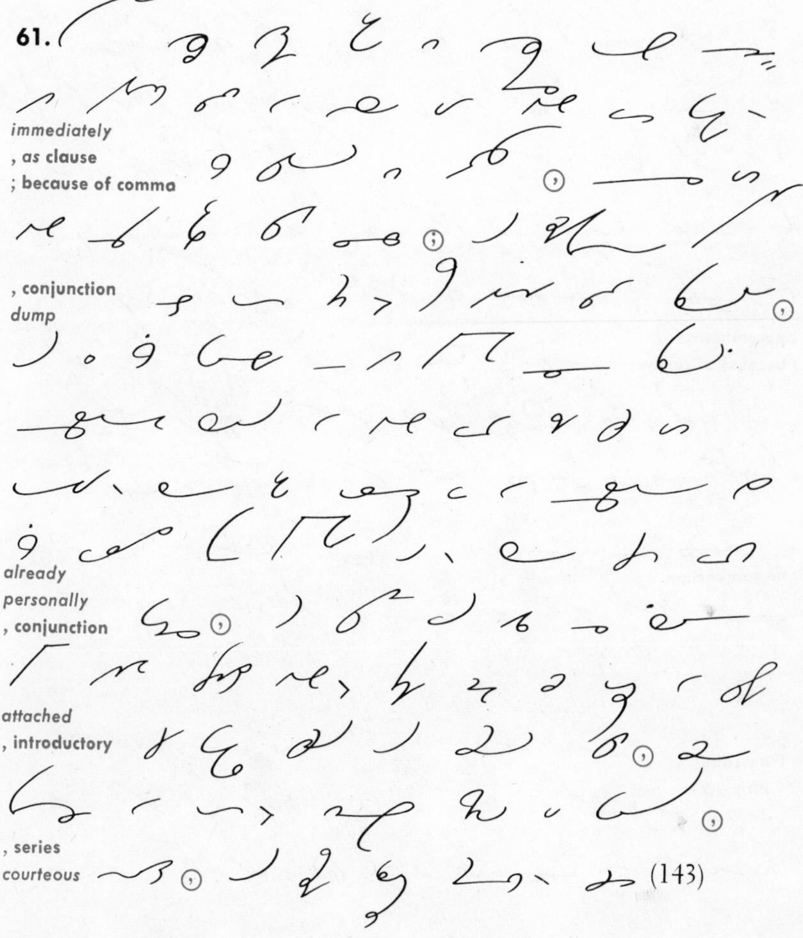

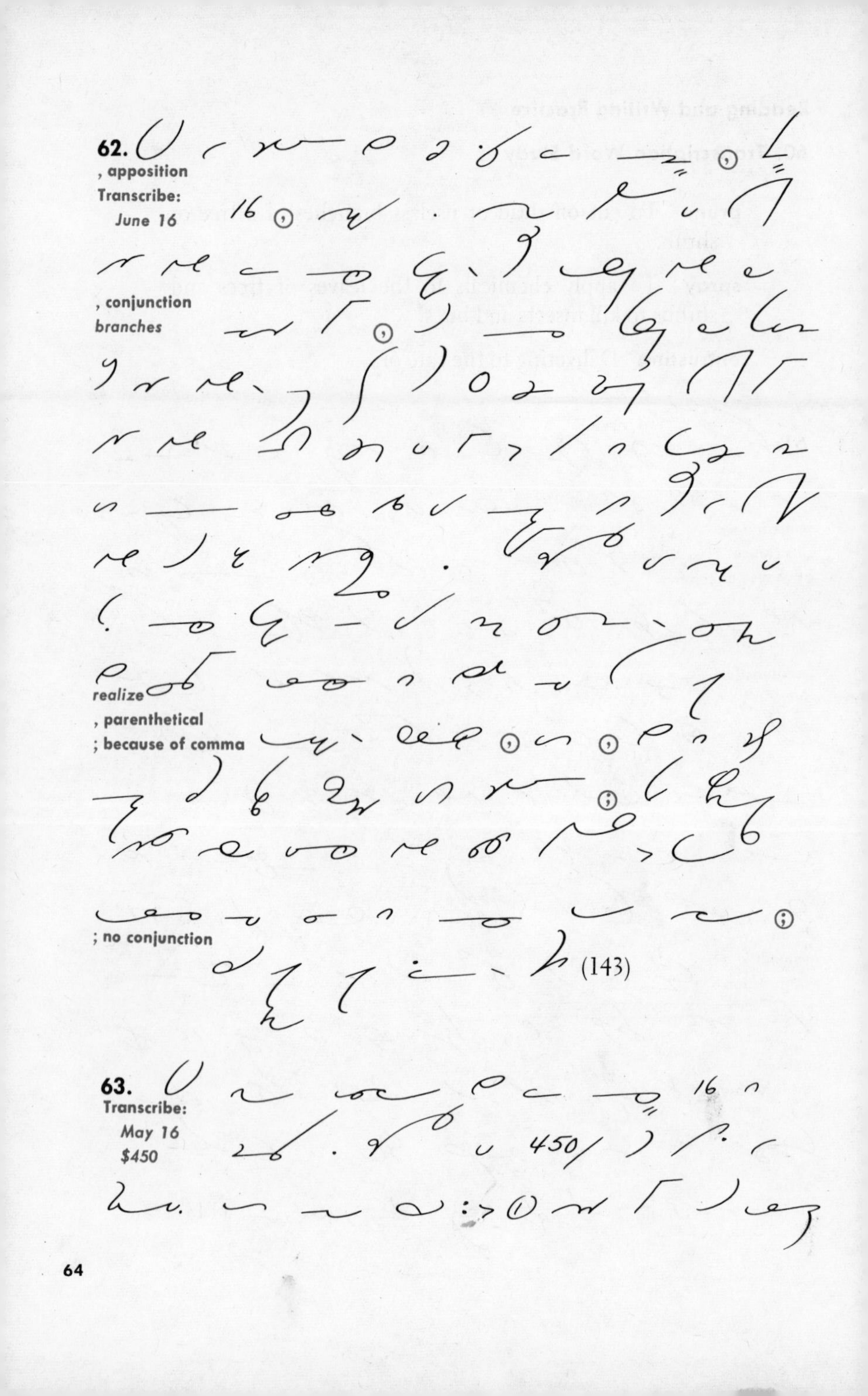

62.

, apposition

Transcribe:

June 16

, conjunction

branches

realize

, parenthetical

; because of comma

; no conjunction

(143)

63.

Transcribe:

May 16

$450

badly diseased
no hyphen after ly

notifying
received
, when clause

, as clause
entitled
explanation

(121)

64.

well-planned
hyphenated before noun
, series

neighbors'

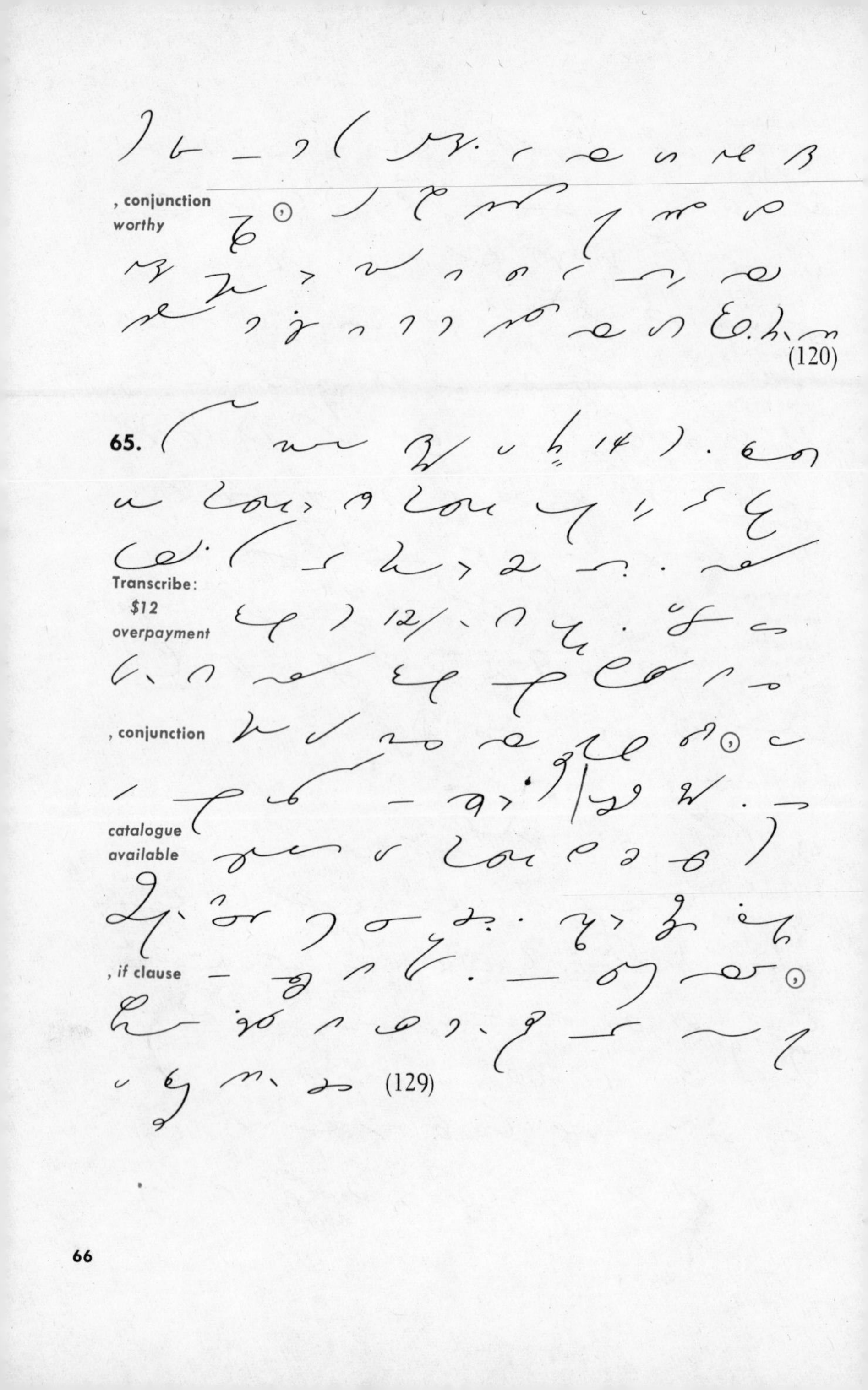

, conjunction
worthy

(120)

65.

Transcribe:
$12
overpayment

, conjunction

catalogue
available

, if clause

(129)

Lesson 10

66. Theory Brushup

Phrases: To

1

Word Beginning: Un-, In-, En-

2

Word Ending: -tion

3

Word Family: -nal

4

Vowel Combinations: Īa, Ĭa

5

1. To serve, to sell, to spare, to spend, to supply, to suppose, to select, to speak.
2. Unfortunate, unpaid, unimportant; install, insured; enjoy, entrust.
3. Co-operation, questionnaire, national, conditions, indication, stationery, hesitation.
4. Nominal, personal, seasonal, internal, journalism.
5. Supplier, drier, trial, diet; piano, aria, negotiate.

Reading and Writing Practice

67. Transcription Word Study

venetian blind A blind having numerous thin parallel wooden or metal slats that can be set simultaneously at any desired angle.

exceed To go beyond. (Be careful not to confuse exceed with *accede*, which means "to give in to.")

68.

high-grade
hyphenated before noun

venetian

whether
inconvenient
, series

. courteous
request

(93)

69.

Transcribe:
$25
; no conjunction

, parenthetical
stopped

local
, introductory

repairing
, if clause

, conjunction

(134)

70.

, apposition
, introductory
suppliers

15

, introductory
assurance

, parenthetical
; because of comma
situation

, introductory
canceled

, *if* clause
elsewhere

, introductory

(153)

71.
, *as* clause
delivery

Transcribe:
September 1
; no conjunction
, parenthetical

; because of comma
, introductory

materials
, parenthetical
fortunately

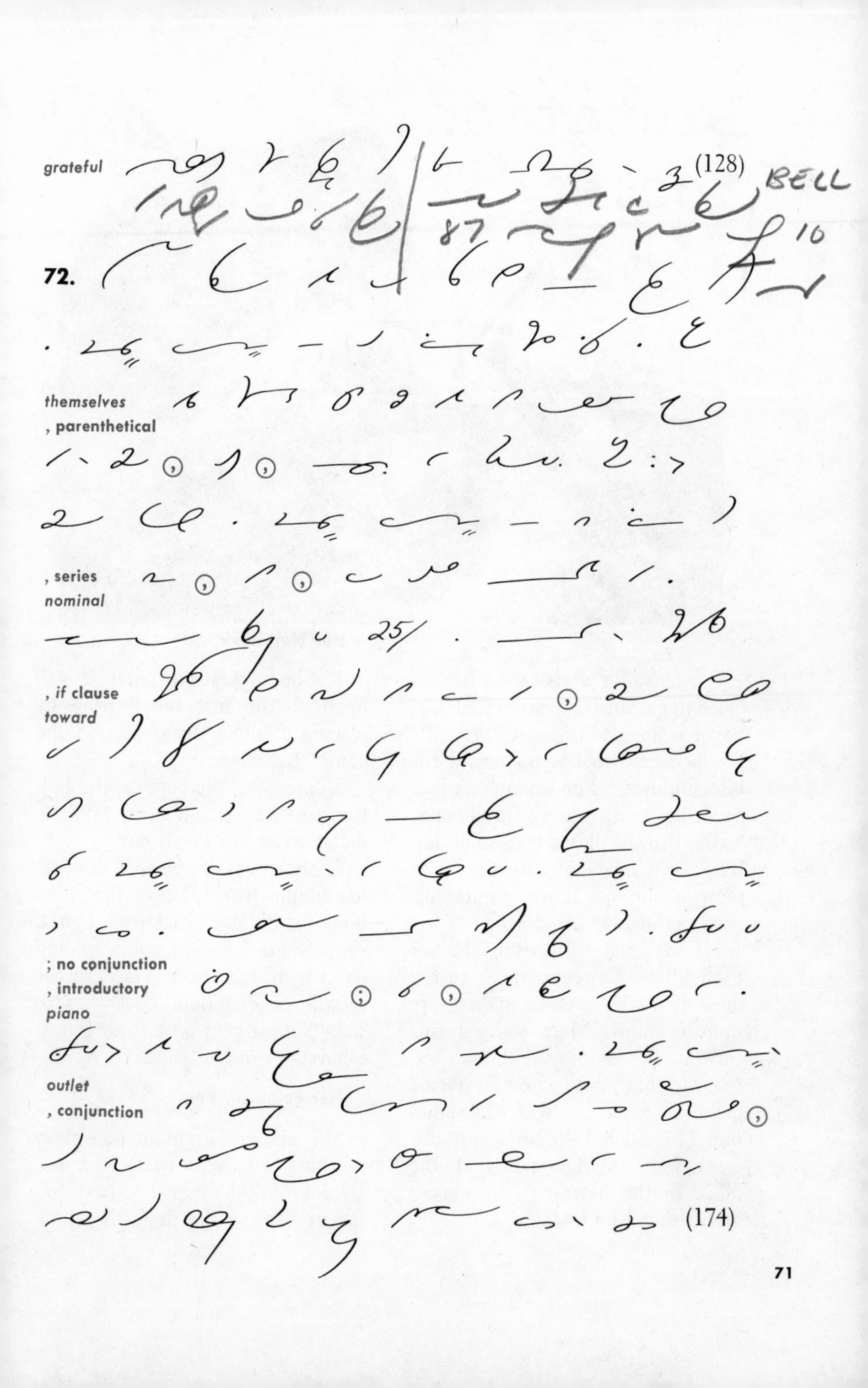

grateful (128)

72.

themselves
, parenthetical

, series
nominal

, if clause
toward

; no conjunction
, introductory
piano

outlet
, conjunction

(174)

Dictation tools

It is easy for a visitor to Mary's office to get the impression that Mr. Baker is an inconsiderate, thoughtless person who has no regard for his employees. For example, when he wishes to dictate, he simply says, "Miss Brown, please take some letters"; and he begins to dictate as soon as she sits down, sometimes even before she sits down.

He is not inconsiderate or thoughtless, however; he is just a busy man who tries to make every minute count. Mary realized this early in her employment and was ready for him, even when he started dictating while she was still standing! This is what she learned to do:

As soon as she arrives at the office in the morning, she checks on her dictation tools.

Her Notebook

1. She makes sure that it will open at the first blank page by placing a rubber band around the completed pages.

2. She dates the page on the bottom so that she can easily find the dictation of any given day.

3. She checks to be sure that she has ample paper left in the notebook for the day's dictation. If not, she obtains a second notebook and dates it on the cover. Mary, in the middle of dictation, never has to say, "I must get another notebook; I have run out of paper."

Her Fountain Pen

She fills her fountain pen every morning, whether it needs it or not. By doing so, she is sure to have sufficient ink for the day's dictation.

In addition, by forcing ink in and out of the barrel several times, she keeps the pen clean. Her pen, consequently, never becomes clogged.

Her Pencils

Even though Mary takes her dictation with a fountain pen (which enables her to write without fatigue for long periods), she always brings along at least one pencil "just in case" and one red pencil that she uses for flagging important letters and telegrams.

These tools she always keeps handy, so that she can immediately place her hands on them when her employer calls her to his office. When that occurs, Mary places her notebook, opened to the proper page, and her pencils and the cap of her fountain pen in her left hand. In her right hand she holds her pen, ready to write. In that way she is ready to take dictation even though Mr. Baker starts dictating while she is still walking to his desk.

Looking after her actual writing tools, however, is not all that Mary does in the morning. She also cleans the type on her typewriter. If the typewriter needs a new ribbon, she puts one on. In addition, she checks to be sure that she has all the stationery items she needs.

Any one of these predictation preparations may seem minor; but, added together, they save a great deal of time.

Marginal reminders, 3

In this chapter you will take up an important use of the colon, another use of the semicolon, and two new uses of the comma. The following simple explanations will help you to understand when these punctuation marks are used; the Reading and Writing exercises will help you master them.

: enumeration

A colon is used after an expression that introduces some following material, such as an explanation of a general statement, a list, or an enumeration.

> There are three requirements: speed, accuracy, and artistry.
>
> The new washing machine has this advantage over other washing machines: it uses very little soap.

Whenever one of these uses of the colon occurs in the Reading and Writing Practice, it is indicated in the margin by ": enumeration."

; illustrative ,

When an illustration is introduced by some such expression as *namely, that is,* or *for example,* the expression should be preceded by a semicolon and followed by a comma.

> Mary has only one ambition; namely, to be a secretary.

, nonrestrictive

Nonrestrictive clauses and phrases are set off by commas. A nonrestrictive clause or phrase is one that may be omitted without changing the meaning of the sentence. The nonrestrictive clause or phrase might be classified as parenthetical. It is important that you follow the meaning of the dictation in order to be able to identify the restrictive and the nonrestrictive clauses and phrases and to punctuate them correctly.

Restrictive – no commas: The automobile that was speeding was completely destroyed.

Nonrestrictive – commas: The automobile, which was speeding, was completely destroyed.

In the first sentence above, *that was speeding* is a restrictive clause and must not be set off by commas. The expression *that was speeding* identifies the particular automobile that was destroyed. In the second sentence, *which was speeding* is a nonrestrictive or descriptive or parenthetical clause that must be set off with commas. It does not identify the particular automobile that was destroyed; it could be omitted without changing the meaning of the sentence.

The use of these commas is determined by the meaning of the sentence. You can always tell the dictator's meaning by the inflection of the voice during dictation. It is almost always possible to decide from the meaning of the dictation whether an expression was intended to be nonrestrictive or restrictive — whether it should be transcribed with or without commas.

, *and* omitted

Usually, two adjectives preceding a noun are separated by a comma.

It is a clear, bright day.

The comma is not used if the first adjective modifies the combined idea of the second adjective plus the noun.

She wore a beautiful green dress.

Lesson 11

73. Theory Brushup

Phrases: *Please*

1

Word Beginning: *De-*

2

Word Ending: *-thern, etc.*

3

Word Family: *-cially*

4

Ngk, Ng

5

1. Please return, please send, please ship, please see, please let us, please write.
2. Decide, decided, decidedly, deposit, depositor, safe-deposit, deposited.
3. Southern, northern, eastern, western, turn, term, determine, modern.
4. Officially, substantially, initially, essentially, financially, specially, especially, partially, confidentially.
5. Bank, trunks, frankly, blanket; strong, wrongly, lengthy.

Chapter 3

Finance

Reading and Writing Practice

74. Transcription Word Study

inherits Comes into possession of by reason of the death of another.

assumes Takes on.

posted Informed.

estate A person's property or possessions.

75.

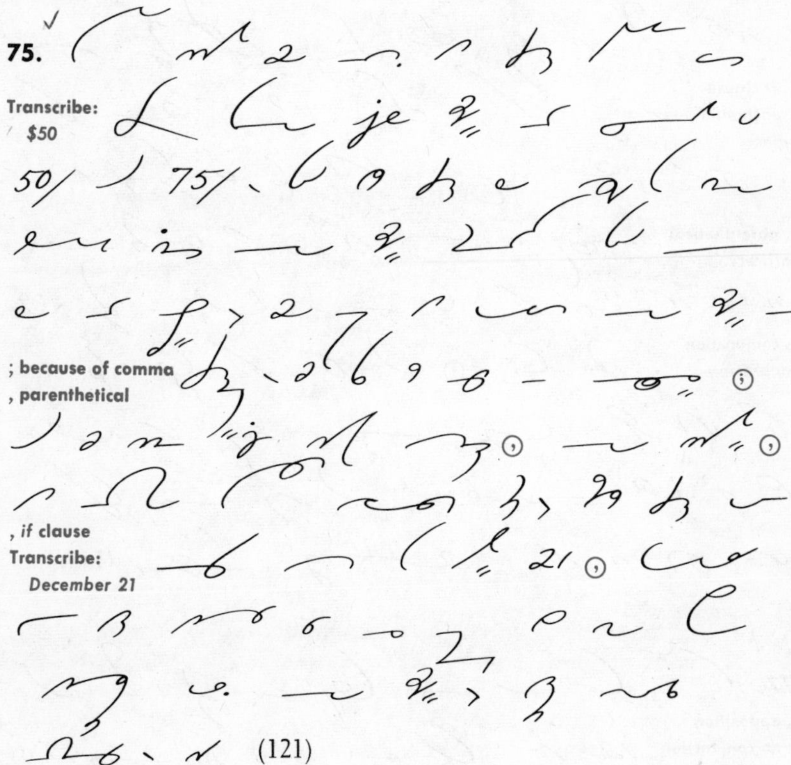

76.

, nonrestrictive
well known
no noun,
no hyphen

, if clause
substantial
piece

, parenthetical
officers

, conjunction
appreciate

(147)

77.

, apposition
; no conjunction
officially

, and omitted
convenient

, if clause
nearby
headquarters

, introductory
equipped

, and omitted
capable

, as clause
welcome

(135)

78.
inherits
substantial
, when clause

; no conjunction
, introductory
someone

investments
bank's

: enumeration
relieve

evenings
; illustrative ,
, series

(157)

79.
inquiring
referred
, conjunction

; illustrative ,
special

requirements
, introductory

pleasure
, parenthetical

(104)

Lesson 12

3/19

80. Theory Brushup

Phrases: We have

1

Word Beginning: Self-

2

Word Ending: -ship

3

Word Family: Out-

4

Omission of T: -ct

5

1. We have, we have not, we have not yet, we have not yet been, we have made, as we have, if we have, we have your order, we have not had.
2. Self-addressed, self-satisfied, self-made, self-respect, self-appointed, selfish, selfishly, selfishness.
3. Ownership, relationships, partnership, fellowship, friendships, hardship.
4. Outline, outlook, outfit, outside, outnumbered, outward, outlived.
5. Select, elected, aspects, unexpected, prospective, respectful, inspector.

Reading and Writing Practice

81. Transcription Word Study

compile To gather together, as records, statistics.

broker A dealer in securities, particularly stocks and bonds.

speculating Buying or selling securities with the expectation of making a profit because of future fluctuations in price.

82.

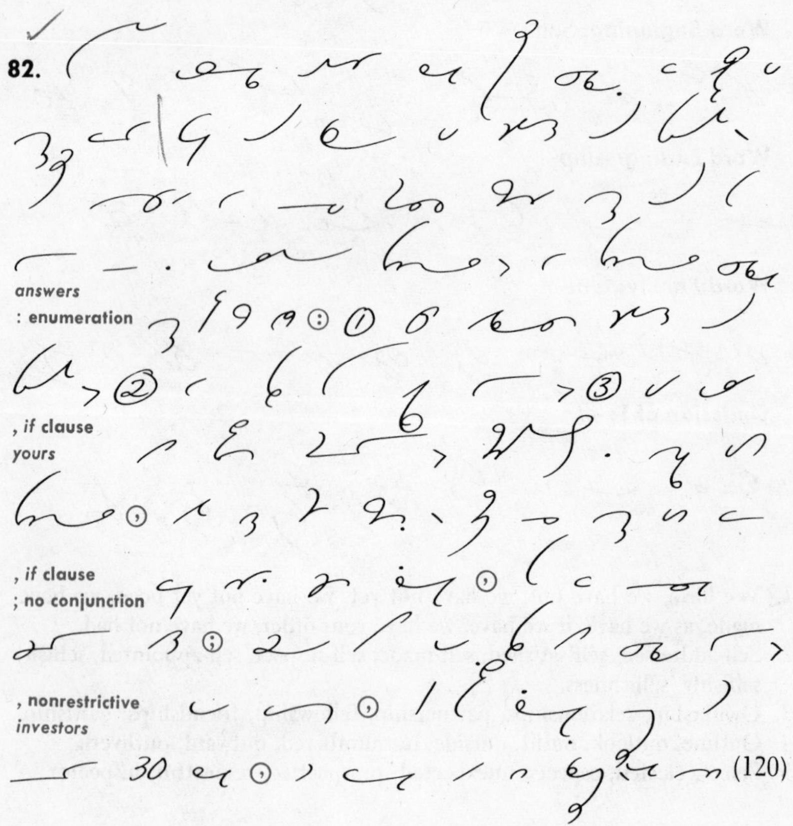

83.

much-needed
hyphenated before noun

questionnaire
; no conjunction
, introductory

, conjunction

, introductory
, *and* omitted
envelope

(150)

84.

company's
, conjunction
, when clause

, conjunction
accepted
recommended

, introductory
organization

(150)

85.
companies
, if clause

; illustrative ,
, series
, parenthetical

broker's

, introductory
report

any one
simply
, conjunction

(144)

86.

low-priced
hyphenated
before noun

worries
, conjunction
, parenthetical

, introductory

(118)

Lesson 13

87. Theory Brushup

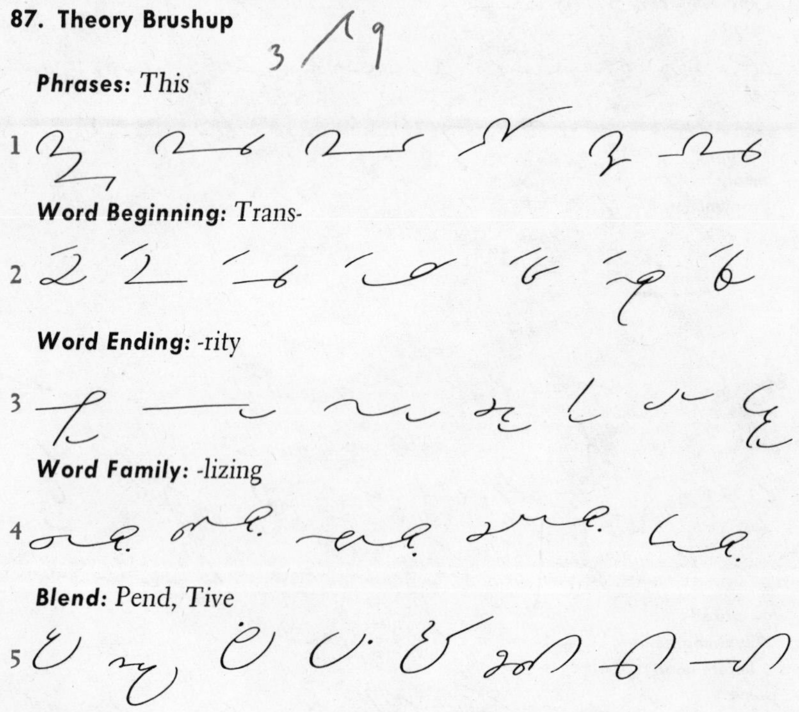

Phrases: This

1

Word Beginning: Trans-

2

Word Ending: -rity

3

Word Family: -lizing

4

Blend: Pend, Tive

5

1. This information, this minute, this month, at this time, this is the, in this matter.
2. Transfer, transform, transmit, translate, transport, transcribe, transpire.
3. Majority, minority, clarity, sincerity, charity, authority, prosperity.
4. Analyzing, utilizing, crystalizing, centralizing, penalizing.
5. Opened, unopened, happened, pending, suspended; executive, native, motive.

Reading and Writing Practice

88. Transcription Word Study

associates Fellow workers.

solution Answer.

systematically According to a regular pattern or method.

89.

, parenthetical
executives

Transcribe:
$21,000,000

, introductory
average

: enumeration
prospects
inquired

(153)

✓
90.

moving

, **introductory**

, **parenthetical**

transferring

; **illustrative**

, *when* **clause**

won't

. **courteous request**

(137)

✓
91.

transferred

Milwaukee

, **nonrestrictive**

available

, **conjunction**

Transcribe:
18 Street
$18,000

financial
, *if* clause
, apposition

anxious
; no conjunction
, introductory

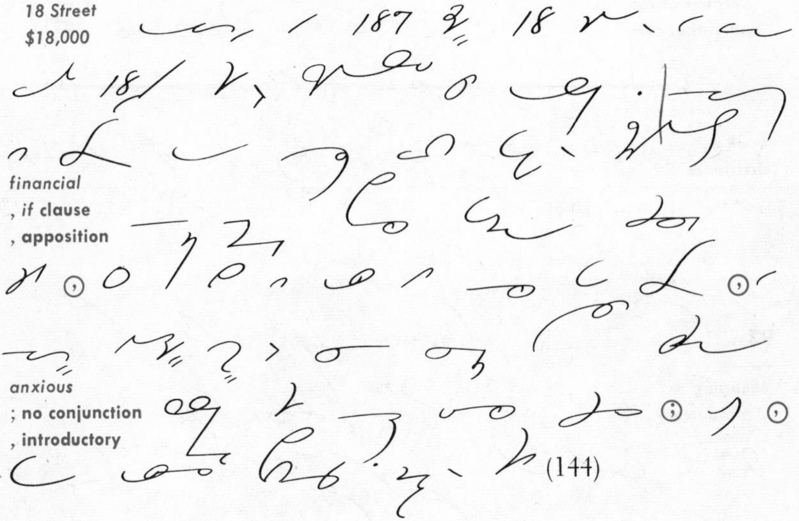

(144)

92.

, apposition
Transcribe:
January 13

worth-while
hyphenated
before noun
, introductory

, as clause
, and omitted
knowledge

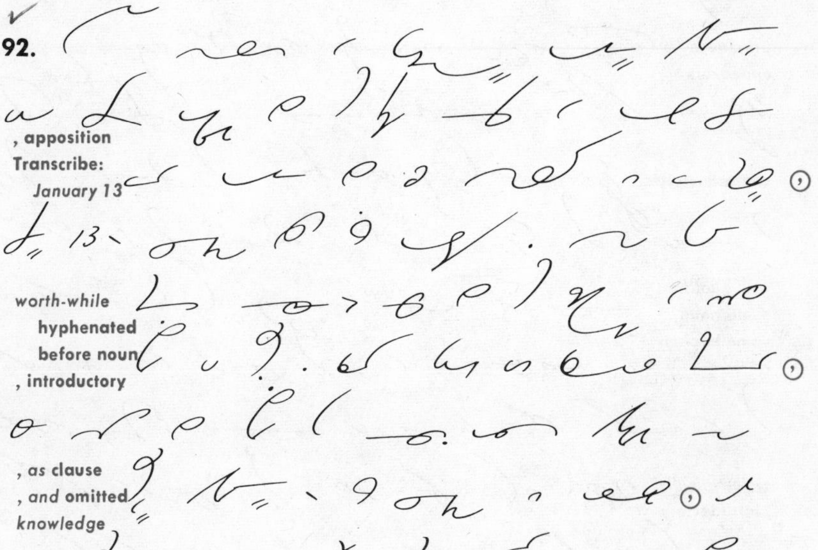

; because of comma
, parenthetical

bank's
assistance

(144)

93.

changing
, introductory

, if clause
endeavors

, introductory

well qualified
no noun,
no hyphen

systematically
, introductory

(162)

Lesson 14

94. Theory Brushup

Phrases: Very

1

Word Beginning: Incl-

2

Word Ending: -ulate

3

Word Family: -pen

4

Figures

5

1. Very much, very well, very important, very good, very little, very glad.
2. Include, including, included, inclusion, incline, inclined, inclination, inclines.
3. Regulate, regulation, regulated, speculate, stipulate, stimulation.
4. Pen, open, happen, cheapen, ripen, dampen, reopen, pencil.
5. One or two, two or three, three or four, 100, \$100; 7,000; \$15,000,000.

Reading and Writing Practice

95. Transcription Word Study

reflection Something that casts discredit or blame.

reputable Enjoying a good reputation; held in high esteem.

active file A file that is currently in use.

96.

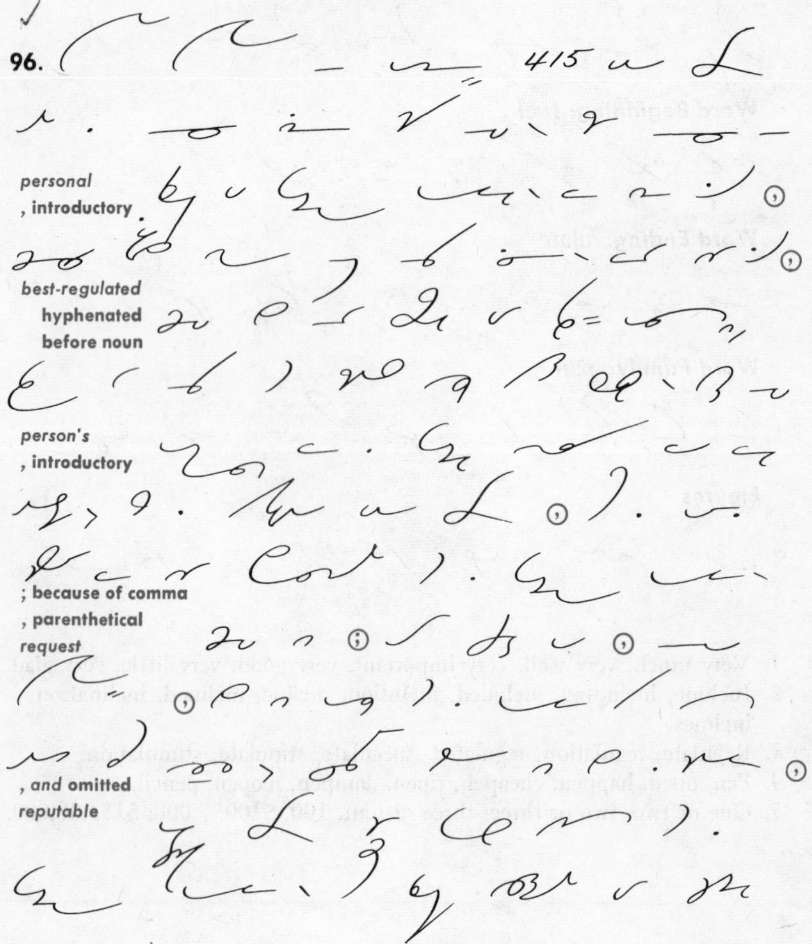

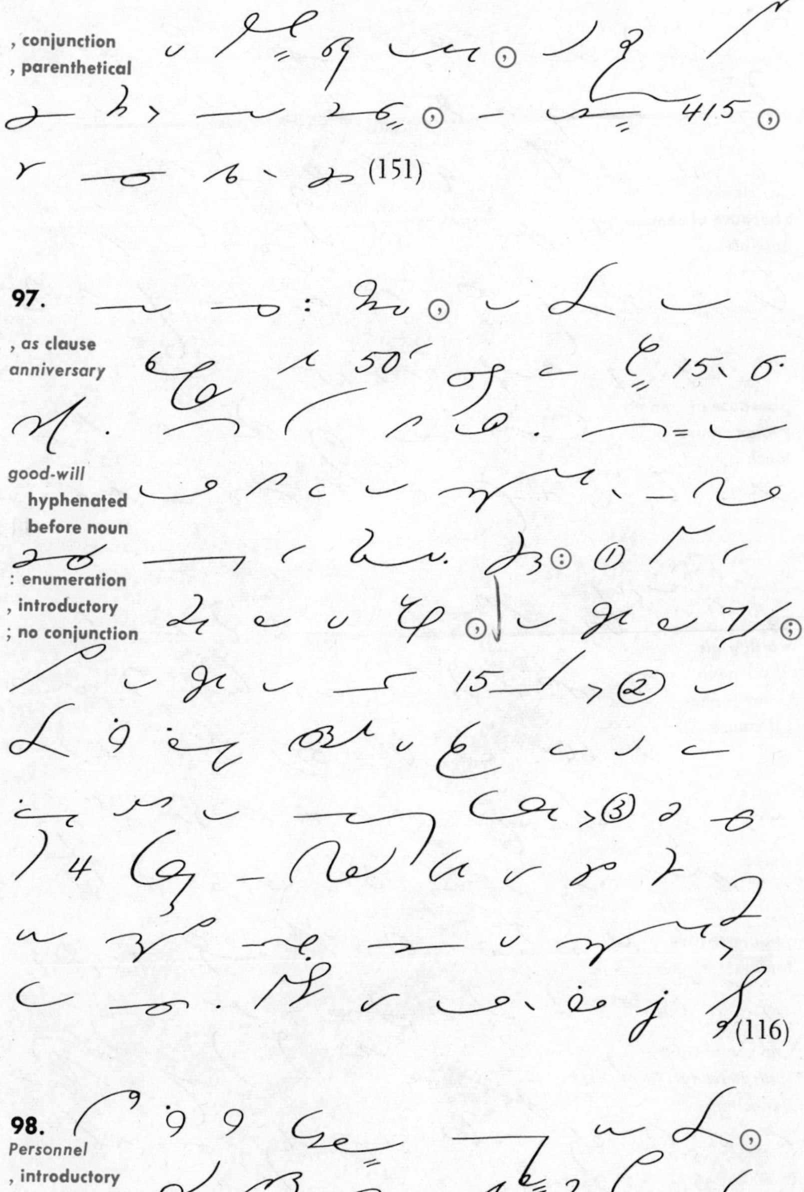

, conjunction
, parenthetical

(151)

97.

, as clause
anniversary

good-will
hyphenated
before noun

: enumeration
, introductory
; no conjunction

(116)

98.

Personnel
, introductory

, as clause
; because of comma
possible

(113)

; because of comma
, *when* clause
touch

99.
worth while
no noun,
no hyphen
, *if* clause

60/ 35) 3^{83}

, nonrestrictive
family

; no conjunction
, introductory
depositor

(114)

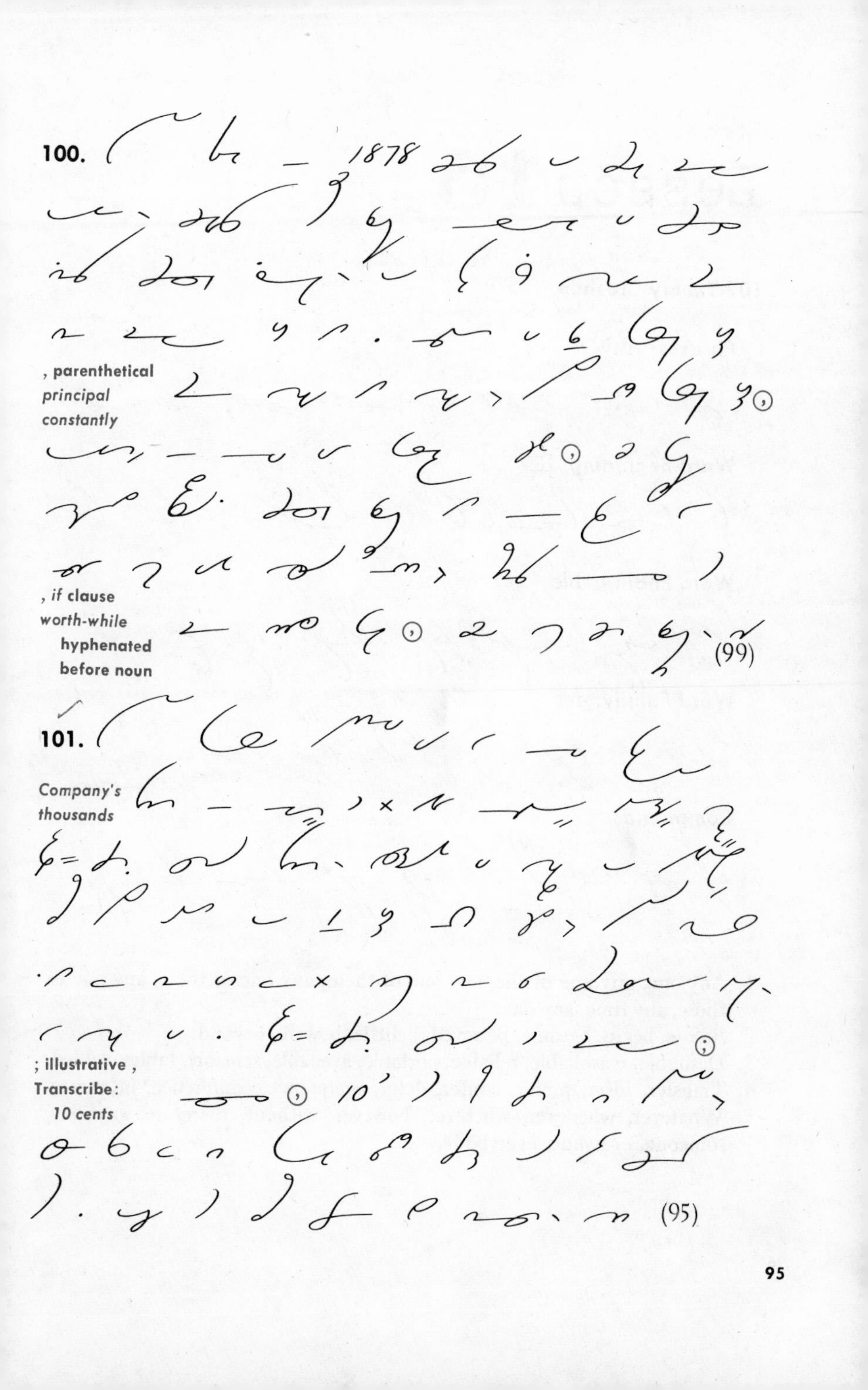

100. 1878

, parenthetical
principal
constantly

, *if clause*
worth-while
hyphenated
before noun

(99)

101.

Company's
thousands

; illustrative ,
Transcribe:
10 cents

10¢

(95)

96

Lesson 15

102. Theory Brushup

Phrases: Any

1

Word Beginning: Be-

2

Word Ending: -ble

3

Word Family: -fer

4

Compounds

5

1. Any one, any one of the, any one of them, any one of these, any one of those, any time, any day.
2. Before, begin, became, betrayed, belittle, beware, beyond.
3. Desirable, reasonable, reliable, portable, available, sensibly, tables, cabled.
4. Transfer, infer, prefer, confer, defer, preference, conference, inference.
5. Whatever, whenever, wherever, however, without, therefore, anybody, someone, everyone, everybody.

Reading and Writing Practice

103. Transcription Word Study

cordial Warm; friendly; sincere.

contractor One who agrees to do a definite job at a specified price.

informative Instructive; supplying information.

104.

drive-in
hyphenated before noun

; illustrative ,

, apposition
, nonrestrictive
deposits

Transcribe:
7 a.m.
6 p.m.

board
; because of comma
, if clause

(133)

105.

family's
requirements
, conjunction

416

Transcribe:
12 Street
$15,000

12

15

, nonrestrictive
mortgage

5

10

15-year
hyphenated
before noun

15

10

, as clause
, introductory
consequently

(150)

106.

16

125 16 150

12

completely
, conjunction

, introductory
, parenthetical
transfer

anyone
, if clause

(147)

107.
, and omitted
economical

, series
up to date
no noun,
no hyphen

estimates
; no conjunction

25

Transcribe:
$100
, conjunction

3^{50}

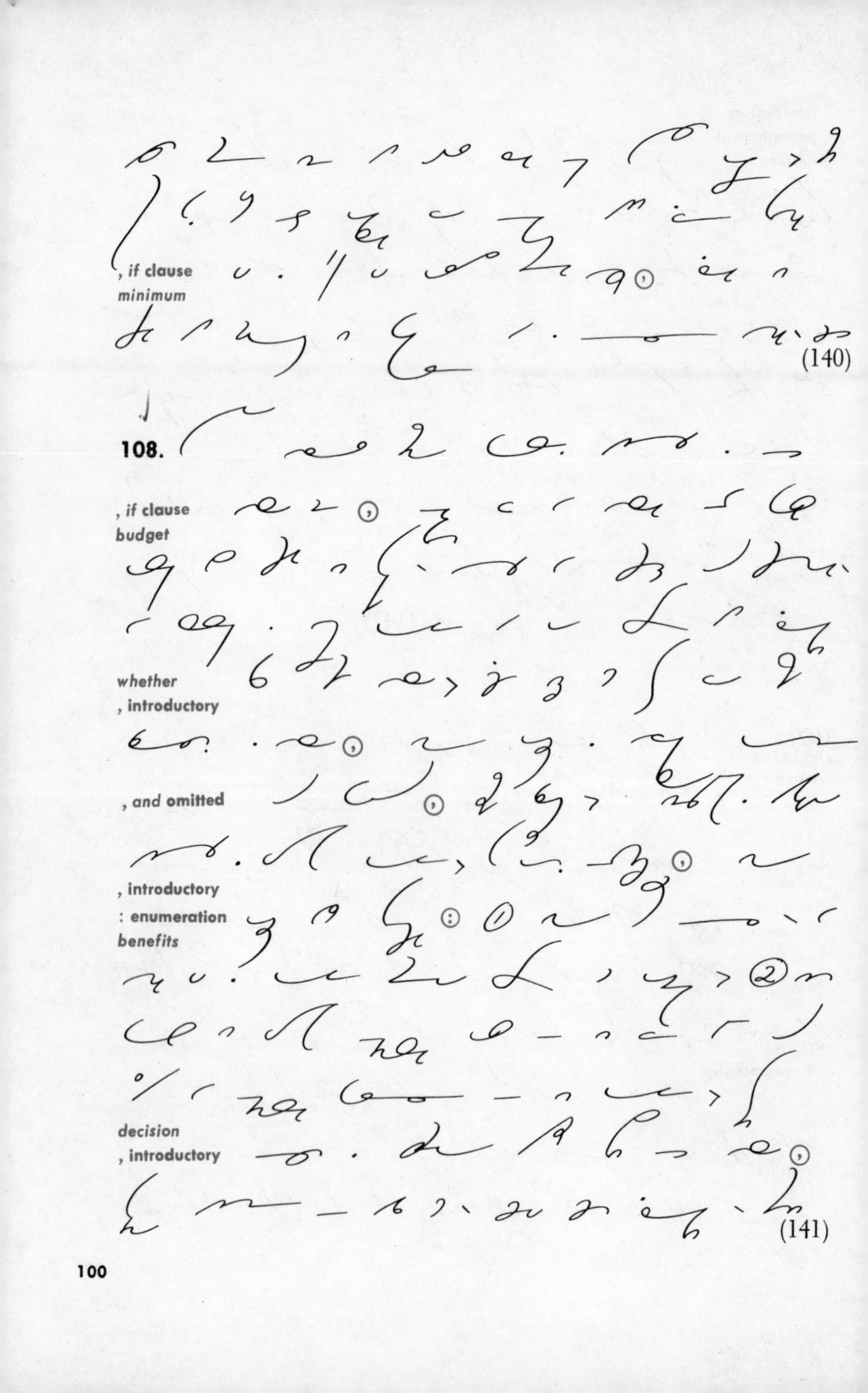

, if clause
minimum

(140)

108.

, if clause
budget

whether
, introductory

, and omitted

, introductory
: enumeration
benefits

decision
, introductory

(141)

109.

Government
, introductory
, series

, introductory

widely held
no hyphen after ly

render
readers'

(146)

Advance information

If you are like most beginners, the chances are that you will be somewhat bewildered during the first few days on your job. You will be particularly "jittery" when you take dictation during those early days, no matter how considerate and thoughtful your employer may try to be. That is only natural. Remember, however, the sooner you get over this jitteriness and become adjusted, the sooner will you be of real value to your employer.

Mary Brown, of course, had to go through this adjustment period, but she took steps to help herself adjust. Here is what she did:

On the day Mr. Baker said, "You're hired," she took home and studied carefully the company's style manual. This manual shows the letter style, salutations, and closings that the company prefers. It shows how to set up an interoffice memorandum.

In addition, it gives the company's preferences in spelling and punctuation. For example, the company prefers *enclosed* to *inclosed*, *theater* to *theatre*, *catalogue* to *catalog*. She learned that dashes are to be avoided whenever possible.

All this information Mary ab-

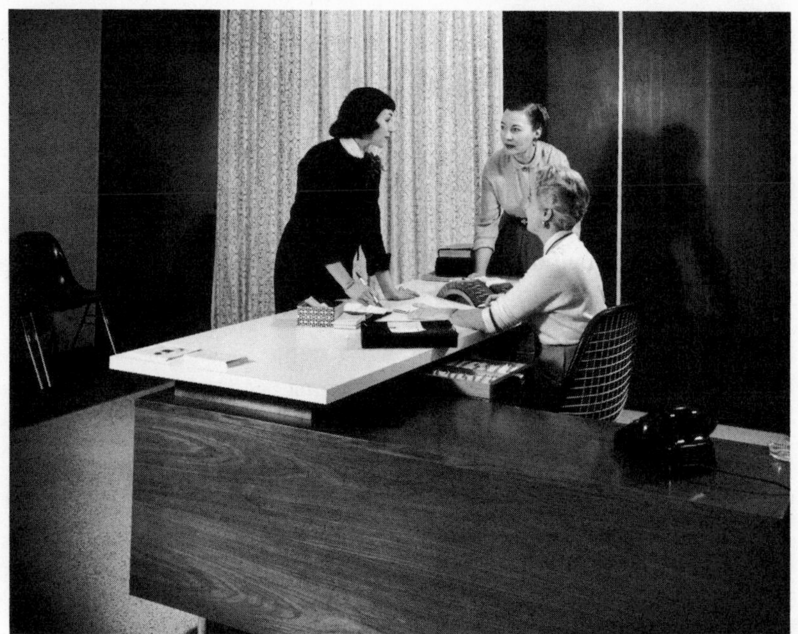

sorbed *before* she had to transcribe her first letter.

The company by whom you are hired may be a small one that does not have a style manual. It will then be your job to learn these things by asking questions, tactfully, of course!

On her first day, Mary asked for and received permission to read some of the letters in the files. By doing so, she had an opportunity to become familiar with the vocabulary of the company and to make note of some of the technical terms used in the business. She was also able to familiarize herself with the names of the persons with whom Mr. Baker frequently corresponded.

Finally, by asking tactful questions of other employees, she learned something about the habits of her employer: whether he dictated with a cigar in his mouth, whether he was a rapid or a deliberate dictator, whether he preferred to have a stenographer interrupt him during dictation or only at the end of a letter.

All this preliminary information helped Mary gain confidence and to get over that critical adjustment period successfully and quickly.

Remember that your employer and everyone on the staff will wish to help you succeed. They, too, were beginners once and realize the problems you face. Consequently, never hesitate to ask when you are in doubt; but be sure that you ask at the right time and in a courteous, tactful manner.

Marginal reminders, 4

The marginal reminders in Chapter 4 deal with the use of punctuation marks with quotations.

, introducing short quote

Short quotations are introduced by a comma.

> The boy said, "I am getting hungry."

: introducing long quote

Long quotations are introduced by a colon.

> The boy said: "I could not get the assignment done because I did not feel well. The doctor said I had a touch of the flu. I will try to make up the assignment."

, inside quote
. inside quote

The comma and the period are *always* typed inside the final quotation mark.

> She said, "I will take the job."
> The booklet, "10 Ways to Reduce," is out of stock.

Question marks are placed inside or outside the final quotation mark according to the sense of the sentence.

> She asked, "Why did he go?"
> Why did she say, "The job is too hard for me"?

Semicolons and colons are *always* placed outside the final quotation mark.

> Be sure to mark that letter "Confidential"; then place the carbon copy in my personal file.
> Shipments of the following goods should be marked "Fragile": china, glassware, ceramics.

Lesson 16

110. Theory Brushup

Phrases: Omission of Words

1

Word Beginning: Post-

2

Word Endings: -ly, -ingly

3

Word Family: -ten

4

Omission of Vowel: Short U

5

1. One of the most, one of the best, up to date, up to the minute, more and more, less and less.
2. Postage, postal, postman, postmaster, postpone, postponement, postdate.
3. Quickly, weekly, monthly, partly, daily; willingly, knowingly, surprisingly.
4. Straighten, lighten, brighten, frighten, gotten, written, tighten.
5. Fun, funny, son, some, summer, ton, done, column, come.

Publishing

Chapter

Reading and Writing Practice

111. Transcription Word Study

extended Stretched or drawn out.

classify To group into classes which have systematic relations.

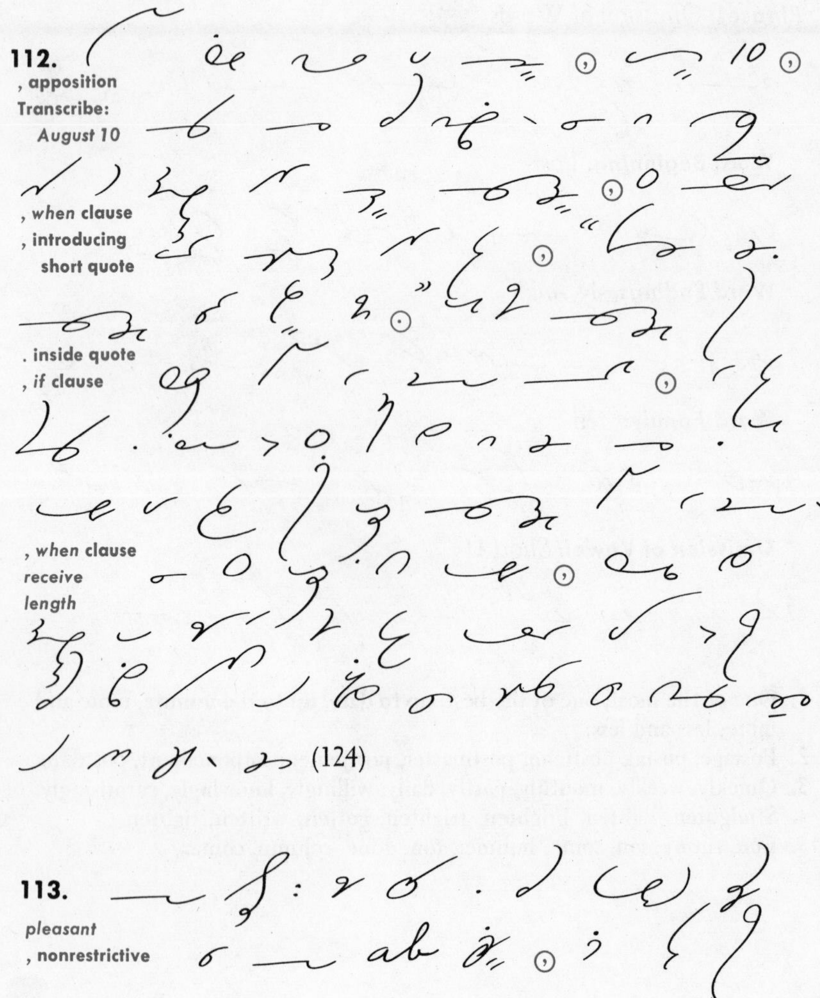

White's
, apposition

, as clause
available

, parenthetical
, introductory
incidentally

(144)

114.

Engineer
; illustrative ,
, series

up to date
no noun,
no hyphen
, conjunction

, as clause
subscription
due

(101)

115.

, parenthetical
becoming

: introducing
long quote
copies

. inside quote

, introductory

worth-while
hyphenated
before noun

, *if clause*
lapse

(168)

116.

; no conjunction
, introductory

up to the minute
no noun,
no hyphen

well-trained
hyphenated
before noun
, and omitted

, introductory
offering

(159)

Lesson 17

117. Theory Brushup

Phrases: Sure

1

Word Beginning: Con-

2

Word Ending: -gram

3

Word Family: -men

4

Omission of Vowel: E in Ū

5

1. I am sure, be sure, to be sure, you may be sure, can be sure, we are sure, must be sure.
2. Contract, congratulations, contained, disconnect, consume, unconcerned.
3. Program, radiogram, monogram, telegram, cablegram.
4. Salesmen, workmen, doormen, statesmen, businessmen.
5. Induce, produce, reduce, manuscript, new, renew, due, subdue.

Reading and Writing Practice

118. Transcription Word Study

induce To persuade.

liberal Generous

admission to the bar Permission to practice law in a state.

119.

; because of comma

, parenthetical

release

balance

exceeds

received

60

routine

overlooked

won't

, when clause

, introducing short quote

. inside quote

(128)

120.

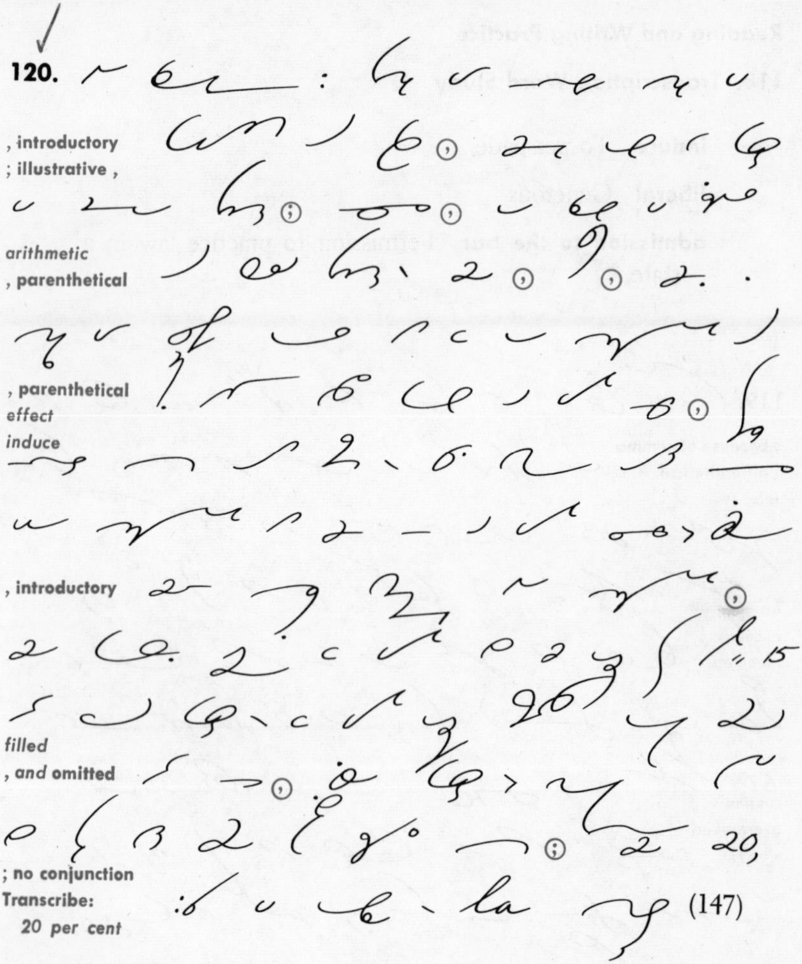

, introductory
; illustrative ,

arithmetic
, parenthetical

, parenthetical
effect
induce

, introductory

filled
, *and* omitted

; no conjunction
Transcribe:
20 per cent

(147)

121.

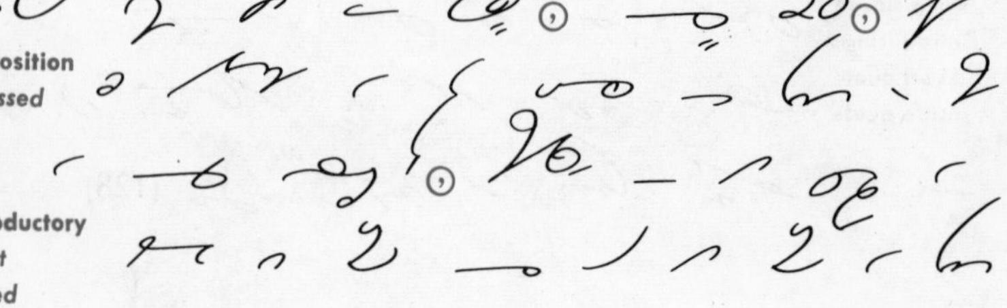

, apposition
discussed

, introductory
accept
offered

, introductory

30 15

, parenthetical
manuscript

(132)

122. 15 10

, *and* omitted
, apposition

28

. inside quote
, nonrestrictive
, *as* clause

, parenthetical
above-mentioned

, *if* clause
: enumeration

, series

receive

, when clause

establish

(141)

123.

congratulations

admission

, introducing short quote

. inside quote

up to date no noun, no hyphen

up-to-date hyphenated before noun

, introductory

(160)

Lesson 18

124. Theory Brushup

Phrases: Several

1

Word Beginning: Super-, Supr-

2

Word Ending: -ual

3

Word Family: -n't

4

Omission of D

5

1. Several months, several months ago, several days, several days ago, several other, several times.
2. Supervise, supervisor, supervision, supreme, supremely, support, supporter, supported.
3. Habitual, gradual, equalize, annually, scheduled, manual.
4. Couldn't, wouldn't, shouldn't, didn't, aren't, weren't, haven't.
5. Command, demand, mind, remind, extend, pretend, recommend.

Reading and Writing Practice

125. Transcription Word Study

habitual Doing something by force of habit.

gesture Something done as an expression of courtesy or thoughtfulness.

packing slip A form that lists the contents of a package or shipment.

compliment *(verb)* To express regard or appreciation for. (Do not confuse *compliment* with *complement*, which means "to complete or to supply a lack.")

; no conjunction
Transcribe:
$3

(151)

127.

, nonrestrictive
Pittsburgh

, parenthetical
gesture

, series
later

(133)

128.

Transcribe:

June 15

, *when* clause

. inside quote

, conjunction

copies

, parenthetical

error

, *as* clause

naturally

first-class

hyphenated before noun

different

, introductory

; because of comma

(162)

129.

prepared

, parenthetical

; illustrative ,

Advertiser's Manual

. inside quote

, parenthetical

: introducing long quote

20

; because of comma

, *when* clause *immediately*

badly needed no hyphen after *ly*

. inside quote

enclosed

(172)

130.

Manual

. inside quote

(48)

Lesson 19

131. Theory Brushup

Phrases: Number

1

Word Beginning: Dis-

2

Word Ending: -sume

3

Word Family: -man

4

Blend: Md

5

1. Number of years, for a number of years, number of the, number of them, number of times.
2. Discuss, dislike, dismiss, distance, disturb, disallow.
3. Assume, assumed, resume, resumed, consume, consumed, presume, presumed.
4. Foreman, salesman, repairman, workman, deliveryman.
5. Performed, informed, conformed, reformed, formed, named, blamed.

Reading and Writing Practice

132. Transcription Word Study

carriage charges The cost of shipping goods.

credit memorandum Allowance for defective or short shipment, for error in billing, or for returned merchandise.

bindery A place where books are bound.

133.

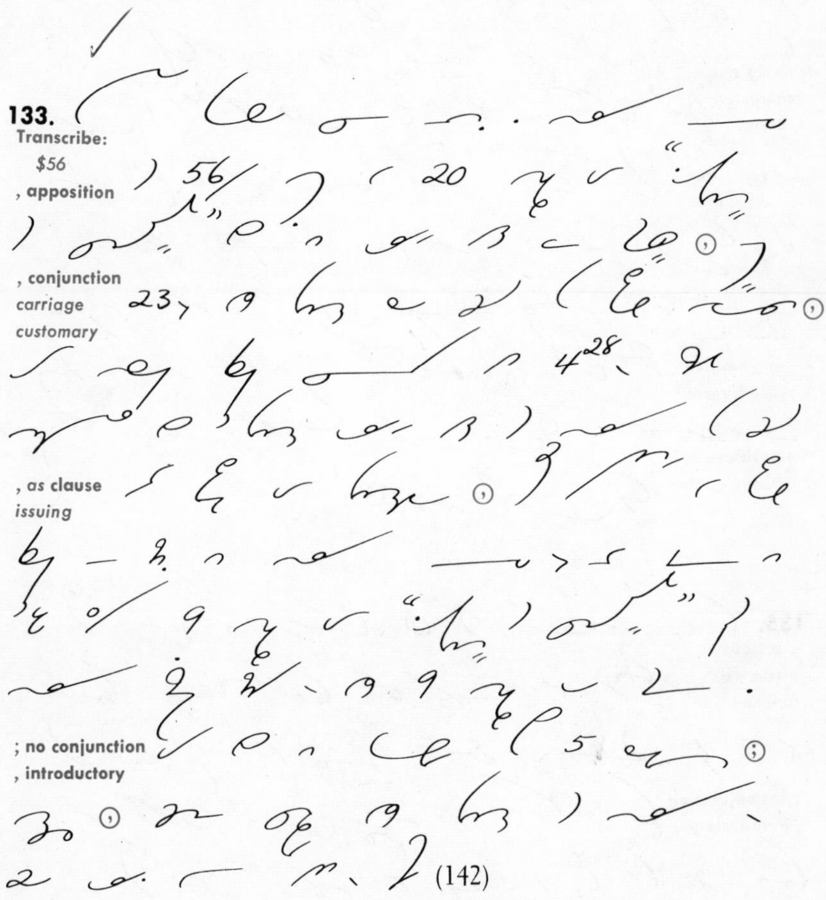

134.

editor

, introducing short quote

, nonrestrictive

. inside quote

appreciate

Henry's

character

, series

, and omitted

self-addressed

, as clause

. inside quote

(138)

135.

, as clause

discussed

foreman

; no conjunction

, introductory

: enumeration
, *if* clause
manuscript

, nonrestrictive
its

, *if* clause

(140)

136.

well-known
hyphenated
before noun
children's
; no conjunction

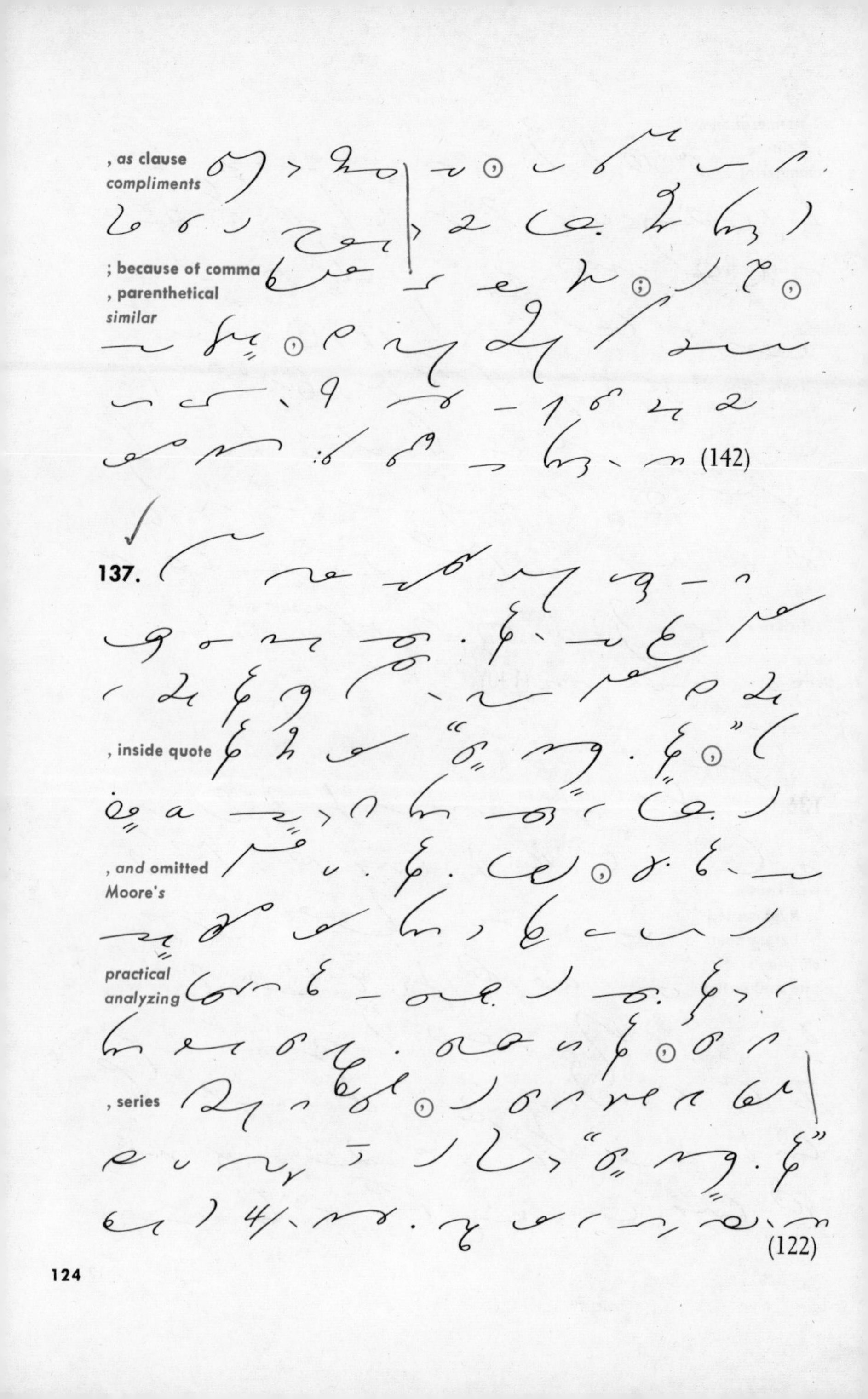

, as clause
compliments

; because of comma
, parenthetical
similar

(142)

137.

, inside quote

, and omitted
Moore's

practical
analyzing

, series

(122)

Lesson 20

138. Theory Brushup

Phrases: Words Modified

1

Word Beginning: Im-, Em-

2

Word Ending: -hood

3

Word Family: -thing

4

Blend: Ted, etc.

5

1. I had, I had not, I had not been, I had been; of course, of course it is, of course it will, of course it will be.
2. Improve, impressive, impart, import; employee, emblem.
3. Childhood, motherhood, parenthood, brotherhood, boyhood, neighborhood.
4. Thing, everything, nothing, something, one thing, plaything, playthings.
5. Interrupted, needed, detail, study, ditto, audit, today, parted.

Reading and Writing Practice

139. Transcription Word Study

drenched Thoroughly wet; soaked.

trying conditions Conditions that are hard to endure.

mailing pieces Catalogues, pamphlets, circulars, and other advertising material that is sent through the mails.

140.

, apposition

totally

destroyed

; illustrative ,

except

, nonrestrictive

purchased

; because of comma

, introductory

suffered

(147)

141.

beginning

reopen

, appos*i*tion

two-week

hyphenated

before noun

, *as* clause

, introductory

interrupted

co-operation

, conjunction

(141)

142.

, apposition

, *when* clause

idea

; introducing

short quote

suggestion

? inside quote
, introductory
, *as* clause

, *if* clause

(98)

143.

: introducing long quote
, and omitted
well-designed hyphenated before noun

, conjunction
campaign

recommended
. inside quote

, *when* clause
printer's
advice

; no conjunction
compliments

(129)

Part II

Dictation on the Job

Notebook techniques

What would you do if you were taking dictation and your employer should suddenly say: "Let's send Mr. Green a carbon of that letter I dictated earlier this morning to Frank Smith. Also, let's send that letter to Green by air mail and get it out today."

That represents a lot of instructions for a letter that had been dictated "earlier this morning." When this happened to Mary Brown, she wasn't disturbed. She simply leafed back in her notebook until she found the letter to Smith and did three things:

1. She wrote in the space that she had *left at the head of the letter*, "cc: Green, Smith letter air mail."

2. She then took her red pencil and drew a line down the page next to the letter to Smith.

3. Finally, she folded over one corner of the notebook page so that she could find the page quickly when she completed her dictation and was ready to transcribe.

You can, of course, immediately see why it was so important for Mary to write these instructions at the *head* of the letter. If she had placed them at the end, she might not have discovered that she needed two carbon copies until it was too late.

The wise stenographer will always leave several blank lines between letters. When the dictator later gives instructions concerning a letter that was previously dictated, the space is available for those instructions where it is needed.

The red line next to the shorthand indicates that the letter should be the first or one of the first to be transcribed. Telegrams and urgent interoffice memoranda would be marked in the same way.

The folded corner of the page makes it possible to locate quickly those letters that get high priority. This device is especially helpful when a stenographer must take 20 or 30 or more notebook pages of dictation at one time, as occasionally happens.

Lesson 21

144. Shorthand Language Study. Many English words are derived from the Greek and Latin. Consequently, an understanding of the meanings of Greek and Latin prefixes and suffixes will often give you the clue to the meaning of words with which you are unfamiliar.

For example, you may never have heard the word *posterity*. However, if you know that *post* means *after*, you may be able to figure out that *posterity* has some reference to those who come after, or descendants.

In each Shorthand Language Study you will be given two or three of the more common prefixes and suffixes, together with their meanings, and a list of words in which they are used. In practicing each Shorthand Language Study, read the definitions carefully and then study the list of words that follows. If you cannot read any words immediately, refer to the key.

Post-: *Something to do with the mail.* POSTMAN, *a mailman. Also after or later.* POSTSCRIPT, *something written after the main part of the letter.*

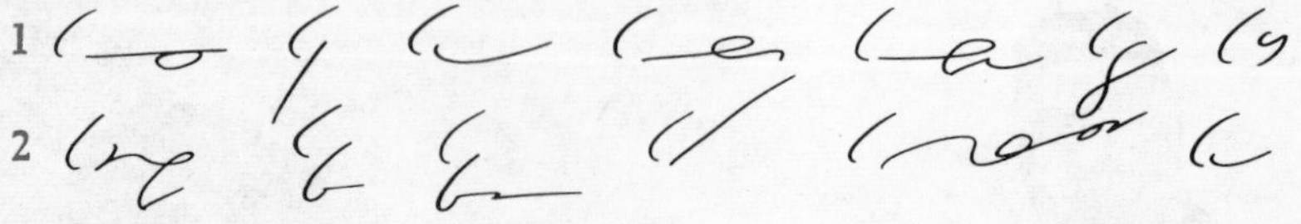

1. **Postman, postage, postal, postmark, postmaster, postpaid, post office.**
2. **Postscript, postpone, postponement, postdate, postgraduate, posterity.**

Pre-: *Before.* PREVIEW, *a viewing before.*

Preview, preliminary, precede, predict, prefix, prearrange, precaution.

Insurance

Reading and Writing Practice

145. Transcription Word Study

cash value (also, *cash-surrender value*) The refund that a life insurance policyholder may receive when he cancels his policy.

urgent Pressing, instantly important.

endowment insurance Insurance providing for the payment of a fixed sum to the insured at the expiration of a term of years or to a beneficiary if the insured should die first.

146.

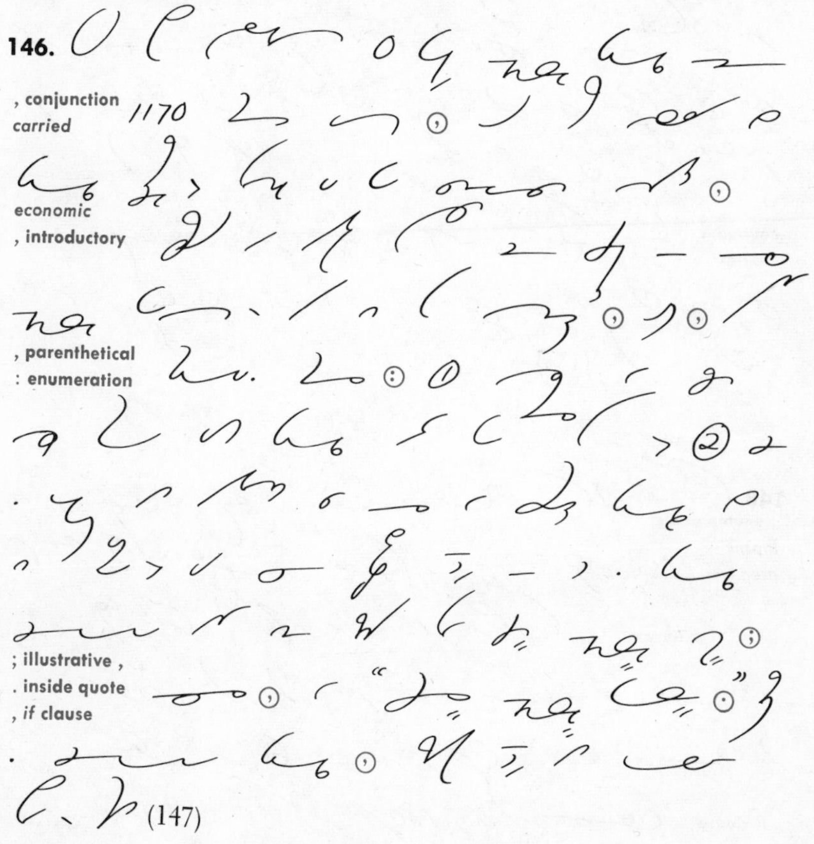

147. 415 ... 615 ...

Transcribe:
21 Street

21 ... 8 ... 166 ...

, introductory
whether
convenient

courteous
, series

(133)

148.
: enumeration
lapses
premium

15 ...

6 ...

, if clause

180 ...

CASPER-CANTRELL COMPANY

CABLE ADDRESS: CASCANCO

223 EAST BROAD STREET • RICHMOND 19, VIRGINIA • PHONE: 2-5822

November 16, 19--

Henderson & Company
1360 East Main Street
Wilmington 4, Delaware

ATTENTION: Mr. Green

Gentlemen:

We are happy to announce a new line of office plastic goods that we believe will be very useful to you. The folder that is enclosed will tell you fully about the five items that we are offering to the trade. These products are the result of many years of research and testing. They were created with the help of nationally known designers.

We suggest that you become familiar with these items by ordering at least one of each. This plan will enable you to test the entire line. Later, you can order such items as you feel you can handle most profitably. The margin of profit is so great and the products so easy to sell that you will find these items will quickly be among your most popular and most profitable items.

For your convenience, we have enclosed some order cards. Simply fill one out and mail it; your shipment will be made as soon as the card arrives.

Yours very truly,

Harold G. Smith
Sales Manager

HGS: MP
Enclosures

Average-Length Letter
Semiblocked Style, with Attention Line
Standard Punctuation

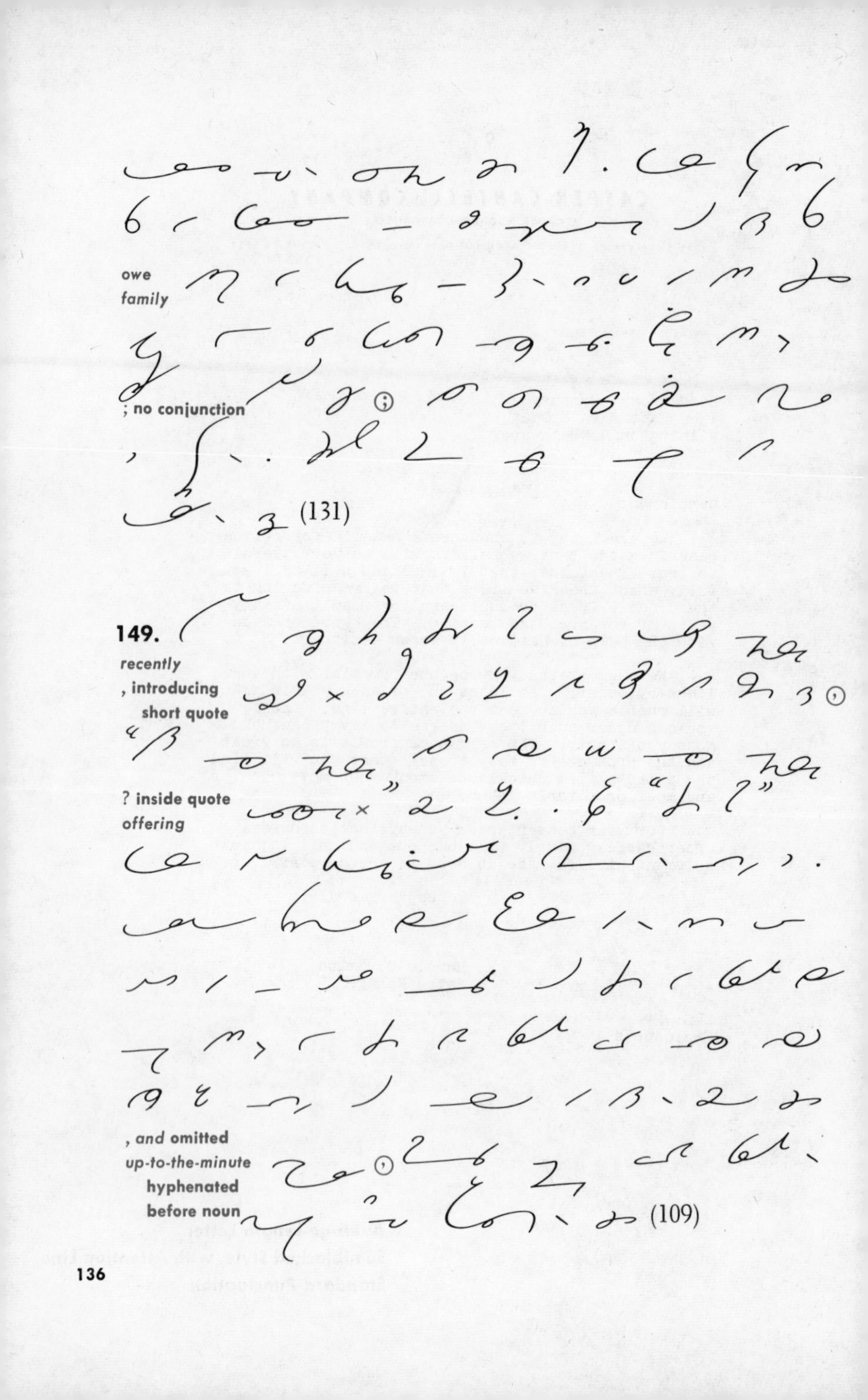

owe
family

; no conjunction

(131)

149.
recently
, introducing short quote

? inside quote
offering

, and omitted
up-to-the-minute
hyphenated before noun

(109)

150.

, apposition

, inside quote

; because of comma

thousands

, introductory

, *if* clause

; no conjunction

, introductory

(108)

151.

, *if* clause

traits

, apposition

20-payment

hyphenated before noun

, nonrestrictive

fully

(85)

Lesson 22

152. Accuracy Practice. Under the stress of rapid writing, certain groups of outlines may cause you difficulty in transcription unless you take special pains to write them accurately and give careful attention to proportion. Usually, the sense of the sentence will enable you to determine the correct transcription of a doubtful outline; but, occasionally, situations may arise where you will have to rely completely on your shorthand outlines.

In this accuracy practice, and those that you will find in later lessons, you will work with a number of these groups.

Practice Procedure. To get the most out of each accuracy practice, follow this practice procedure:

1. Write the words in group 1 slowly, watching your proportions carefully.
2. Write the words in group 1 once again, writing as rapidly as you can.
3. Read and copy the sentences for group 1 in the Practice Drill.
4. Repeat steps 1 through 3 for groups 2 and 3.

Group 1	Group 2	Group 3
any	no	order
many	most	audit

Practice Drill

1

2

1. He will not bring <u>any</u> friends to the party. He will not bring <u>many</u> friends to the party.
2. <u>No</u> boys are permitted to use the pool. <u>Most</u> boys are permitted to use the pool.
3. The accountant will <u>order</u> the books tomorrow. The accountant will <u>audit</u> the books tomorrow.

Reading and Writing Practice

153. Transcription Word Study

replacement value The amount that would be required to rebuild a house or to replace property at today's prices.

fiscal year The uniform period between one balancing of accounts and the next. The *calendar* year runs from January 1 to December 31. A fiscal year may begin on any day of the year and end one year from that day.

audit An official examination of accounts.

154.

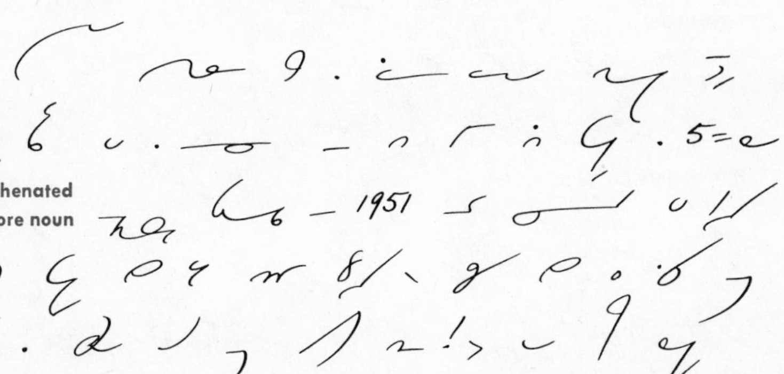

5-year
hyphenated before noun

, parenthetical
; no conjunction
preferred

promptly
, parenthetical
; because of comma

pennies
, conjunction

(174)

155.
, apposition
Transcribe:
May 29

, introductory
friend's
handle

, as clause
follow-up

(122)

156.

privilege
liberal
fiscal

, nonrestrictive
, introductory

31

past due
no noun,
no hyphen

. courteous
request
balance

120

(121)

157.

: introducing long quote

property

382 ... 24 ... 150 ...

. inside quote

, conjunction

... 24 ...

, introductory

reinsure

broader

, and omitted

... 3-4211 ...

(138)

158.

Transcribe: 20 per cent

... 20 ...

... 105 ...

renewal

, conjunction

... 20 ...

, *if clause*
Mutual

, *introducing short quote*
. *inside quote*

(117)

159.

; *no conjunction*
different

; *illustrative* ,
difficult

, *introductory*
experienced

up to date no noun, no hyphen
, *apposition*

(140)

Lesson 23

160. Office-Style Dictation. When a businessman is answering a routine letter, he will often dictate the entire answer without making any changes or insertions. When he dictates an important letter, where every word is important, he may change words or phrases, transpose sentences, and even revise entire paragraphs. It will be your job to make all these changes and insertions in your notes quickly and in such a way that you will be able to transcribe the letter exactly as the businessman wishes it transcribed.

If you have a good shorthand speed, you will have no difficulty making the transition from the timed dictation that you have been taking in class to the office-style dictation of your employer. The more shorthand speed you possess, the easier office-style dictation will be for you. In addition, if you are alert, you will soon "spot" the types of changes that your employer frequently makes and develop skill in handling them.

In this chapter and each chapter hereafter, you will take up one of the more common problems of office-style dictation. Read the explanation of the problem carefully, and study the illustrations that accompany it. Then read the shorthand letter that follows the explanation, to see how the problem would be handled in your shorthand notes.

Perhaps your teacher will dictate an occasional letter to you as a businessman might dictate. Thus, you will have an opportunity to apply the office-style suggestions that will be presented to you.

A businessman will occasionally decide to take out a word or a phrase or even a sentence that he has dictated. He may, for example, say:

> The pamphlet describes completely the insurance that
> we are urging parents to buy—take out *completely*.

To indicate this deletion, you would simply strike a heavy downward line through the word completely.

Sometimes he may simply repeat the sentence without the word or phrase that he wishes to omit. He may say:

> The enclosed pamphlet describes and illustrates the policy—no, *the enclosed pamphlet describes the policy.*

To indicate this deletion, you would mark out in your notes not only the word *illustrates* but the word *and* as well.

If only one word is to be taken out, use a heavy downward line; if several words are to be taken out, a wavy line will save time.

817

17

Illustration of Office-Style Dictation

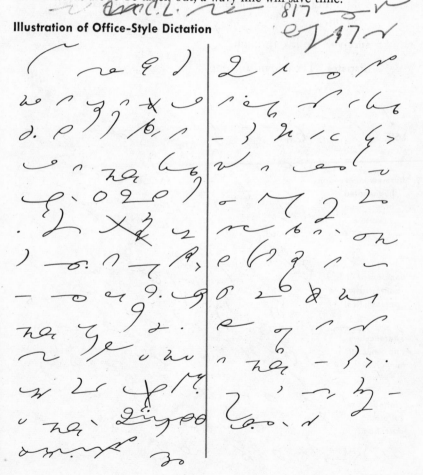

30

Reading and Writing Practice

161. Transcription Word Study

business-interruption insurance Insurance that compensates the insured for loss of earnings or profits during the period that his business cannot operate because of fire, flood, or other cause.

fixtures Things that are firmly attached to a house or building, such as radiators, electric lights, furnaces, and so on.

survive To live through.

disaster Terrible misfortune.

162.

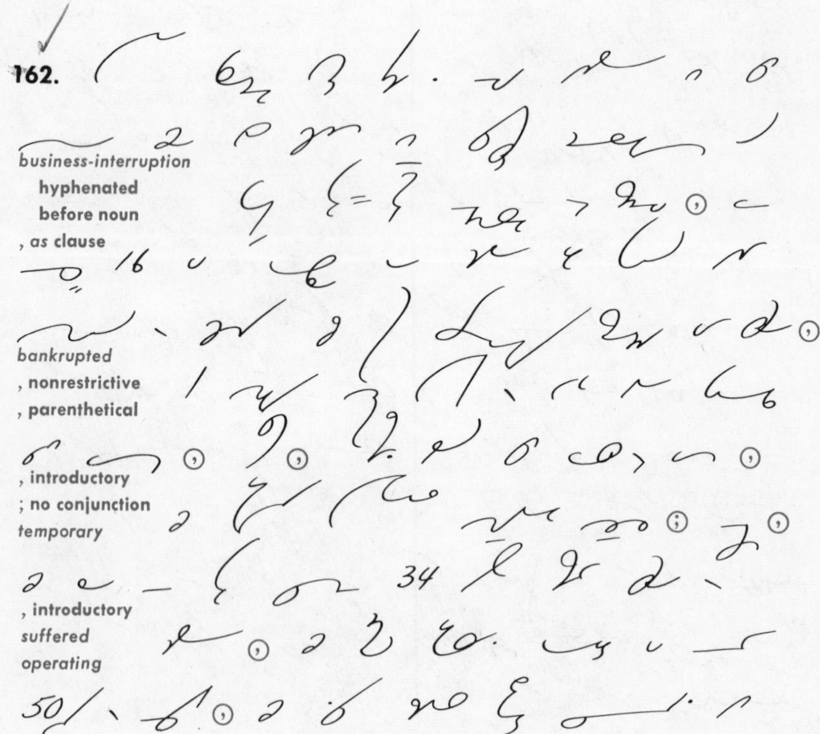

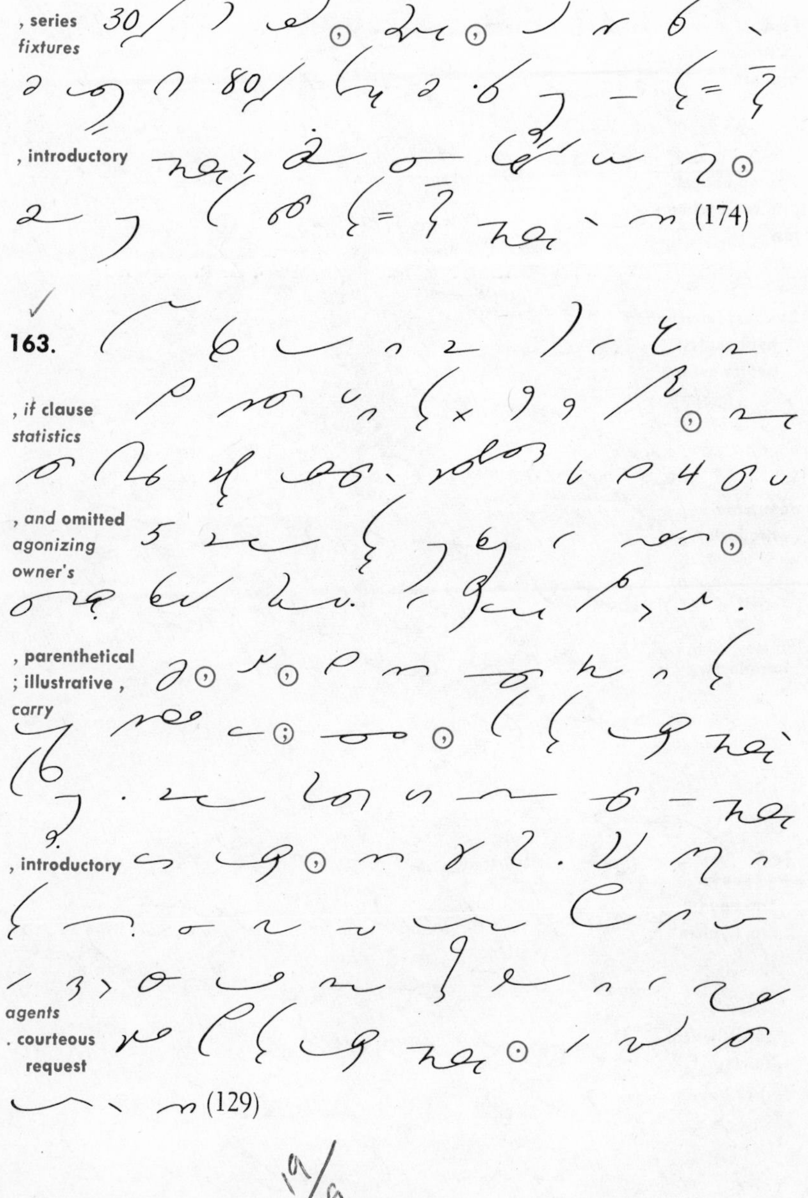
, series
fixtures
, introductory
(174)
163.
, if clause
statistics
, and omitted
agonizing
owner's
, parenthetical
; illustrative ,
carry
, introductory
agents
. courteous
request
(129)

164.

, introductory
against

, parenthetical
; no conjunction
loss

business-interruption
hyphenated
before noun

determine
, introductory

, introductory

(118)

165.

well known
no noun,
no hyphen

, series
, parenthetical
receiving

known

total

loss

. courteous

request

, introducing

short quote

. inside quote

(154)

Review Tip

Beginning on page 481 you will find complete lists of the word beginnings and endings, phrases, and brief forms of Gregg Shorthand.

You are already familiar with the words and phrases in those lists; but to be sure that they do not become hazy in your mind, you should review them frequently.

Consequently, plan to set aside a few minutes each day to read from those lists. Time spent on those lists will be time well spent.

After you have read all the lists from left to right, read them again from right to left.

At this stage of your shorthand course, you should be able to read the lists very rapidly.

Lesson 24

166. Shorthand Spelling Drill. It is helpful to practice shorthand outlines in related groups. It is also helpful to practice spelling words in related groups. It is doubly helpful to practice groups of words from which you will benefit both in longhand spelling and in shorthand skill.

To help you fix in your mind the correct longhand spelling of these groups in the Shorthand Spelling Drills, spell each word aloud as you read it from the shorthand.

Words Ending in L: *When the last syllable of a word ending in* L, *preceded by a single vowel, is accented, the* L *is doubled in forming derivatives in* -ING *and* -ED.

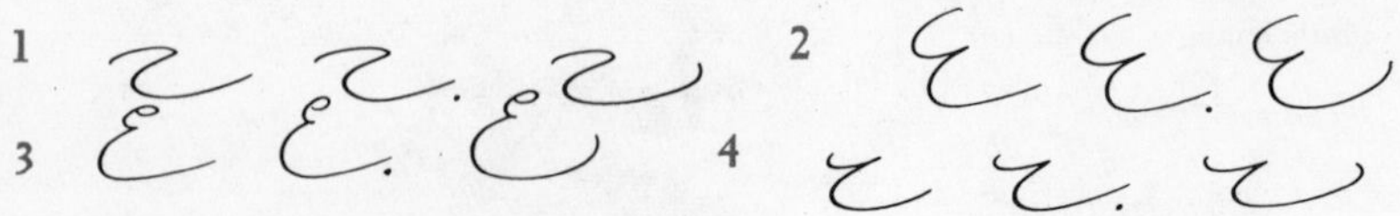

1. **Compel, compelling, compelled.**
2. **Propel, propelling, propelled.**
3. **Expel, expelling, expelled.**
4. **Repel, repelling, repelled.**

When the last syllable is not accented, the L *is not doubled.*

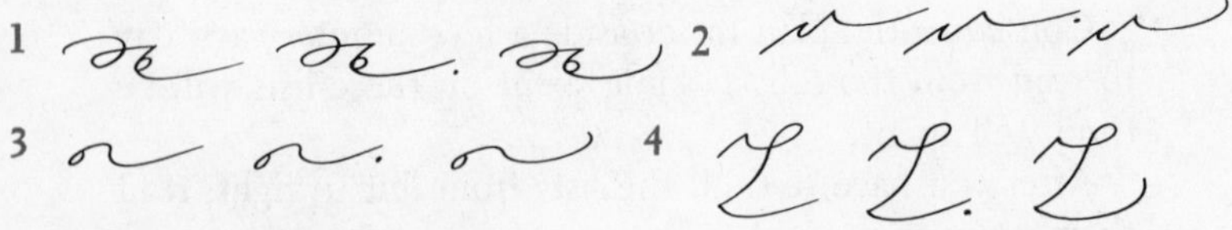

1. **Cancel, canceling, canceled.**
2. **Total, totaling, totaled.**
3. **Equal, equaling, equaled.**
4. **Travel, traveling, traveled.**

Reading and Writing Practice

167. Transcription Word Study

hurricane A severe storm in which there are winds up to 100 miles an hour, usually accompanied by rain, thunder, and lightning.

modest circumstances Not poor, not rich, but having enough to get along.

claim adjuster One who determines the amount payable under a policy for loss resulting from fire or some other cause.

168.

Transcribe:
January 10
, apposition

whether
decision

, as clause
thousands
country

; because of comma
policies

(122)

169.

, and omitted
accident

, introductory
hospital

, when clause

, parenthetical
carry

part-time
hyphenated
before noun

; no conjunction

(121)

170.

hurricane
, as clause
, apposition

, nonrestrictive
: enumeration

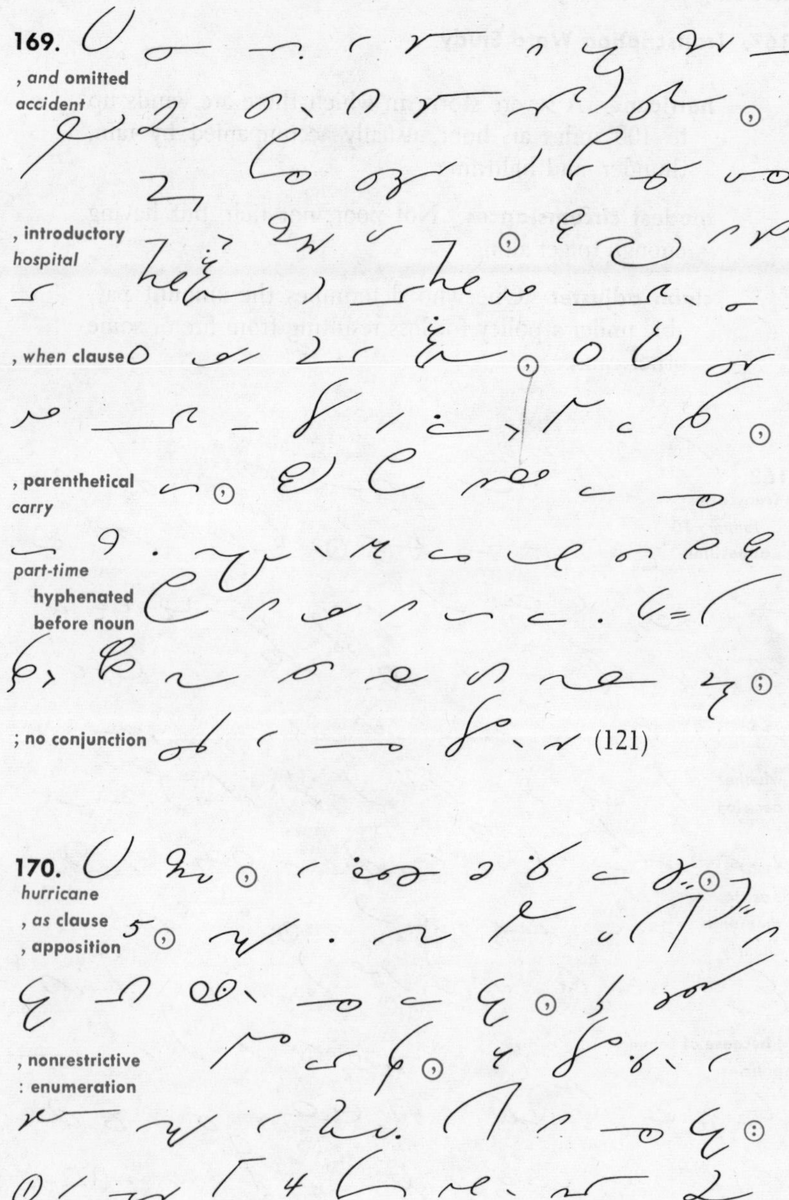

local
, conjunction

rereading
, introductory

(150)

171.

compliment
, introducing short quote

handle
? inside quote

adjusters
character

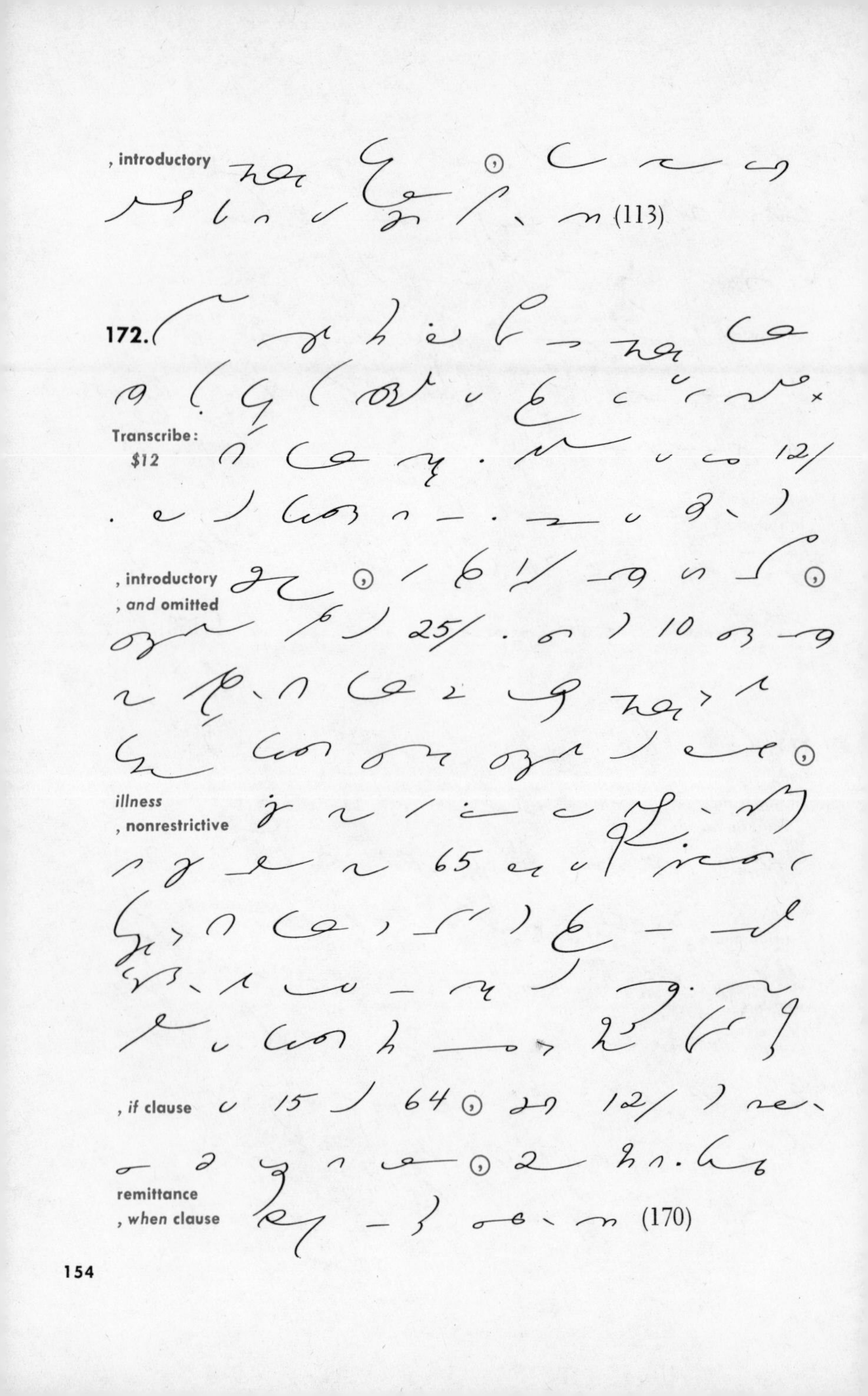

, introductory

(113)

172.

Transcribe:
$12

, introductory
, *and* omitted

illness
, nonrestrictive

, *if* clause

remittance
, *when* clause

(170)

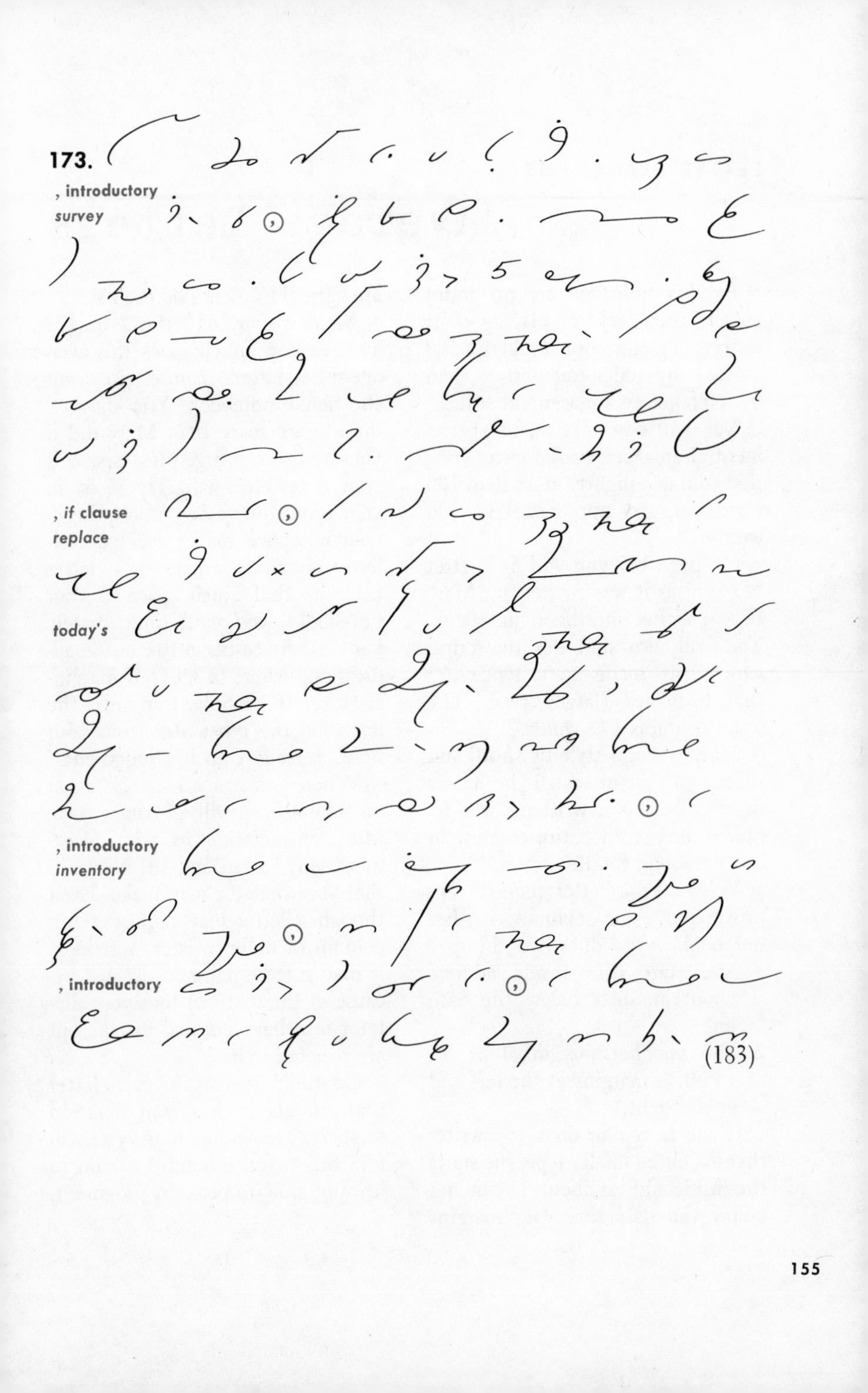

173.

, introductory
survey

, if clause
replace

today's

, introductory
inventory

, introductory

(183)

Average Letters

By this time you are no doubt getting the "feel" of placing short letters (up to approximately 100 words) by judgment rather than by reference to a placement scale.

You will now take up the placement of an average-sized letter (one that contains slightly more than 100 words, up to approximately 200 words).

On page 157 you will find letter No. 172 as it was written by Mary Brown in her shorthand notebook. You will also find her transcript, which was made on a typewriter that had pica (large) type. The letter contains 174 words.

Mary writes a style of shorthand similar to that in which the letters in this book are written. She required almost an entire column in her notebook for this letter.

Whenever a letter requires approximately one column in her notebook, Mary does two things:

1. She starts the inside address about an inch below the date line.
2. She sets her margin stops for 1½-inch margins at the left and at the right.

If she is typing on a typewriter that has elite (small) type, she starts the inside address about 1½ inches below the date line. Her margins are again 1½ inches on each side.

Make a copy of letter No. 172 and see how much space this average-sized letter requires in your shorthand notebook. You may require more space than Mary did if your notes are large; less space if your notes are small. Try to fix in your mind the space you require in your notebook for an average-sized letter so that, whenever a letter takes up that much space in your notebook, you will immediately know where to begin the inside address and where to set your marginal stops. If possible, transcribe the letter on the typewriter from your notes, setting it up by "judgment."

When you are taking dictation on the job, you will, of course, take into consideration in your placement any insertions or deletions that your dictator may make. Even though a letter may require a full column or more in your notebook, it may still be a "short letter" because of the material that your dictator may have decided to take out after dictating it.

Continue to classify each letter that you take in class from dictation as short, average, or long; you will find this practice helpful to you in learning how to place by judgment.

The Gorman Corporation

SERVICE BASED ON RESEARCH

Executive Offices . . . . 2 East 34th Street, NEW YORK 16, N. Y.

June 18, 195-

Mr. James E. Gates
313 Grand River Avenue
Detroit 8, Michigan

Dear Mr. Gates:

Have you heard abou[illegible]
is being purchased by th[illegible]
country? This plan cost[illegible]
and protects you in a nu[illegible]
pays $1,000 in case of y[illegible]
and $25 a week for ten we[illegible]

This plan is not li[illegible]
protection against accid[illegible]
are at home or traveling[illegible]
until you are sixty-five [illegible]
benefits.

This plan is intend[illegible]
cumstances. It is low i[illegible]
of protection for your m[illegible]

If you are between [illegible]
five, send us $12 for one [illegible]
remittance, we will issue [illegible]
force immediately.

ABH/id

Lesson 25

174. Brief Forms and Derivatives. By this time, you should have good command of the brief forms and their derivatives. Consequently, you should be able to read the brief-form drill in this and following lessons in a half minute or less.

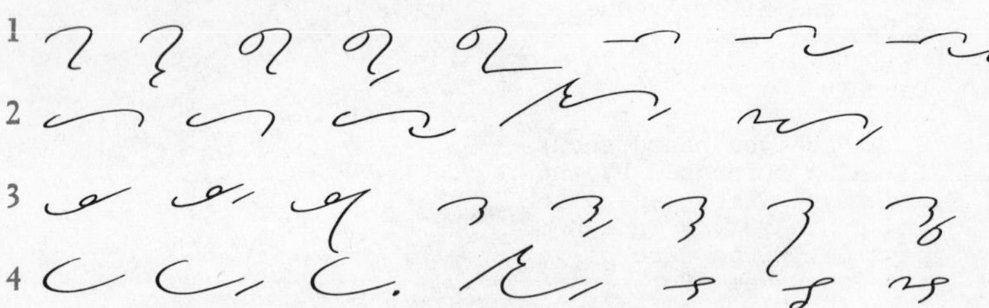

1. Company-keep, companies-keeps, accompany, accompanied, accompaniment; enclose, enclosure, enclosures.
2. Organize, organization, organizer, disorganized, unorganized.
3. Return, returned, returnable; consider-consideration, considered, considers-considerations, considerable, considerate.
4. Please, pleased, pleasing, displeased; necessary, necessarily, unnecessary.

Reading and Writing Practice

175. Transcription Word Study

typical Conforming to type; having the characteristics possessed by a group.

padded Filled out or stuffed with needless matter.

176.
, if clause
Transcribe:
$1,200

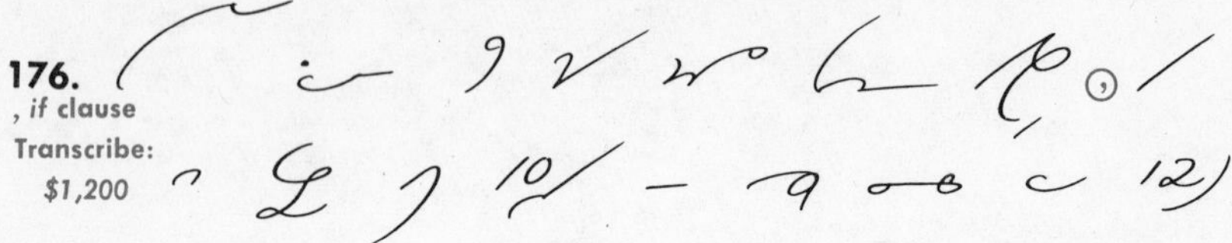

company's
, introductory

permanently
: enumeration

, if clause
requirements

(150)

177.
, as clause
premium

; because of comma
, series
telephone

, if clause
automatically
lapse

, parenthetical

worth-while
hyphenated before noun
; no conjunction
, *if* clause

(127)

178.

helpful
, apposition
, introductory

low-cost
hyphenated before noun
, introductory

recommendations
, *when* clause

, introductory
low cost
no noun, no hyphen

, nonrestrictive
typical

, *if clause*
, *and omitted*
client

(167)

179.

: **introducing long quote**
steals

, **conjunction**
gambling

. **inside quote**
, **introductory**

10/

90/

discussed
, *if clause*

flaws

, *if clause*
. **courteous request**

(158)

Writing

When Mary Brown was studying shorthand in school, she took dictation under ideal conditions. She had her own comfortable desk and chair, with plenty of room and light. That was as it should be, because Mary was learning a skill; and her teacher knew that she would progress most rapidly if she practiced under ideal conditions.

Mary realized, however, that when she took dictation on the job, the conditions under which she would have to write might not be ideal. During the first few months, Mary counted six different positions in which she had to take dictation. Here they are:

1. The most frequent position, and a fairly comfortable one for Mary, is writing with her notebook on the ledge of Mr. Baker's desk.

2. Once in a while, however, Mr. Baker has papers or books on the ledge, and she does not wish to disturb them. On such occasions, Mary writes with her notebook on her knee.

3. On a few occasions, Mary can take dictation in real comfort. That is when she can place a chair on the side of the desk facing Mr. Baker and write on the desk itself. This does not happen often, however, because Mr. Baker's desk is usually too full of papers and other materials.

4. On rare occasions, Mary has to write while standing up or even while walking. There was the oc-

positions

casion, for example, when Mr. Baker had an office full of people and all chairs were occupied. Mr. Baker called Mary in and asked her to take a memorandum on an agreement that had been reached. Of course, no employer would ask his secretary to write in a standing position unless it was an emergency.

5. Every month Mary has the job of taking minutes of the meeting of the board of directors. That is the most difficult shorthand assignment of her job; but, as a compensating factor, she is able to write under the most comfortable conditions, sitting at the head of the table.

6. Finally, Mary often takes dictation over the telephone. Sometimes she takes an order or makes a few simple notes. On occasion, she takes entire letters or memoranda. For this purpose, she always has handy near the telephone a pencil and a notebook for which she reaches almost automatically when she answers the phone.

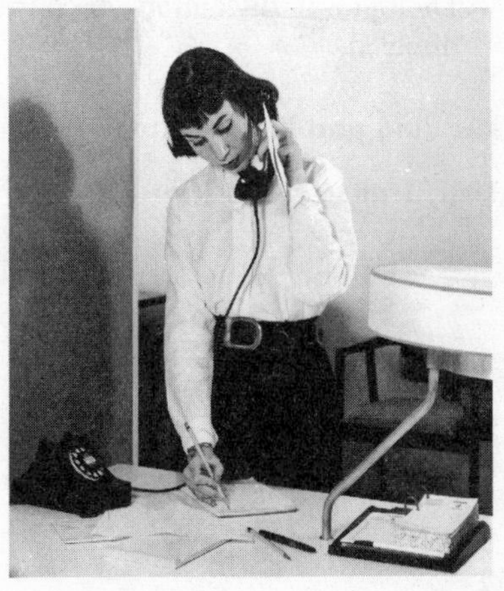

Lesson 26

180. Shorthand Language Study

Mis-: Wrong. MISINFORMED, *gave the wrong information.*

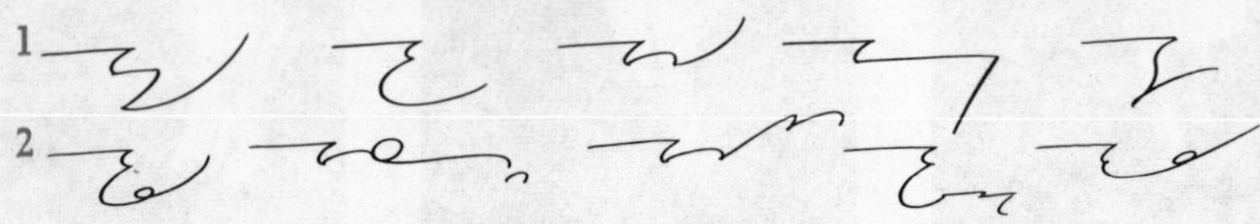

1. **Misinformed, misspell, miscount, mismanage, misfortune.**
2. **Misprint, miscalculate, misconduct, mispronounce, mislead.**

Dis-: *The opposite or absence of.* DISAPPROVAL, *opposite or absence of approval.*

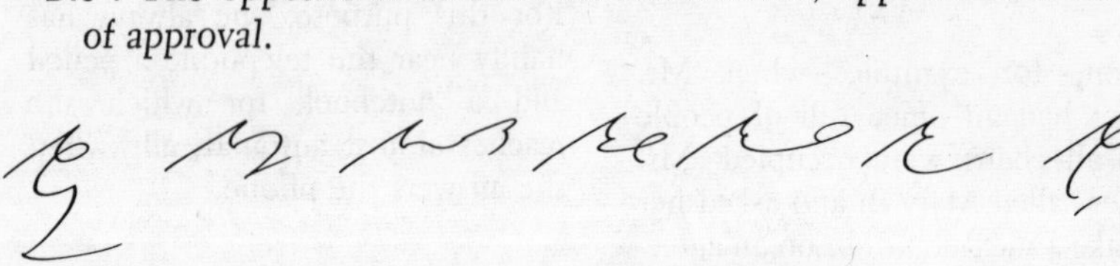

Disapproval, discomfort, discourteous, dishonest, dislike, displease, disabled.

Reading and Writing Practice

181. Transcription Word Study

bail bond A document that releases a person from prison and is security for his appearance at his trial.

expiration End.

182.

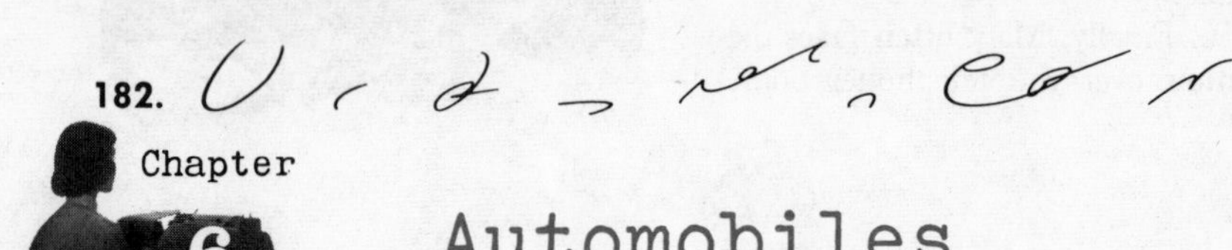

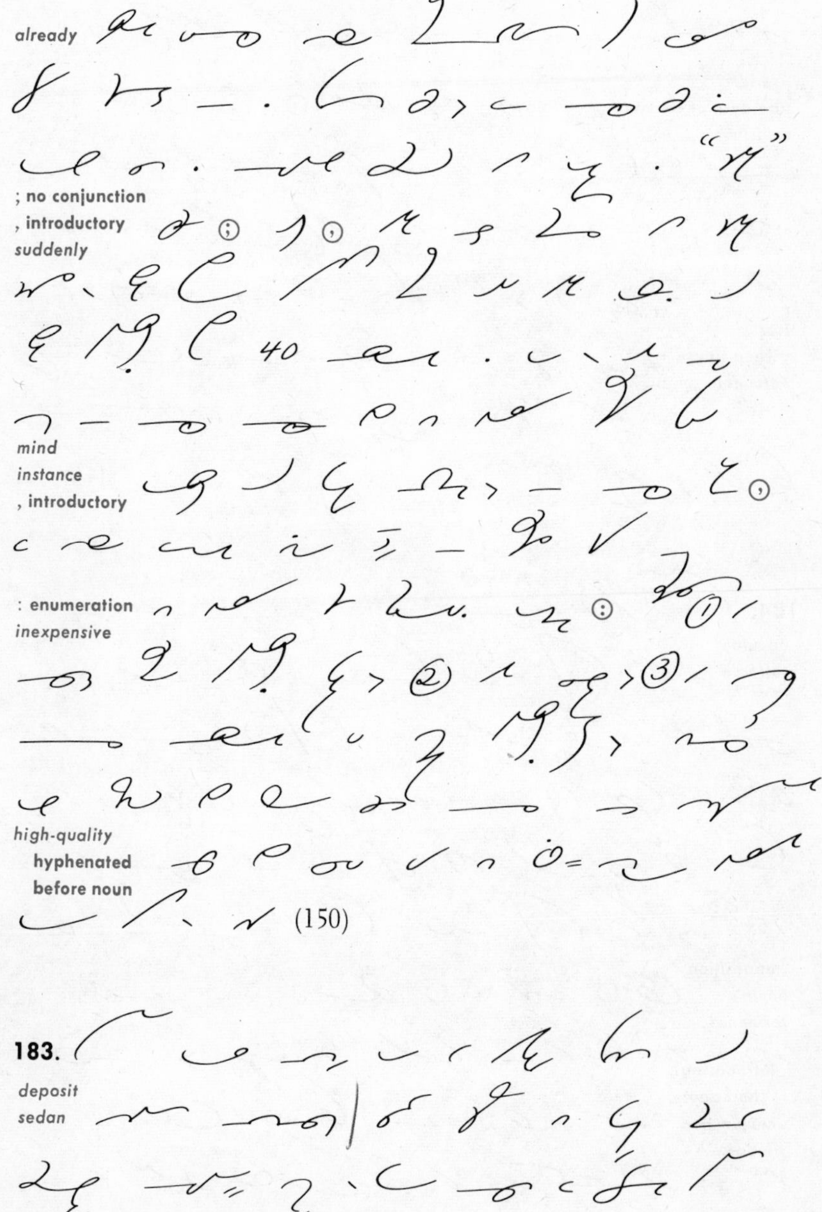
already
; no conjunction
, introductory
suddenly
mind
instance
, introductory
: enumeration
inexpensive
high-quality
hyphenated
before noun
(150)

183.

deposit
sedan

, series
; because of comma
collision

loss
, when clause
Terminal

(118)

184.

damage
suffered

, apposition
Smith's
residence

, introducing
short quote
, conjunction
window

. inside quote

(140)

185.

; illustrative ,

, series

specifically

; no conjunction

, introductory

immediately

operator's

(90)

186.

driver's

license

, if clause

(67)

Lesson 27

187. Accuracy Practice. Follow the practice procedures outlined on page 138.

Group 1		Group 2		Group 3	
I was		say		as	
he was		see		if	

Practice Drill

1

2

3

1. I was glad to take care of the matter. He was glad to take care of the matter.
2. Can you say whether he made all the changes? Can you see whether he made all the changes?
3. As you are attending the meeting, I shall not go. If you are attending the meeting, I shall not go.

Reading and Writing Practice

188. Transcription Word Study

automobile accessories Such items as radios, heaters, cigarette lighters, and white-wall tires.

durability Power or ability to last or endure.

minor Of less importance. (Do not confuse *minor* with *miner*, which means "one who digs in a mine.")

189.

accessories

, introductory

: enumeration

, conjunction

conveniently

, if clause

, introductory

delighted

(124)

190.

, nonrestrictive
bread
knocked

fully loaded
no hyphen
after *ly*
principal
scratching
, conjunction

, introductory
garage

Transcribe:
$80

, and omitted
unusual
tribute

(148)

191.
high-grade
hyphenated
before noun

, introductory
level
appears

absorbed
minor

10

effective
, parenthetical
; illustrative ,

, introductory
honored

(155)

192.
, apposition
, introducing short quote
Jackson's
. inside quote

, nonrestrictive
materials

, when clause
yours
, parenthetical

; because of comma
, parenthetical
foresee

(132)

193.

inquiry
referred

, as clause
, and omitted
economical

inasmuch as
freight
, series

; no conjunction

, when clause

(106)

Lesson 28

194. Office-Style Dictation. Occasionally, a businessman will dictate a word or a phrase and, on reflection, decide to substitute another word or phrase. He may say:

> Next month our school will be sending into the business world more than – make that *approximately* 300 girls.

In your notebook you would simply place a heavy downward line through the phrase *more than* and write *approximately* next to the outline you crossed out.

Sometimes the dictator may change his mind about a word or a phrase after completing a sentence. He may say:

> Next month our school will be sending into the business world more than 300 girls – make that *approximately*.

You must be on the alert to notice that it is the phrase *more than* that is to be changed to *approximately*. You then place a line through the phrase *more than* and above it write the word *approximately*.

Illustration of Office-Style Dictation

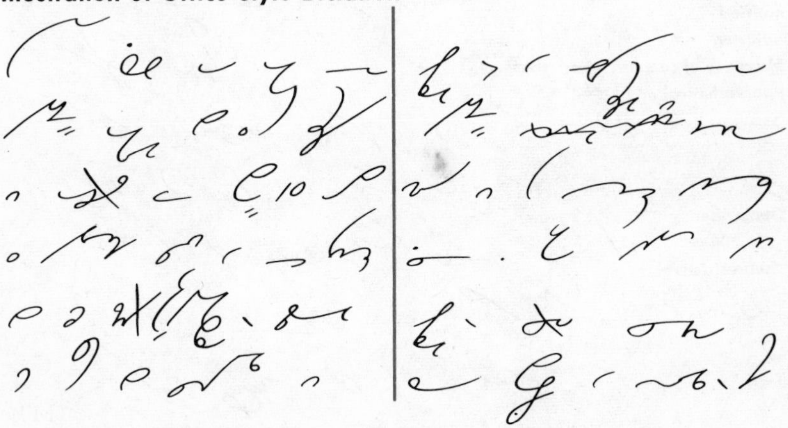

Reading and Writing Practice

195. Transcription Word Study

tubeless tires Tires in which the air is held by the casing of the tire rather than in an inner tube.

project A planned undertaking.

counselors Advisers.

196.

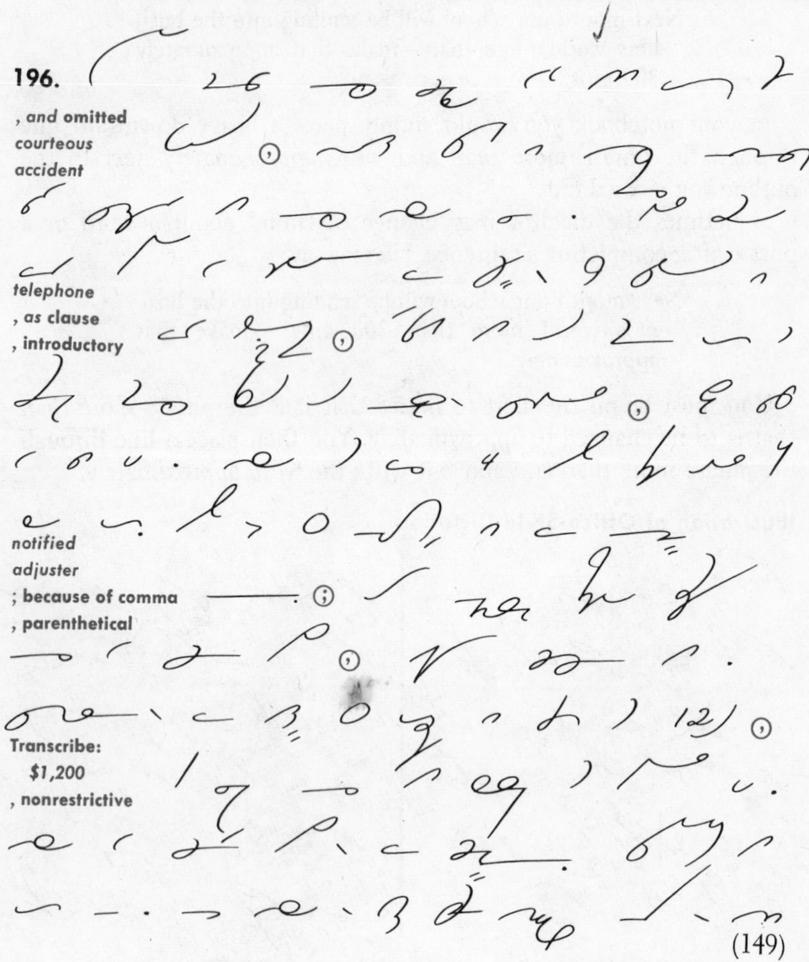

197.

, apposition
equipped

, nonrestrictive
high-quality
hyphenated
before noun

, introductory
surprised

, parenthetical
worn

, introductory
; because of comma
similar

, introductory
past
sometimes

, introductory

(150)

198.
, as clause
vacant
occupies

enough
: enumeration

proceed
; no conjunction
, introductory

(126)

199.

year's
dealers'

, conjunction

; illustrative ,
loan

, introducing short quote

. inside quote

(111)

200.

, introductory

, parenthetical

counselors

, series

application

envelope

, parenthetical

Transcribe:

$15

(133)

Lesson 29

201. Shorthand Spelling Drill. Remember, you will derive the greatest benefit from these drills if you spell each word aloud as you read it from the shorthand.

Words Ending in R: *When the last syllable of a word ending in* R, *preceded by a single vowel, is accented, the* R *is doubled in forming derivatives in* -ING *and* -ED.

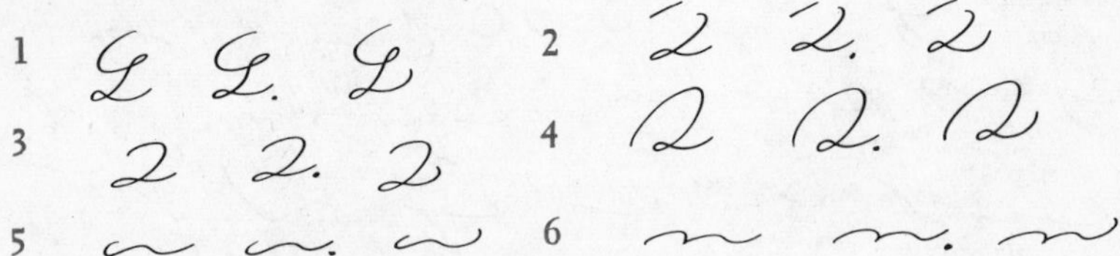

1. Prefer, preferring, preferred.
2. Transfer, transferring, transferred.
3. Confer, conferring, conferred.
4. Defer, deferring, deferred.
5. Occur, occurring, occurred.
6. Concur, concurring, concurred.

When the last syllable is not accented, the R *is not doubled in forming derivatives in* -ING *and* -ED.

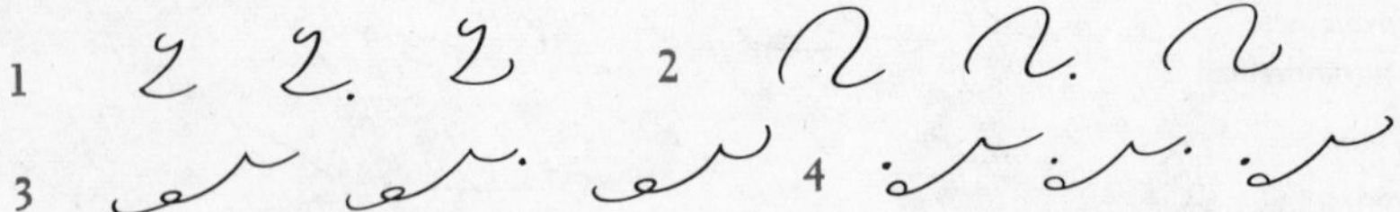

1. Offer, offering, offered.
2. Differ, differing, differed.
3. Render, rendering, rendered.
4. Hinder, hindering, hindered.

Reading and Writing Practice

202. Transcription Word Study

squad car A police automobile especially equipped with a short-wave radiotelephone that is connected with headquarters.

stable Firmly established.

patrons Customers.

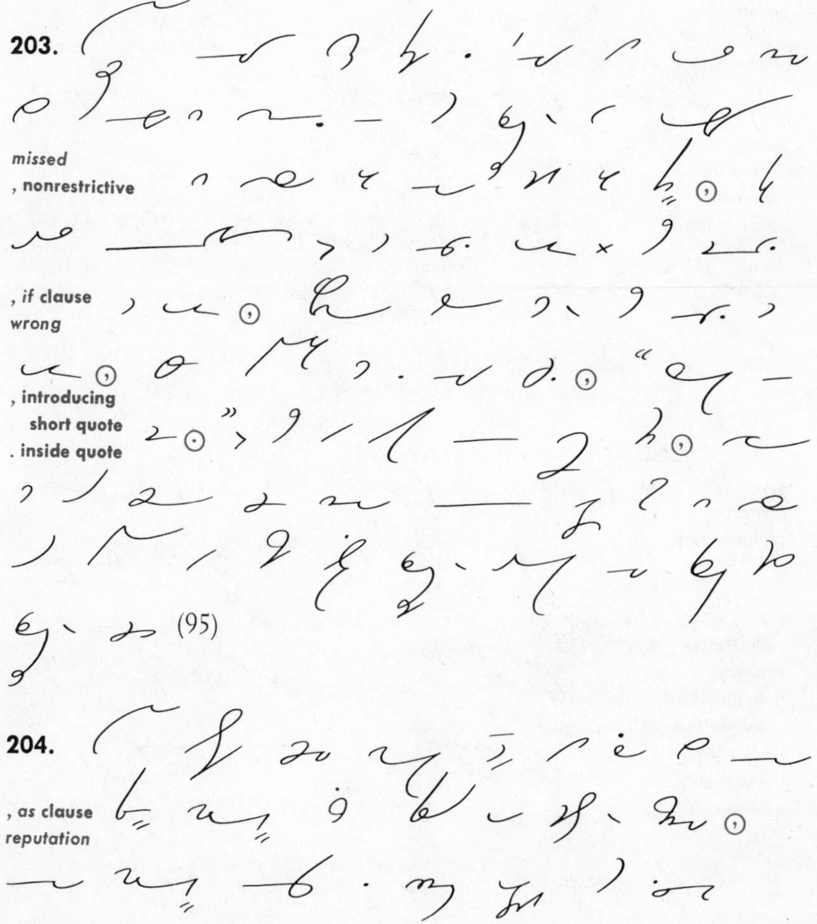

, introductory

Walsh's
county
undertaking

up to date
no noun,
no hyphen

(137)

205.
operator
, introductory

; illustrative ,
two-way
hyphenated
before noun

, introductory
vehicles
chief

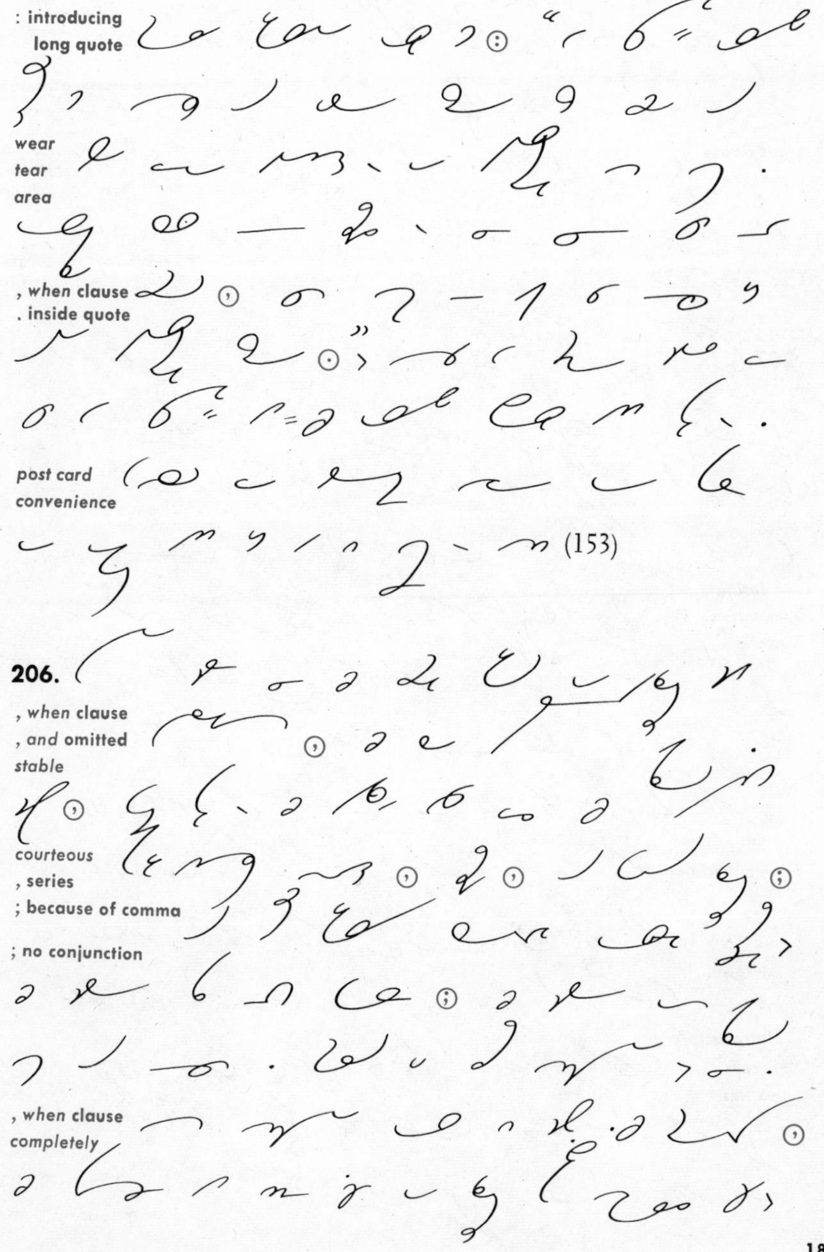
: introducing long quote
wear
tear
area
, when clause
. inside quote
post card
convenience
(153)
206.
, when clause
, and omitted
stable
courteous
, series
; because of comma
; no conjunction
, when clause
completely

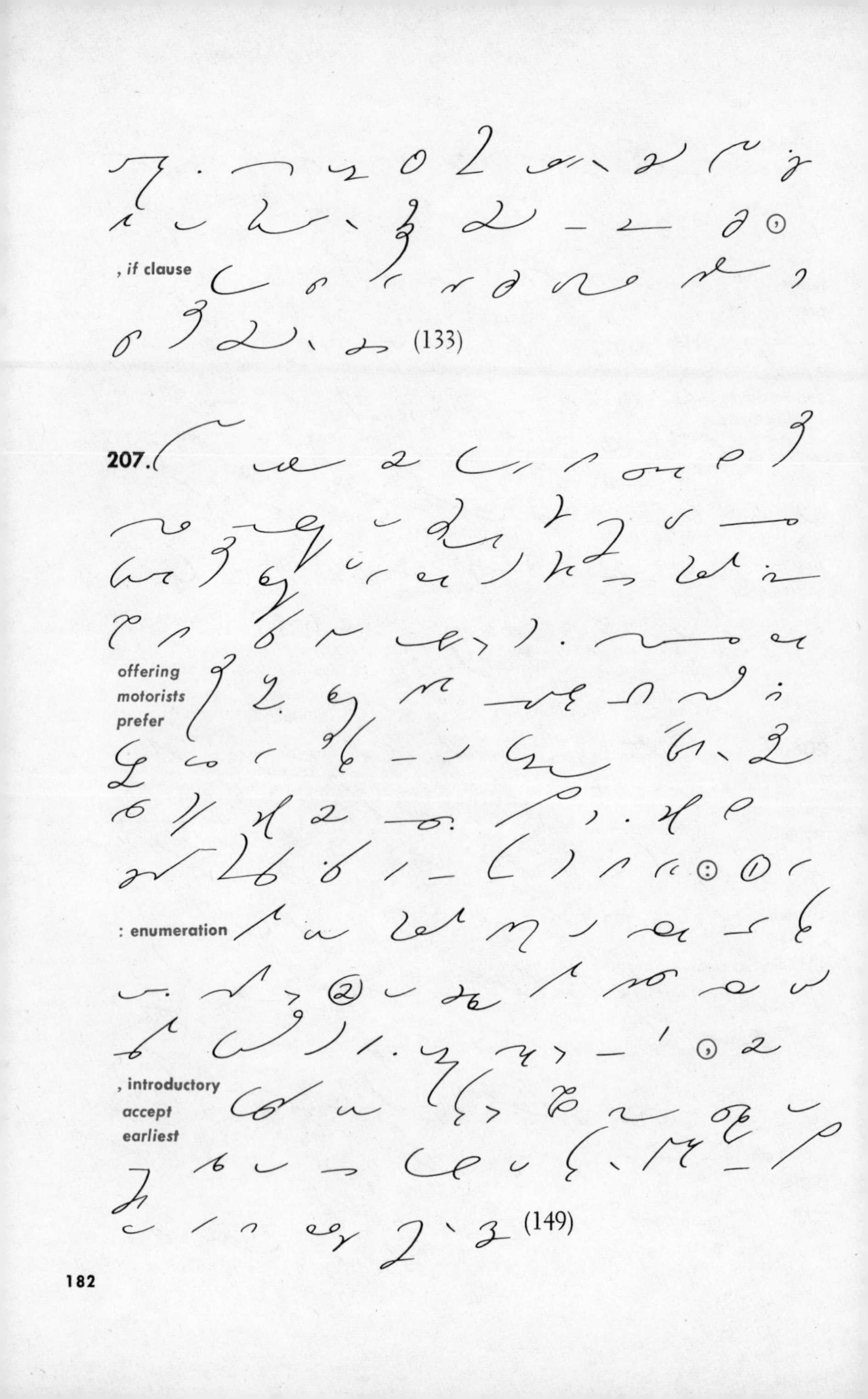

, if clause

(133)

207.

offering motorists prefer

: enumeration

, introductory accept earliest

(149)

Lesson 30

208. Brief Forms and Derivatives

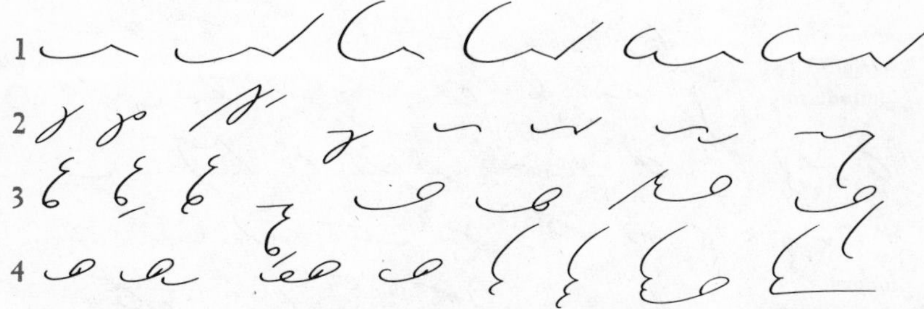

1. Long, longed, belong, belonged, prolong, prolonged.
2. Satisfy-satisfactory, satisfactorily, dissatisfied, unsatisfactory; work, worked, worker, unworkable.
3. Experience, experienced, experiences, inexperienced; like, likely, dislike, likable.
4. Write-right, writer, rewrite, all right; business, businesses, businesslike, businessmen.

Reading and Writing Practice

209. Transcription Word Study

fatigue Weariness from labor; tiredness.

maintenance costs The amount necessary for upkeep; in the case of a car or truck, such items as gas, oil, and repairs.

sturdy Strong.

210.

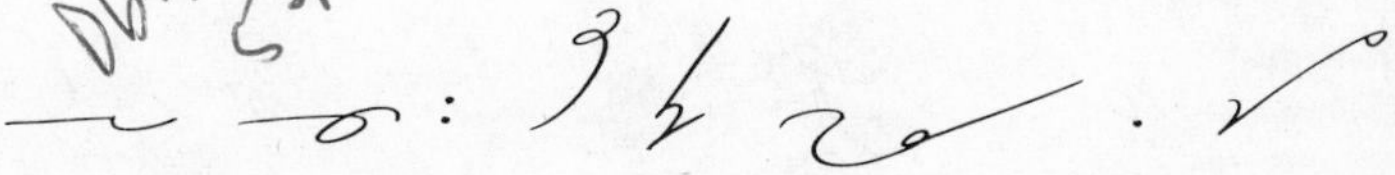

effect
installation
foam

: enumeration
penny

formerly
, introductory

fatigue
, nonrestrictive

, introductory
recommend

(134)

211.

frequency
accidents

, parenthetical
; because of comma
effort

Transcribe:
40 cents

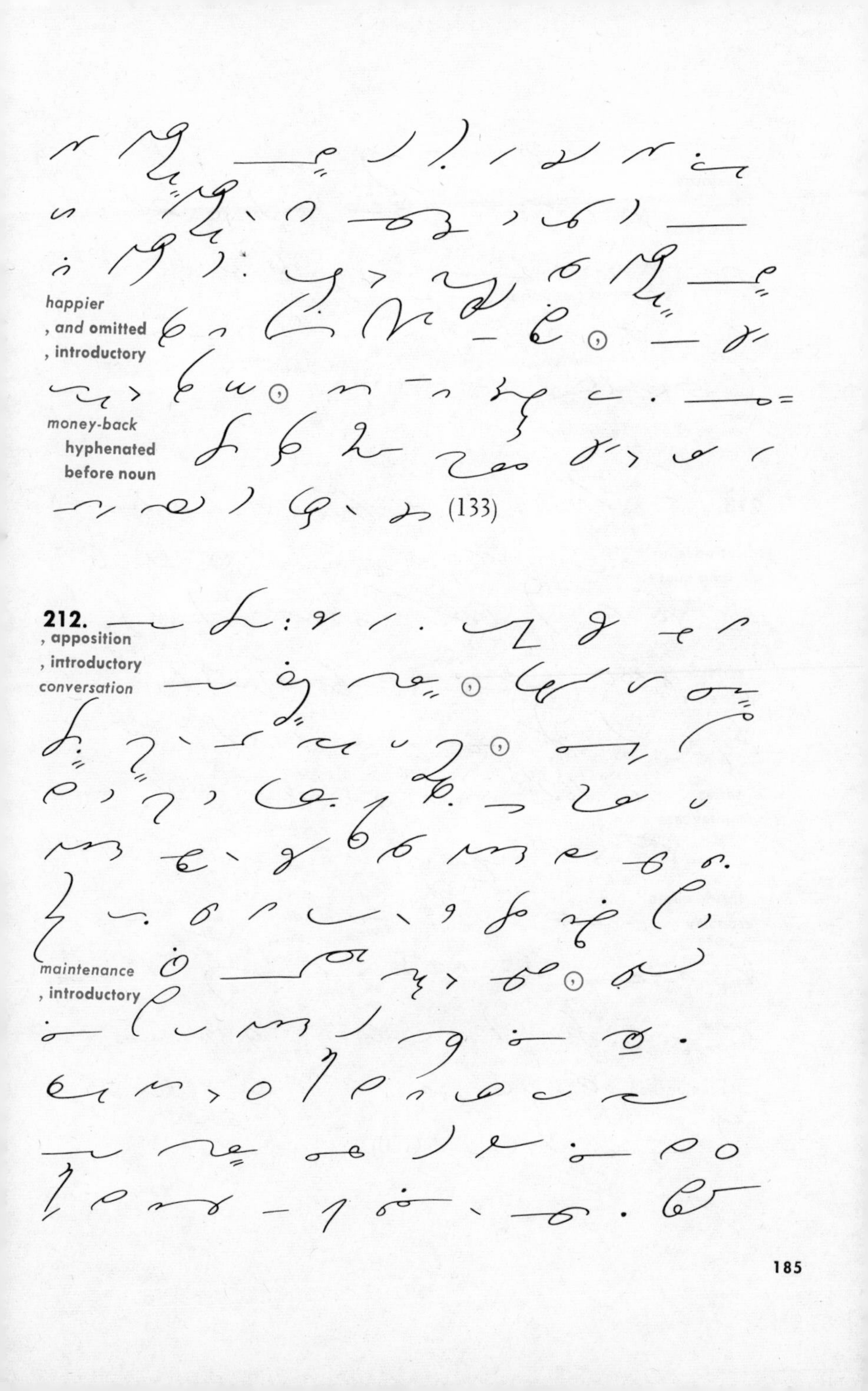

happier
, and omitted
, introductory

money-back
hyphenated
before noun

(133)

212.
, apposition
, introductory
conversation

maintenance
, introductory

, *if clause*
piece
commission

(154)

213.

: *introducing long quote*

, *series*
deliveries

8,350 17,339

, *series*
maintenance

162[13] 1.94

. *inside quote*
economy

; *no conjunction*

(120)

214.

vehicles
company's

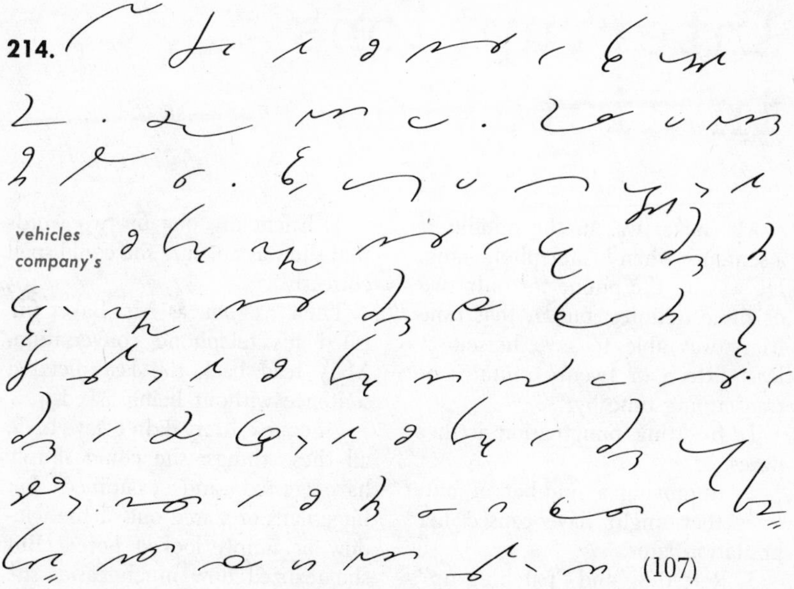

(107)

215.

, introductory
dependent
transportation
, conjunction
, introductory

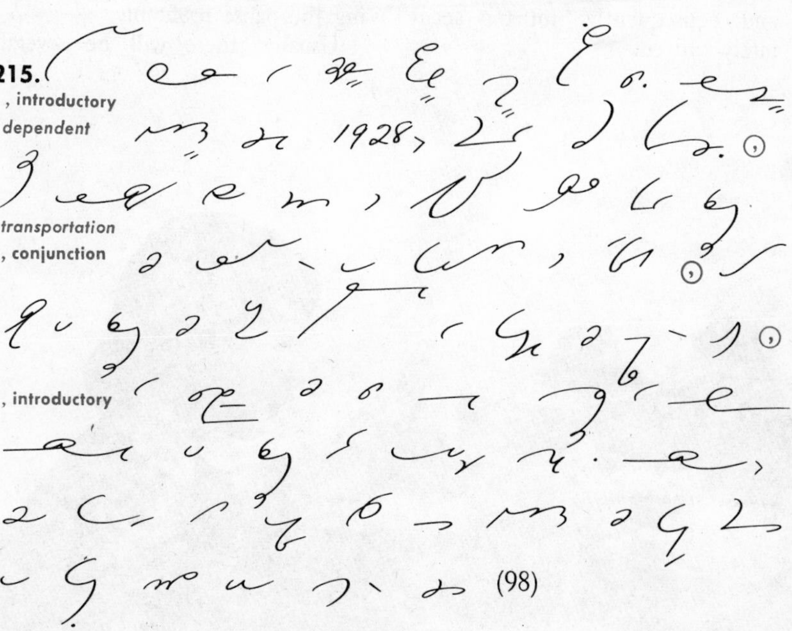

(98)

Interruptions in dictation

Mr. Baker was in the middle of a sentence when his telephone rang. He was on the phone for only two or three minutes, but in that time Mary was able to save herself at least fifteen or twenty minutes of transcribing time by:

1. Inserting punctuation in her notes.
2. Improving a number of outlines that might have caused her hesitation later.
3. Rereading and "patching up" a sentence that was rapidly dictated and, consequently, not too accurately written.
4. Encircling one or two words that she was not sure she could spell correctly.

Then, as soon as Mr. Baker finished his telephone conversation, Mary read back the last dictated sentence without being asked.

Of course, Mary didn't *have* to do all these things; she could simply have rested and examined her fingernails or stared out of the window or simply looked bored! But she realized how much easier she could make her transcribing by using the pause profitably.

Usually, there will be several

interruptions during a dictating period. For example, the dictator may have a visitor with whom he will chat briefly. He may stop for a few moments to fill his pipe or light a cigarette. He may read previous correspondence relating to the letter that he is about to answer. All these pauses represent priceless opportunities for the stenographer to simplify her task of transcription.

Mary does not always sit at her employer's desk during an interruption. Sometimes she realizes that the interruption will be a lengthy one and that she can use her time better doing her regular work. For example, one day Mr. Baker's phone rang in the middle of dictation; and she heard him say, "Let me tell you about the meeting I attended." She knew that the conversation would take some time; therefore, she returned to her desk and started to transcribe, keeping one eye on her employer. When she saw him hang up the receiver, she immediately returned to his desk and read back the last sentence that he had dictated.

The experienced stenographer soon comes to welcome these breaks in dictation, especially if her employer dictates for long periods of time. Aside from the opportunity they give her to patch up her notes, they also provide a brief respite from shorthand writing.

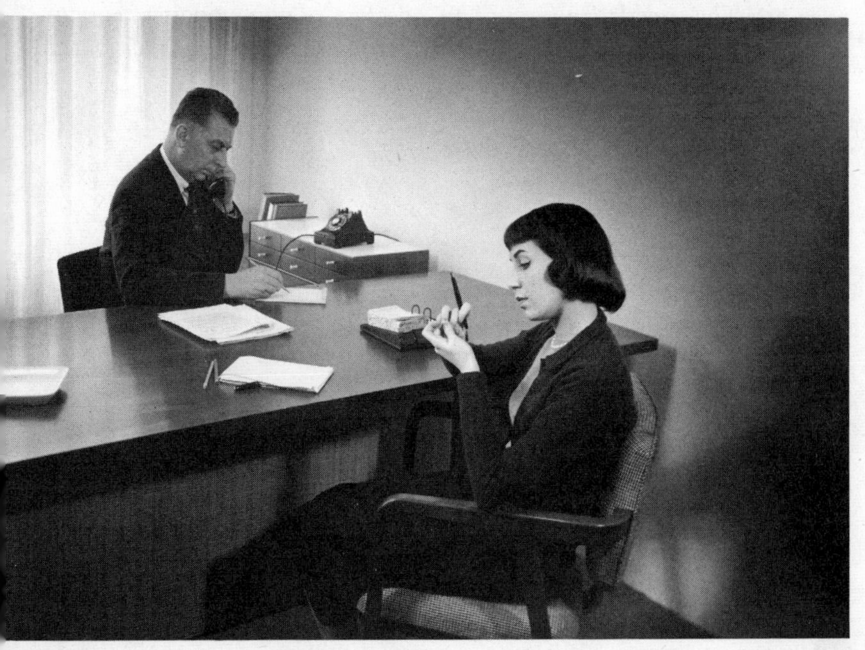

Lesson 31

216. Shorthand Language Study

-ist: *One who is or one who does.* MOTORIST, *one who drives a car.*

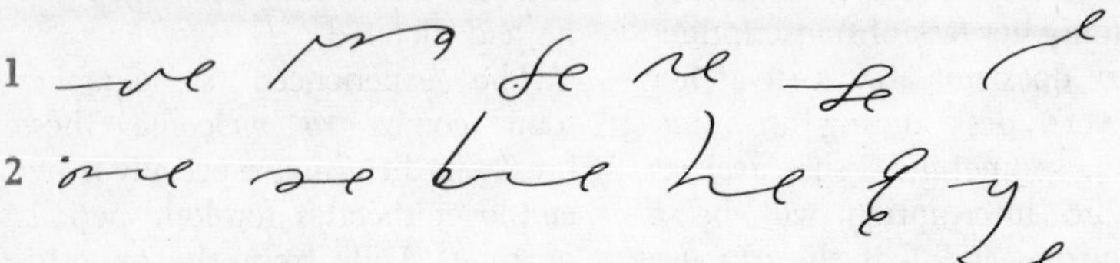

1. Motorist, druggist, pianist, tourist, machinist, dentist.
2. Humorist, chemist, journalist, vocalist, typist, novelist.

-est: *The superlative form of an adjective.* ROUGH, ROUGHER, ROUGHEST. *In shorthand, the ending is joined after consonants, disjoined after vowels.*

1. Roughest, kindest, smoothest, nearest, fastest, slightest, broadest, largest.
2. Happiest, healthiest, earliest, prettiest, heaviest, lowest, newest.

Reading and Writing Practice

217. Transcription Word Study

tentative Not final.

fundamentals Essentials.

outgrowth A by-product.

Chapter 7 Education

218.

, nonrestrictive
well known
no noun,
no hyphen

receive
intensive
tentative

reaction
, introductory

(145)

219.
sales-training
hyphenated
before noun
: enumeration

, and omitted
on-the-job
hyphenated
before noun

performance
, if clause

25

, introductory
essential

hundreds
, conjunction

(147)

220.

offered
probably

spare
, if clause

borrow
demand

; no conjunction
, introductory

, series
, conjunction

worth while
no noun,
no hyphen

(129)

221.
, introductory
; because of comma
, *if* clause

outgrowth

, introductory
practical

; no conjunction
thorough

, introducing short quote
, if clause
. inside quote
coupon

. courteous request

(167)

222.

company's
correspondents
, series

, and omitted

business-letter hyphenated before noun

: enumeration
, series

25%

20%

, if clause

(123)

Lesson 32

223. Accuracy Practice. Follow the practice procedures outlined on page 138.

Group 1	**Group 2**	**Group 3**
written	get	job
regular	gather	position

Practice Drill

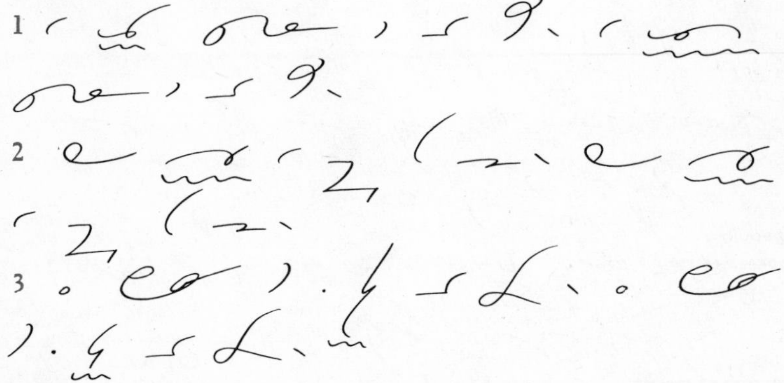

1. The written agreement is in the safe. The regular agreement is in the safe.
2. I will get the information by noon. I will gather the information by noon.
3. He applied for a job in the bank. He applied for a position in the bank.

Reading and Writing Practice

224. Transcription Word Study

clerical Pertaining to general office workers.

resolution A formal expression of opinion adopted by a vote.

reject To refuse.

confidential Given in confidence; private.

225.

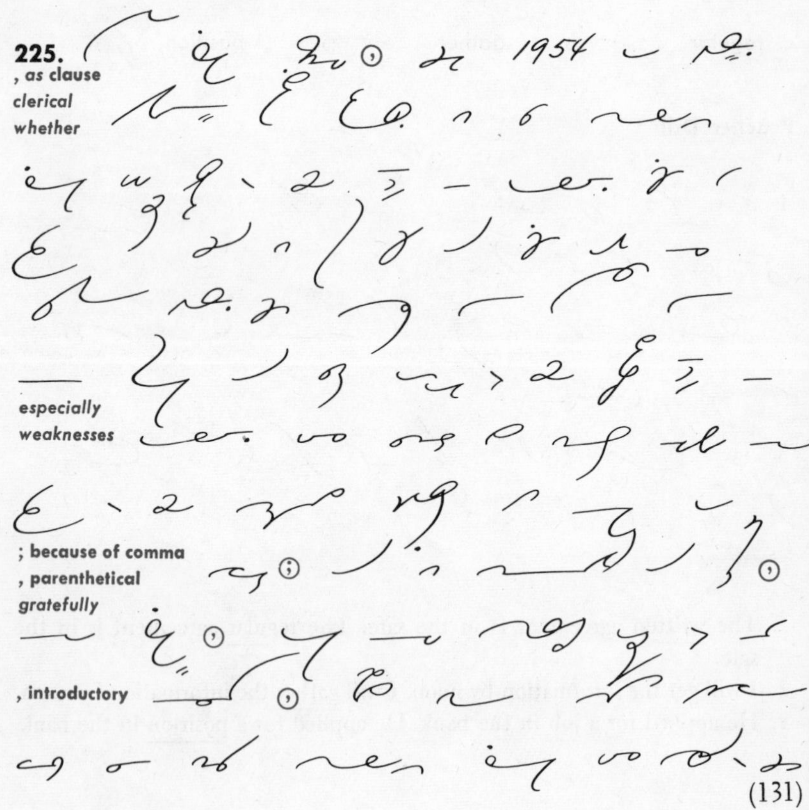

226.

scheduled
, apposition

Committee's
belief

discuss
, introductory

resolution
postponement
enclosed

. courteous
request

(159)

227.

, as clause
announcement

, nonrestrictive

Transcribe:
9 a.m.
$25

co-operation
, conjunction

acceptance
, when clause

(129)

228.

admission
, introducing short quote

. inside quote

enrolled
, parenthetical

, and omitted
confidential

two-year
hyphenated
before noun

(147)

229.

, introductory
, series
annuals

; no conjunction
, introductory
budget

, introductory
fair

(143)

Lesson 33

230. Office-Style Dictation. Sometimes a businessman will use a word or a phrase but will change his mind and substitute another word or phrase. Then, on further reflection, he will decide that the first word or phrase was better. He may say:

> I thought the food served in the hotel was excellent – make that *out of this world;* oh, perhaps we should leave it *excellent.*

When the businessman says, "Make that out of this world," you will strike a heavy downward line through *excellent* and write *out of this world.* Then, when he says, "Oh, perhaps we should leave it *excellent,*" you will write the word *excellent* again.

Do not try to indicate in your notes that the original *excellent* is to be restored. This may take you longer than writing the word again. In addition, it may lead to confusion when you come to transcribe.

Illustration of Office-Style Dictation

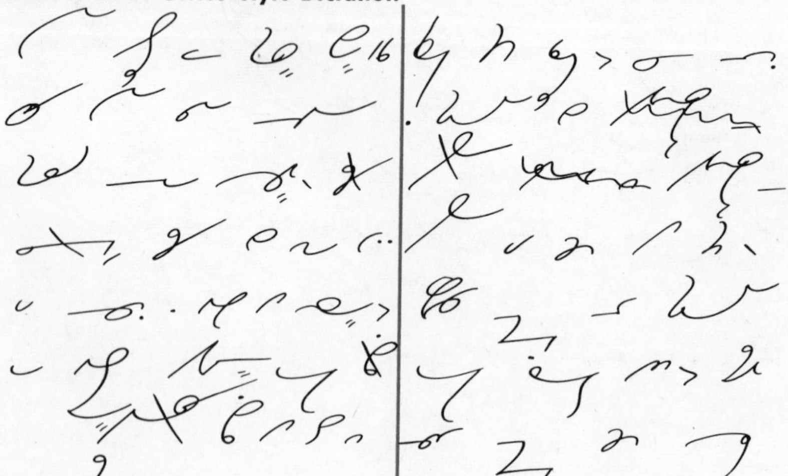

Reading and Writing Practice

231. Transcription Word Study

restrict To limit.

nonresident One who does not live in a particular place.

232.

, apposition

, as clause

recommended

replacement

, if clause

(103)

233.

, apposition

principal

specifically

; illustrative ,

, introductory

, parenthetical
whether

, parenthetical
; because of comma

1956

, and omitted
up-to-the-minute
hyphenated
before noun
Hoffman's

(147)

234. **Transcribe:**
April 16
referred

16

, nonrestrictive
worth while
no noun,
no hyphen

, *if* clause
suitable

(111)

235.

, *as* clause
, introductory

father
, parenthetical

, introducing short quote
? inside quote

four-year hyphenated before noun
, parenthetical

: enumeration
; no conjunction
children's

(137)

236.

son's
admission

nonresident
, parenthetical

: introducing
long quote

entrance
. inside quote

, if clause
proper

(137)

237.

, as clause
tuition

, if clause
immediately

(69)

Lesson 34

238. Shorthand Spelling Drill

Over- and Under-: *The words* OVER *and* UNDER *are joined without a hyphen at the beginning of words.*

Over-

1. Overcome, oversight, overlook, overhead, overconfident, overflow.
2. Overrule, oversee, overwork, overtake, overcoat, overstock, overdraft.

Under-

1. Undertake, underscore, underneath, undergraduate, underbid, undersigned, underwater.
2. Underwent, underdone, undergo, underline, undersell, understand, undersized.

Reading and Writing Practice

239. Transcription Word Study

stimulating Exciting.

testimonial A statement vouching for the quality or character of a thing, person, or action.

indispensable Essential, necessary.

240.

preliminary announcement

; no conjunction

, introductory

question-and-answer

hyphenated before noun

, *if* clause

enrolling

, apposition

(147)

241.

offered

; because of comma

, apposition

, introductory qualifications

, and omitted

well-paying hyphenated before noun

testimonial

, if clause

(161)

242.

approaching

assemble

eighth-grade hyphenated before noun

, apposition

, conjunction

assembly

, parenthetical

, introductory

(138)

243.

, apposition

: introducing long quote

, when clause

instrument

. inside quote

, nonrestrictive

world-famous

hyphenated before noun

child's
, if clause

(130)

244.

, apposition
. inside quote
, when clause
, worth while
no noun,
no hyphen

, if clause
overwhelmingly

: enumeration
; no conjunction
indispensable

(157)

Lesson 35

245. Brief Forms and Derivatives

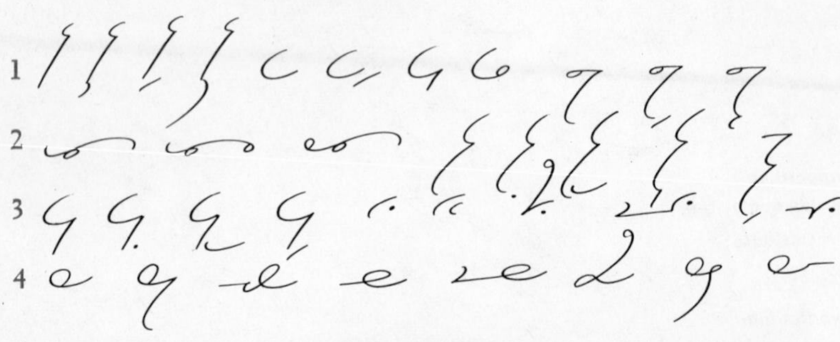

1. Subject, subjects, subjected, subjective; presence–present, presented, presentation, presently; enable, enabled, enables.
2. Regular, regularly, irregular; publish-public, publishing, publisher, publication, unpublished.
3. Purchase, purchasing, purchaser, purchased; thing-think, things-thinks, everything, something, nothing.
4. Where, whereby, nowhere, anywhere, somewhere, everywhere, wherever, wherein.

Reading and Writing Practice

246. Transcription Word Study

adult education The teaching of grownups.

educator A teacher.

incurred Brought on oneself.

247.

Newark
, apposition

, series
grammar
punctuation

grasp
, if clause

appreciate
aids

choice
, as clause

(137)

248.
, as clause
, and omitted
well-planned
hyphenated
before noun

radio
, series

, conjunction
available
experienced
, parenthetical
; because of comma

(144)

249.

procedure
: enumeration

, introductory
, series

; no conjunction
registrations

(151)

250.

, introducing short quote

. inside quote
noises

, conjunction
, *when* clause

analysis
, introductory

(134)

251.

, nonrestrictive
offered
medical

1950

; illustrative ,
nurses'
doctors'
surgeons'

, series
, introductory

, if clause
attached

; no conjunction
until

(141)

252.
energy
; no conjunction

, introductory
principal

assemblies
bulletins

pictured
ideal
medium

, introductory

(161)

Interrupting the dictator

Early in her stenographic career, Mary Brown had an experience she never forgot.

Mr. Baker was dictating a complicated report and was so absorbed in the subject matter that he did not realize that he was dictating rapidly, much more rapidly than Mary could write. Mary naturally was not getting it all, but she could not get up her courage to stop him. She was afraid that, if she stopped him, it would be a reflection on her ability. That was her first mistake.

When she sat down to transcribe, she tried to reconstruct what Mr. Baker had said. That was her second mistake.

When Mr. Baker read the report, he "blew his top," and Mary dissolved into tears as he stormed:

"In the first place, if I was going too fast for you, why didn't you tell me? I know that I concentrate so hard on what I am dictating that I don't always realize how fast I am going. In the second place, don't ever hand anything to me that doesn't make sense. If you are not sure about something, ask me. Now you will have to do this entire report over. You have wasted my time, your time, and company money as well."

Mary never made those mistakes again. Thereafter, whenever Mr. Baker started to dictate so rapidly that she could not get it, she would say, "I am sorry, Mr. Baker, but could you dictate a little more slowly." Whenever she wasn't sure whether she had taken something down correctly—that is, it didn't sound right—she would say, "May

I read this last sentence to you as I have it?" Whenever Mr. Baker used an expression with which she was unfamiliar and that she thought she might not be able to locate in a reference book, she would say, "That expression is new to me. Would you mind spelling it for me?" Mr. Baker was always glad to oblige.

A businessman realizes that occasionally a stenographer may have trouble with his dictation, especially a beginner. Consequently, he is always glad to do anything that will enable her to turn out a correct transcript the *first time!*

Just one suggestion: Some businessmen like to be interrupted as soon as the stenographer has a question. Others like to complete a sentence or a thought. Perhaps the wisest thing for you to do, as you are about to take your first dictation from your employer, is to ask him his preference.

Lesson 36

253. Shorthand Language Study

Tele-: *Far; usually includes the idea of operating at a distance.* TELEVISION, *vision at a distance;* TELEPHONE, *sound at a distance.*

Television, telecast, telephone, telegram, telescope, teletype.

-port: *Carry.* EXPORT, *means literally to carry out, because* EX- *means out. The business meaning of* EXPORT *is to send abroad in the way of commerce.*

Export, import, transport, deport, passport, purport, report, comport.

Reading and Writing Practice

254. Transcription Word Study

transcontinental Crossing from the Atlantic to the Pacific.

impartial Not favoring one side more than the other.

advocated Supported.

Chapter 8

Travel and transportation

255.

scheduled
transcontinental
impartial

experienced
traveler
, introductory

; illustrative ,
telephone

, parenthetical
; no conjunction
, introductory

, conjunction
rewarded

self-addressed
, and omitted
envelope

(127)

256.

, apposition
Reconfirmation

burden
travelers

, introductory
advocated
dropping

air-transport hyphenated before noun
, introductory

(127)

257. round-trip hyphenated before noun

; because of comma
, when clause

, nonrestrictive
Kansas City

weeks'
, conjunction

. courteous request

(133)

258.

, introducing short quote

. inside quote

sun-filled hyphenated before noun

, introductory

describes

, introductory

(149)

259.

: enumeration

standpoint
, introductory

despite
leveling
generally

, conjunction
forward
co-operation

(167)

260.

, introductory
Guide

(57)

Lesson 37

261. Accuracy Practice. Follow the practice procedures outlined on page 138.

Group 1		Group 2		Group 3	
theirs		satisfactory		at the	
ours		fit		in the	

Practice Drill

1
2
3

1. These books are theirs. These books are ours.
2. After a month's trial, I find he is not fit for this heavy work. After a month's trial, I find he is not satisfactory for this heavy work.
3. I will meet you at the railroad station. I will meet you in the railroad station.

Reading and Writing Practice

262. Transcription Word Study

tourist cabins Cabins, usually along highways, at which automobile travelers may spend the night. (Also called *motels.*)

lodge A cabin, usually in a forest.

263.

, as clause
some time
whereby

, conjunction

, introductory
, series
expenses

, introductory
personally

; because of comma
facilities

(132)

264.

confirm

, introducing short quote

. inside quote

, *if clause*

occupied

hard-earned hyphenated before noun

(73)

265.

up-to-the-minute hyphenated before noun

tourist

, *when clause*

up to date no noun, no hyphen

(101)

266.

, conjunction
; illustrative ,
everyone's

lodge
, conjunction

, if clause
accommodations

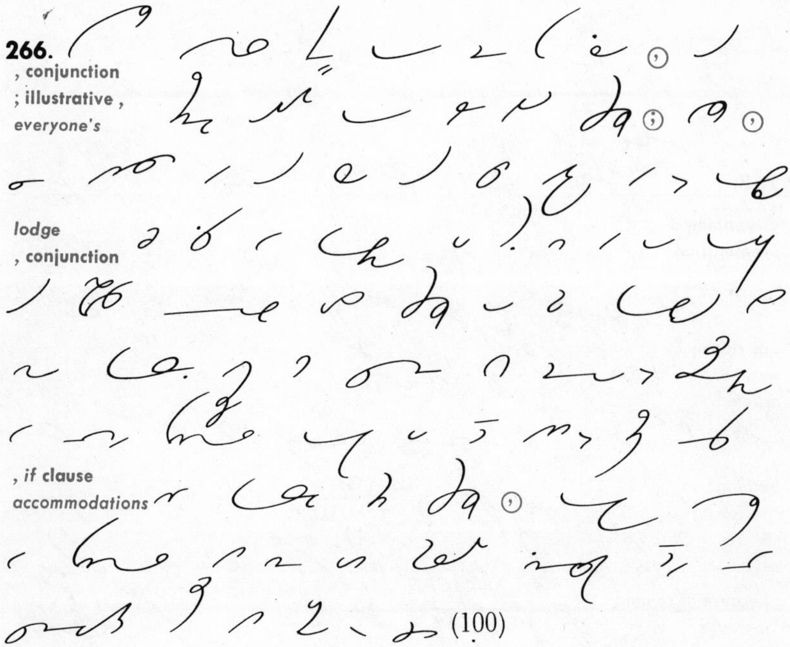

(100)

267.

; because of comma
, parenthetical

traveling
area
, when clause

, apposition
, and omitted
modern

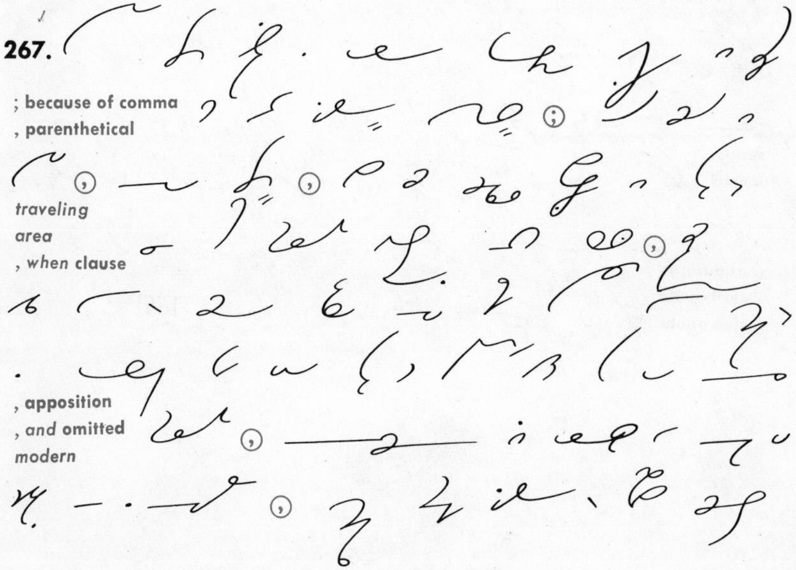

(107)

268.

disappointed

, conjunction

, *as* clause

weather

relief

bathing

, series

; because of comma

, *if* clause

requirements

, series

forward

7/, 15/, 20/.

, introducing short quote

. inside quote

(155)

Lesson 38

269. Office-Style Dictation. A businessman may occasionally decide to transpose words or phrases for emphasis or for some other reason. The easiest way to indicate the transposition of a word or a phrase is to use the regular printer's sign for transposition.

The dictator may say:

> We are conducting an advertising campaign for our cars in both weekly and monthly magazines–make that *monthly and weekly magazines.*

In your shorthand notes, you would indicate this transposition in this way:

You would then be careful, when you transcribe, to type the word *and* after the word *monthly*.

Illustration of Office-Style Dictation

Reading and Writing Practice

270. Transcription Word Study

in transit In the hands of a carrier.

unprejudiced Not having an opinion for or against something before knowing all the facts.

identical Same.

271.

acknowledge
berth

, introductory
, parenthetical
: enumeration

facilities
accommodations

(132)

272.

transit
Denver
referred

occurred
, *if* clause

anywhere
, introductory

(132)

273.

, parenthetical
, *and* omitted

, apposition
. inside quote
Manual

year's
; because of comma
, series

1,190

55

, *when* clause
widely used
no hyphen
after *ly*
, introducing
short quote
. inside quote

30

days'
, introductory

, nonrestrictive
5

(160)

274.

, *if* clause
, series

, *and* omitted
up-to-date
hyphenated
before noun

; illustrative ,

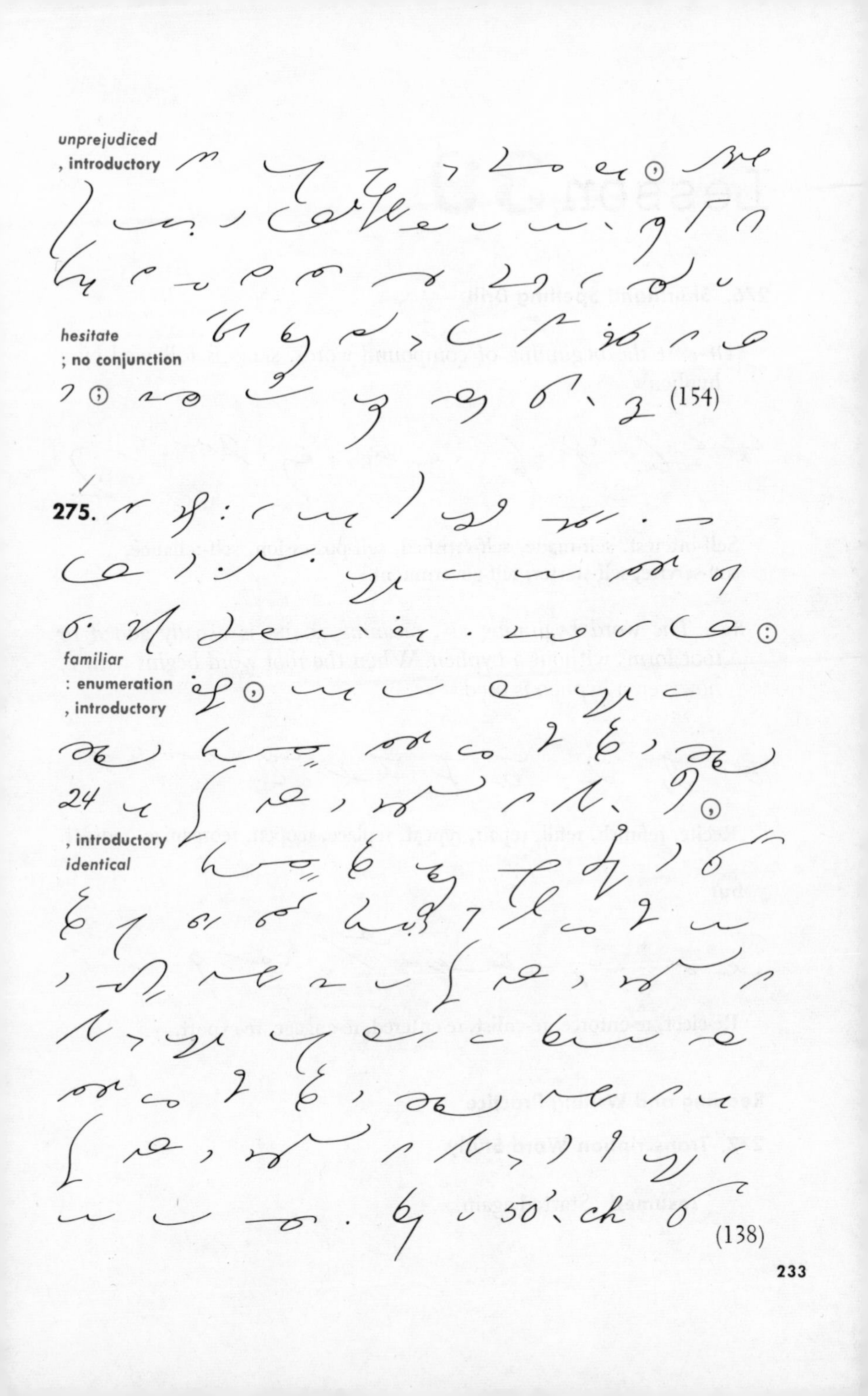

unprejudiced
, introductory

hesitate
; no conjunction

(154)

275.

familiar
: enumeration
, introductory

24

, introductory
identical

50

(138)

Lesson 39

276. Shorthand Spelling Drill

Self-: *At the beginning of compound words,* SELF- *is followed by a hyphen.*

Self-interest, self-made, self-satisfied, self-possession, self-reliance, self-service, self-starter, self-government.

Re-: *The word beginning* RE-, *meaning* AGAIN, *is usually added to root forms without a hyphen. When the root word begins with* E, *however, a hyphen is used.*

Recite, refinish, refill, repair, repeat, replace, reopen, reorganize, reorder.

but

Re-elect, re-enforce, re-enlist, re-entered, re-engage, re-export.

Reading and Writing Practice

277. Transcription Word Study

resumed Started again.

heavily booked Having a large demand for accommodations.

itinerary A traveler's outline of his trip.

278.

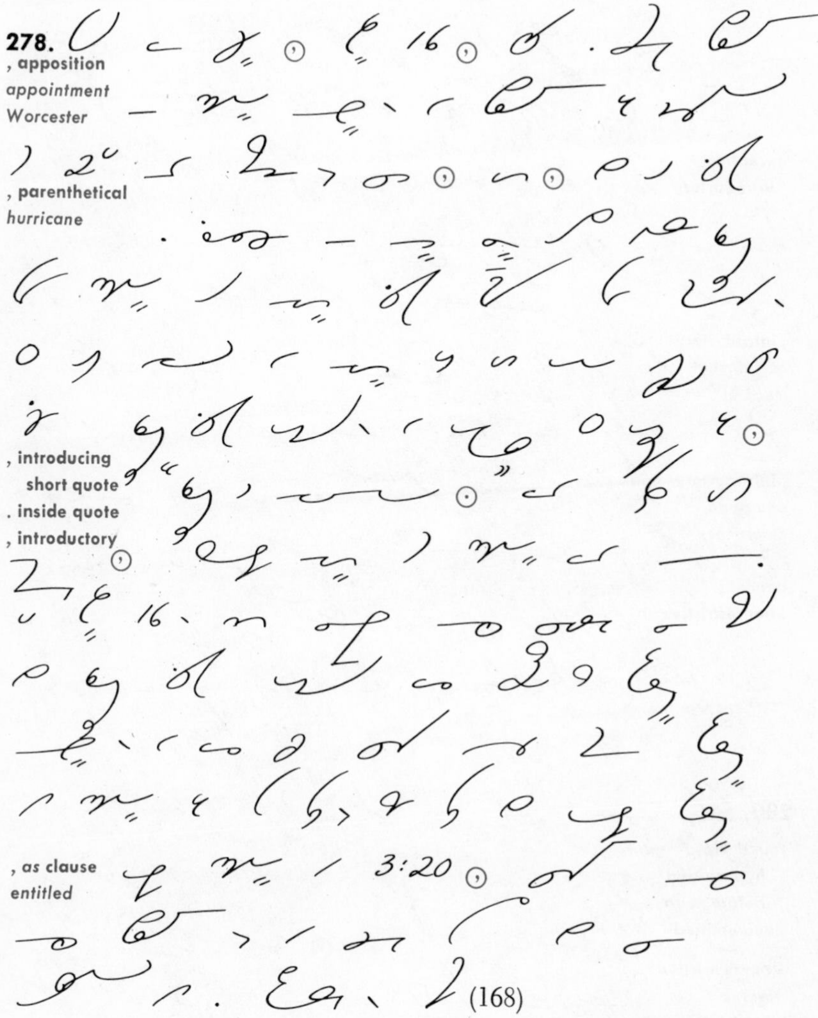

279.

, inside quote

exception

, introductory

, introductory

compliment

medical

, introductory

equipped

emergency

peace

, nonrestrictive

(135)

280.

round-trip

hyphenated

before noun

, and omitted

, nonrestrictive

Nassau

, conjunction

653

13

mind

, conjunction

18 x 7

co-operate

accommodations

(106)

281.

Pacific

, as clause

; illustrative ,

. inside quote

, parenthetical

; because of comma

, introductory

voyage

, introductory

earliest

(127)

282.

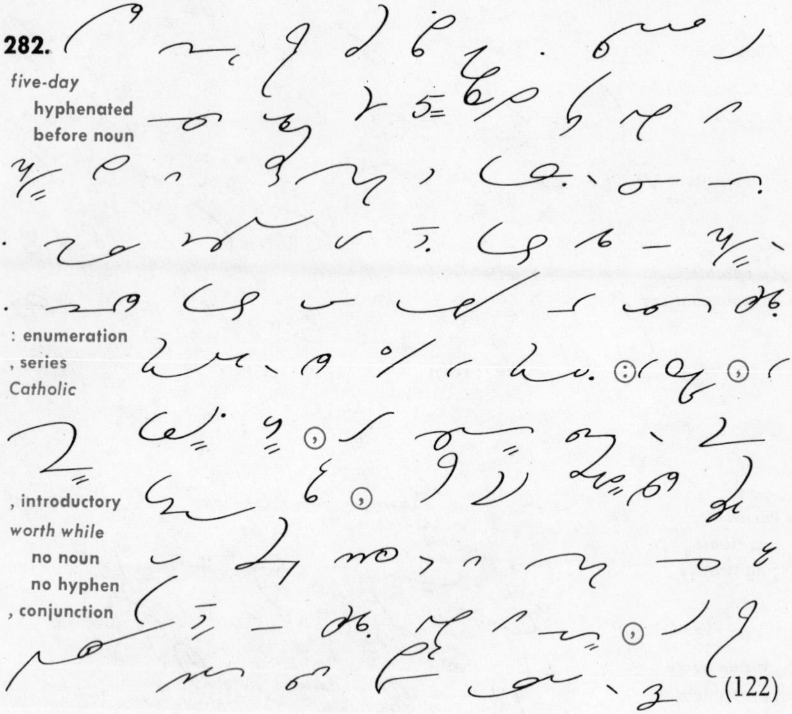

five-day
hyphenated
before noun

: enumeration
, series
Catholic

, introductory
worth while
no noun
no hyphen
, conjunction

(122)

283.

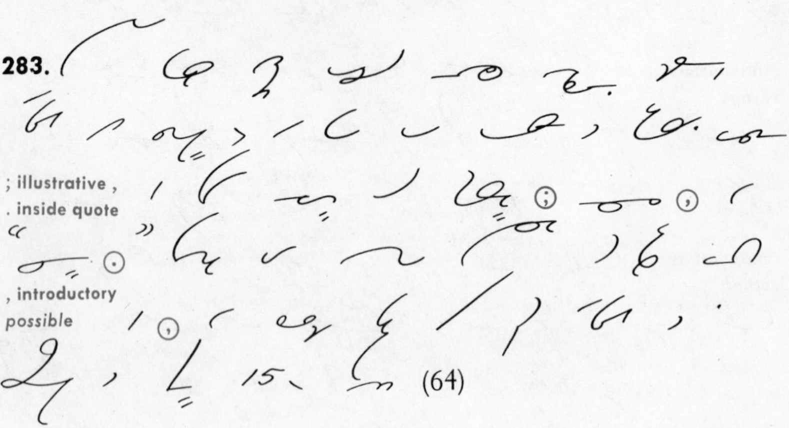

; illustrative ,
. inside quote
" "

, introductory
possible

15

(64)

Lesson 40

284. Brief Forms and Derivatives

1. Immediate, immediately; considerable, considerably; order, orderly; ordinary, ordinarily.
2. Deliver, delivery, deliveries, undeliverable; worth, worthy, unworthy.
3. Ever, everlasting, everlastingly, forever, whenever, whatever, wherever.
4. More, moreover, furthermore; glad, gladly, gladness.

Reading and Writing Practice

285. Transcription Word Study

everlastingly Continuing indefinitely.

council A body assembled to give advice. (Do not confuse with *counsel*, which means "to give advice.")

soloing Flying a plane alone.

286.

, as clause
Los Angeles
serious

; because of comma
, introductory
lose

, nonrestrictive

, conjunction
, introductory
fleet

everlastingly
grateful
, conjunction

(154)

287.

Council
, apposition

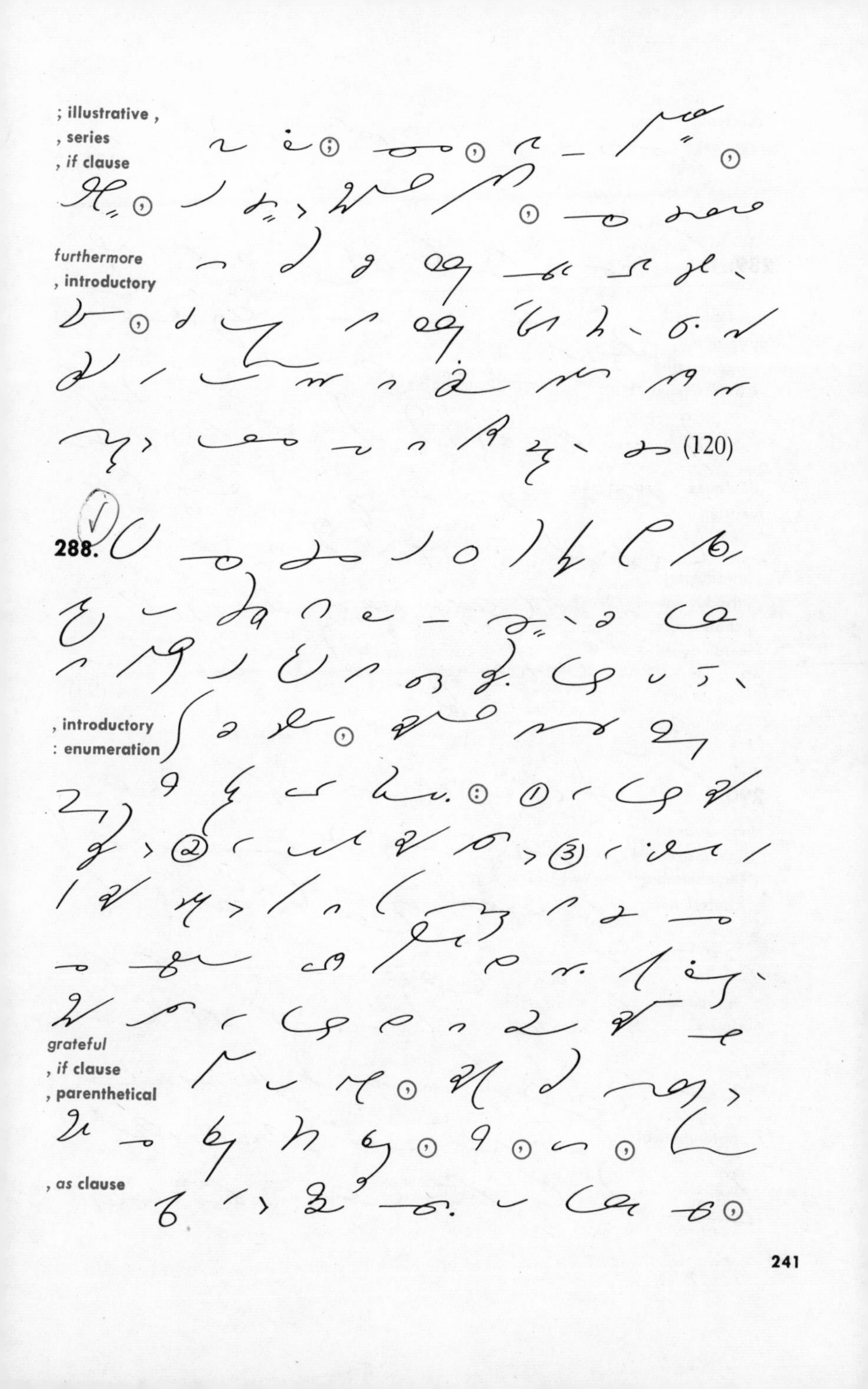

; illustrative ,
, series
, if clause

furthermore
, introductory

(120)

288.

, introductory
: enumeration

grateful
, if clause
, parenthetical

, as clause

. courteous
request

(131)

289.

, and omitted
up-to-date
hyphenated
before noun

, if clause
pleasant

.

, introductory
, introducing
short quote
. inside quote

(94)

290.

long-awaited
flight-instruction
hyphenated
before noun

, introductory
soloing

, parenthetical

, *and* omitted
, parenthetical

, *and* omitted
; no conjunction
, introductory

(132)

291.

well known
no noun,
no hyphen

coast-to-coast
hyphenated
before noun
, *and* omitted

, series
dependability

, introductory
contribution

, introductory

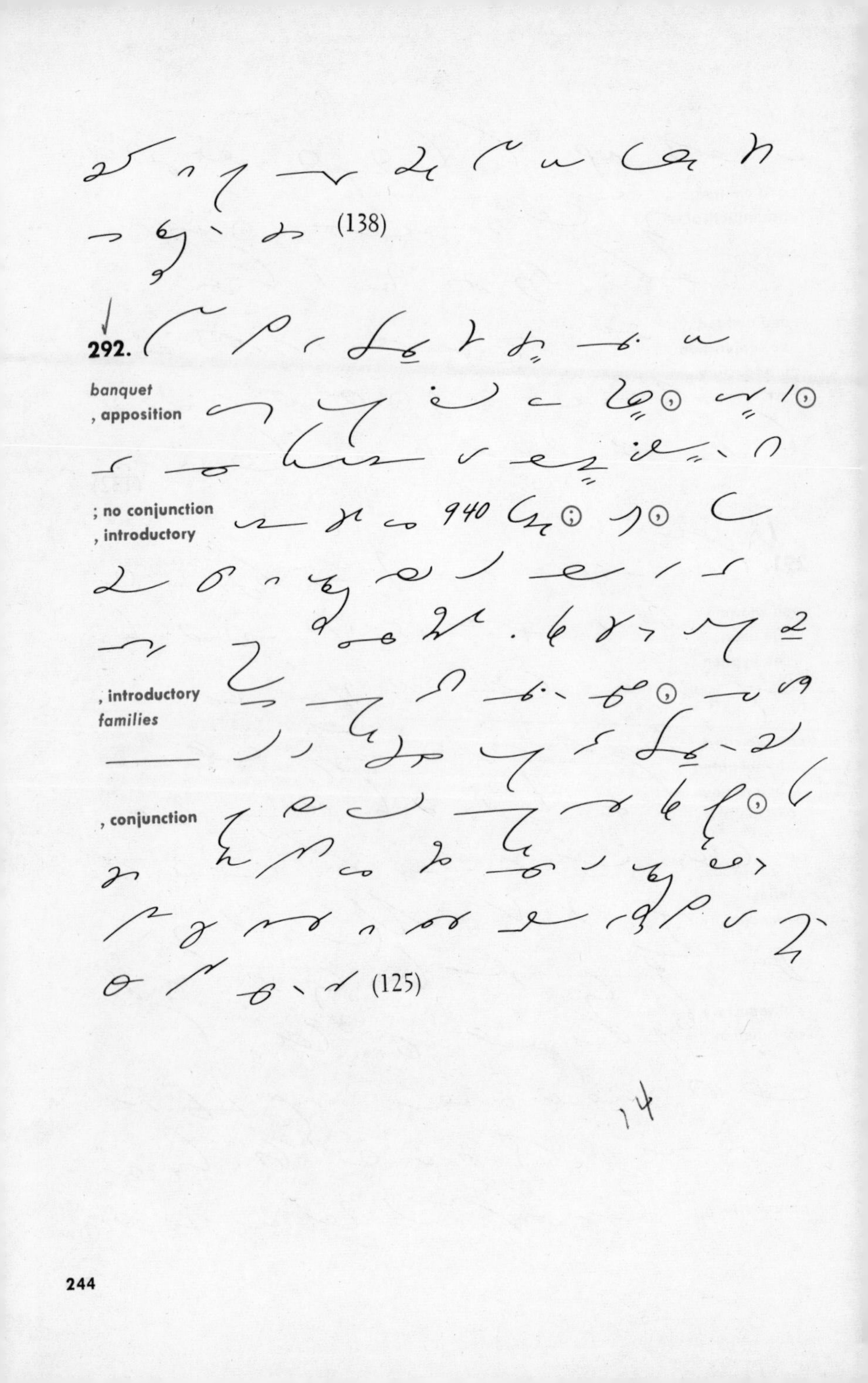

(138)

292.

banquet

, apposition

; no conjunction

, introductory

, introductory

families

, conjunction

(125)

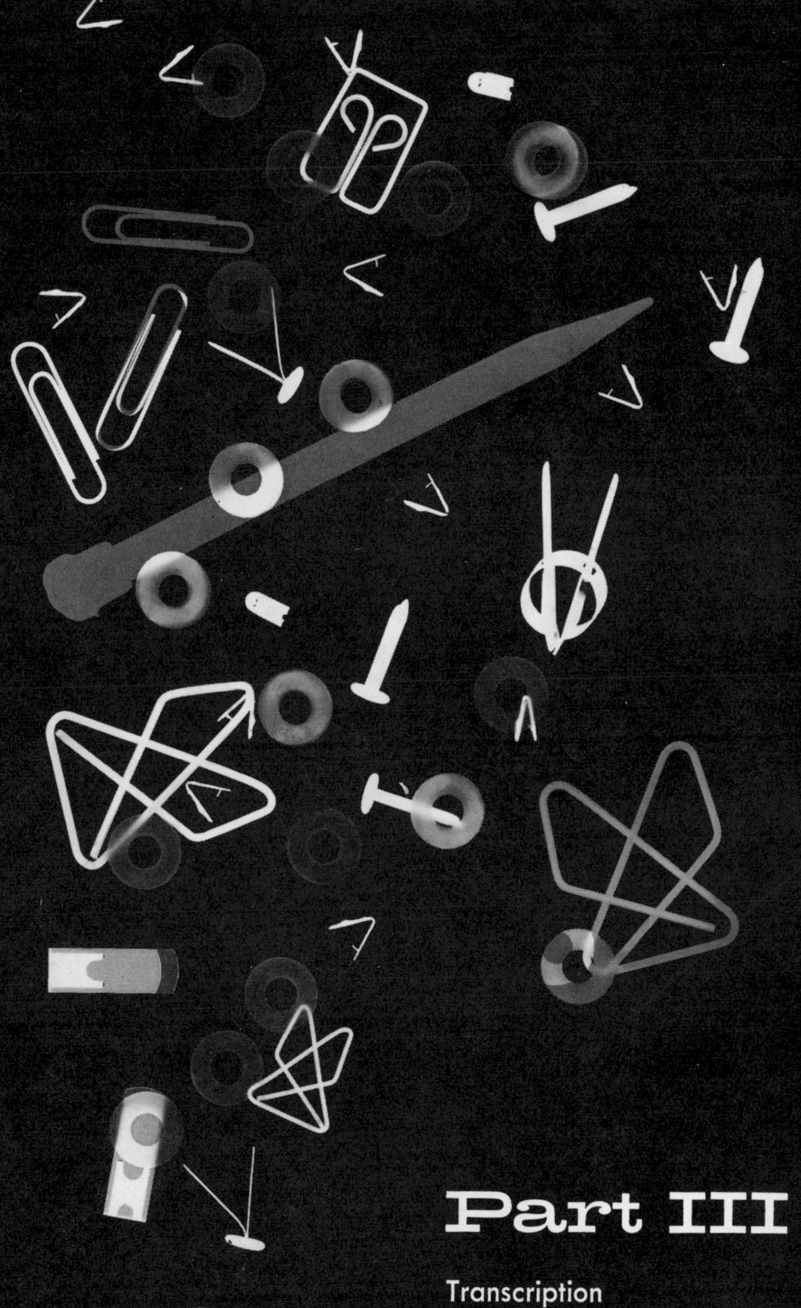

Part III

Transcription on the Job

Carbon paper

Mr. Baker has just completed his day's dictation, and Mary is ready to transcribe. To be sure that she can transcribe uninterruptedly and not have to jump up and down, she has gathered all the material and information she will need, such as catalogues and booklets to be enclosed, lists for verifying the spelling of names, and other useful material.

She is now ready to insert the paper and start transcribing.

Her first consideration is the number of copies that she will have to make—an original and how many carbons? Many a careless stenographer completes the typing of a long letter with one carbon, only to find that she should have made two!

In selecting the type of carbon paper to use, there are two things to take into consideration:

1. The kind of typewriter: standard, electric, or noiseless.
2. The number of copies to be made. In general, a heavier weight carbon should be chosen when only one carbon is to be made than when four or five carbons are to be made.

Before Mary actually inserts the carbon paper, she checks to see that it is in good condition, so that it will give a legible reproduction.

Finally, she inserts the pack into the machine. Before she types a stroke, however, she takes one final precaution: she looks to be sure that the carbons have been correctly inserted. She will be much embarrassed, on completion of the letter, if she finds that she has typed the carbon on the back of the original.

A conscientious stenographer will take pride in her carbons. They are a more or less permanent record of the quality of her work for all to see.

Lesson 41

293. Shorthand Language Study

Super- (or Supr-): *Over, above, more than.* SUPERVISE, *to oversee.*

Supervise, supervision, superintendent, superior, superimpose, supersede, superhuman, supreme.

Sub-: *Under, inferior, or less than.* SUBMERGE, *to place under water.*

Submerge, submit, submission, substandard, subdue, substitute, subsidiary.

Reading and Writing Practice

294. Transcription Word Study

French cuffs Cuffs that are folded over and that usually require cuff links.

wardrobe Clothes or clothing.

significance Meaning.

295.

Chapter

9

Clothing

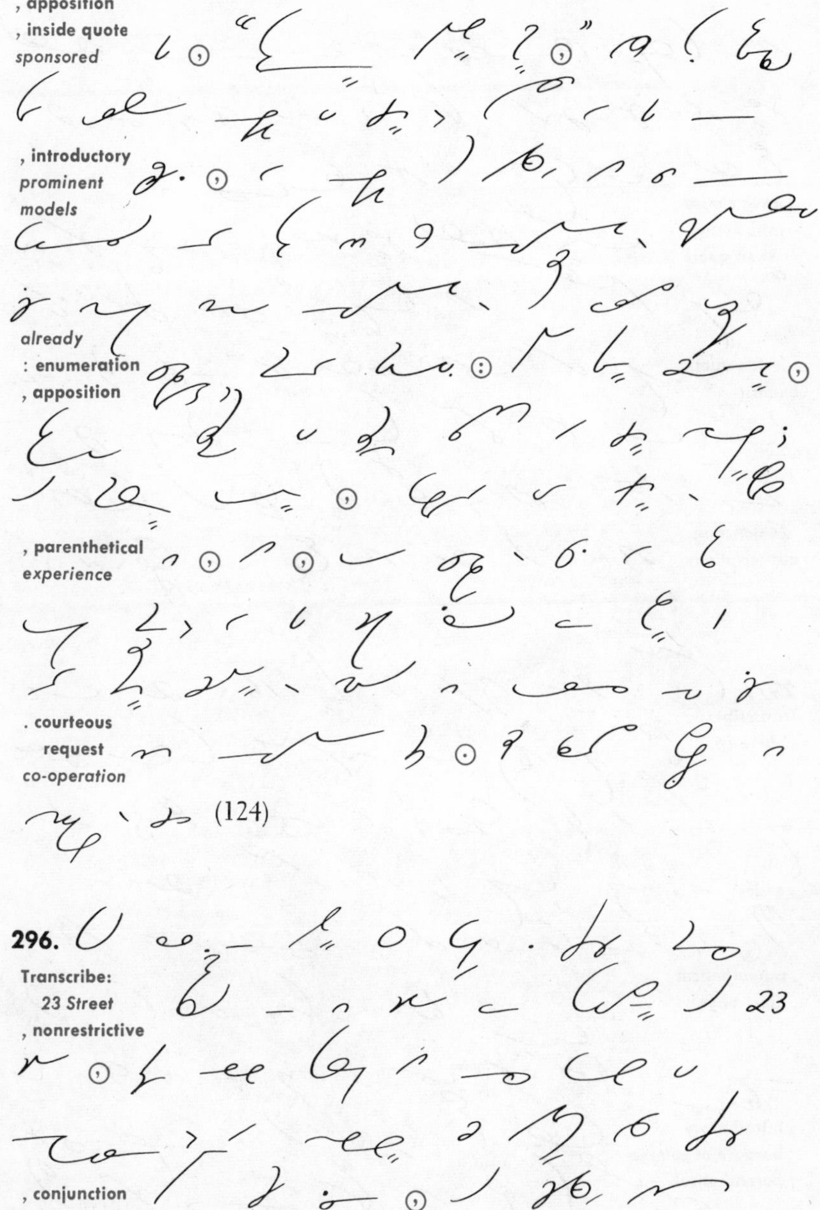
, apposition
, inside quote
sponsored
, introductory
prominent
models
already
: enumeration
, apposition
, parenthetical
experience
. courteous request
co-operation
(124)
296.
Transcribe:
23 Street
, nonrestrictive
23
, conjunction

, *when* clause
, introducing short quote
. inside quote
benefit
, conjunction
appreciation

(137)

297. Transcribe: *June 16*

ties
, series
, parenthetical
; illustrative ,
, introductory
; because of comma
, parenthetical

STEPHEN SAMPSON & SONS 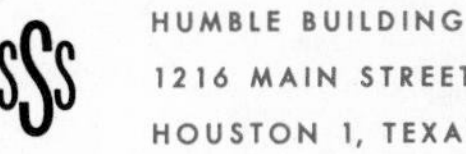 HUMBLE BUILDING
1216 MAIN STREET
HOUSTON 1, TEXAS

April 14, 19--

Mrs. Charles R. Gray
3313 Western Parkway
Houston 4, Texas

Dear Mrs. Gray:

I must make a confession. When I arrived here last fall to take over the Houston branch of Stephen Sampson & Sons, I was sure that it would be easy to sell a great deal of furniture in a short time. The sight of the beautiful homes here in Houston must have caused me to be overoptimistic.

In anticipation of the business that I expected, I bought large quantities of fine furniture. In spite of the quality of the furniture and the appeal of our low prices, however, sales fell far below my expectations. Now I have a warehouse full of merchandise that must be moved. What's more, there are new shipments on the way from several manufacturers.

The time for action has arrived. On Saturday, May 6, you will see in all the Houston papers an announcement of stock-disposal sales. Prices will be low. In many cases, furniture will be offered at cost and even less. Of course, we expect a great response. Because of this, I feel that you and a few other preferred customers should have the opportunity to shop in comfort before public announcement is made of the sale.

Therefore, please consider this a personal invitation for you to shop at your convenience on May 3, 4, or 5. When you arrive, please give the enclosed card to any of our salesmen. He will then take you to the floor where the sale is held.

Very truly yours,

STEPHEN SAMPSON & SONS

Martin A. Foster
Manager

MAF:CS
Enclosure

Long Letter
Indented Style
Standard Punctuation

Imperial

4.50

high-quality hyphenated before noun

30

, if clause

, and omitted

self-addressed

(167)

298. *Men's wardrobe*

Transcribe: $60

60/ 70/

orlon

nylon

35/ 60/

; no conjunction
, *if* clause

(140)

299.

significance
, conjunction

Men's

; because of comma
, introductory
merchandise

, conjunction

pleasant
mutually

(130)

Lesson 42

300. Accuracy Practice. Follow the practice procedures outlined on page 138.

Group 1	Group 2	Group 3
fear	your	would
feel	this	did

Practice Drill

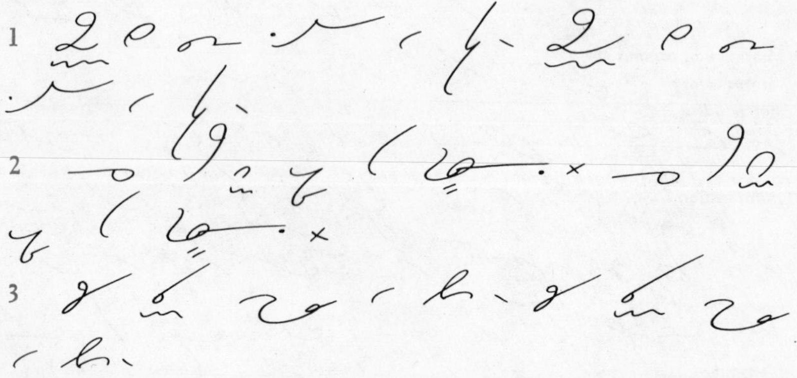

1. I fear that he cannot handle the job. I feel that he cannot handle the job.
2. May I have your report by Friday morning. May I have this report by Friday morning.
3. He said he would complete the task. He said he did complete the task.

Reading and Writing Practice

301. Transcription Word Study

preview *(noun)* A private showing beforehand; before a public presentation.

dispelled Cleared up.

fallacy A foolish or incorrect idea or impression.

302.

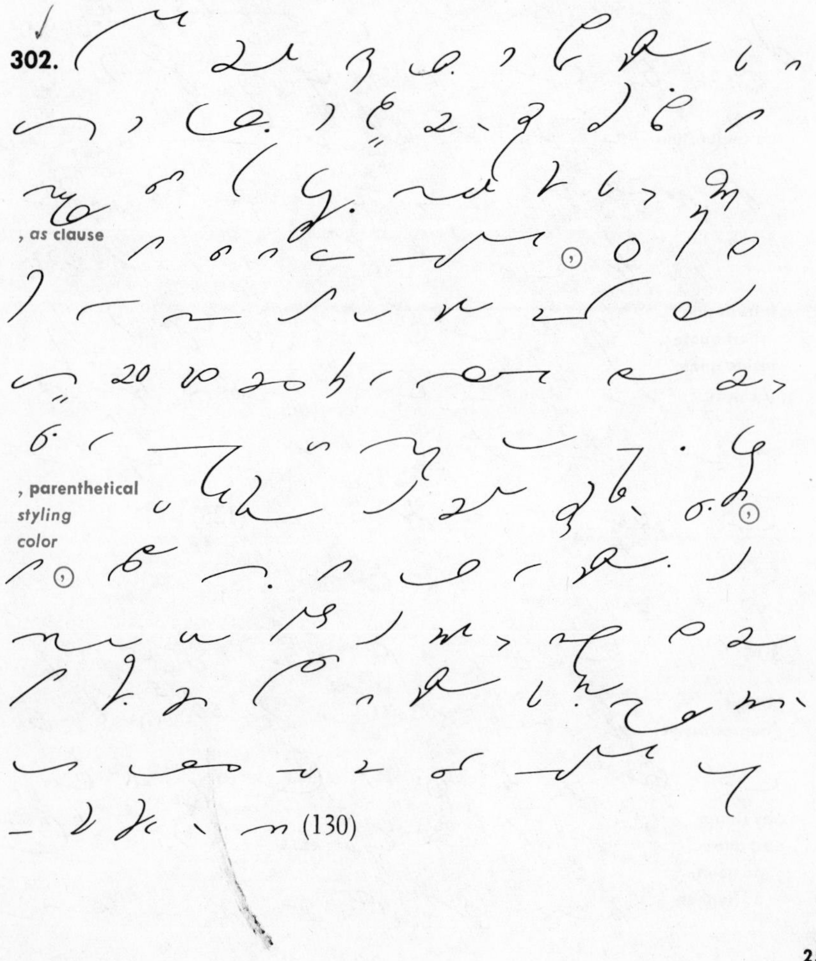

303.

, conjunction
appreciate

, parenthetical
; because of comma
convenience

; no conjunction

, introducing short quote
. inside quote
, *if* clause

(125)

304.

patient
, nonrestrictive

, *as* clause
past due
no noun, no hyphen

, introductory
, and omitted
disagreeable

. courteous request

(125)

305.

Women's

, when clause

, as clause

, parenthetical

, introductory

: enumeration

clothing

10

high quality
no noun
no hyphen

(133)

306.

Ladies'

, conjunction
women's

buyer
, nonrestrictive

, *and* omitted
well-known
hyphenated
before noun

; illustrative ,
assemble

, conjunction
souvenir

, parenthetical

(141)

Lesson 43

307. Office-Style Dictation. Occasionally, a dictator will decide that an entire sentence or even a paragraph would be more effective if it were transposed to another part of the letter. When this happens, the simplest way to show the transposition is to encircle the material to be transposed and indicate the new position by an arrow.

Illustration of Office-Style Dictation

SIMMS

472

715

Reading and Writing Practice

308. Transcription Word Study

C.O.D. Cash on delivery.

deviate To turn aside from a course; to stray.

tailoring Cutting and fitting by a tailor.

309.

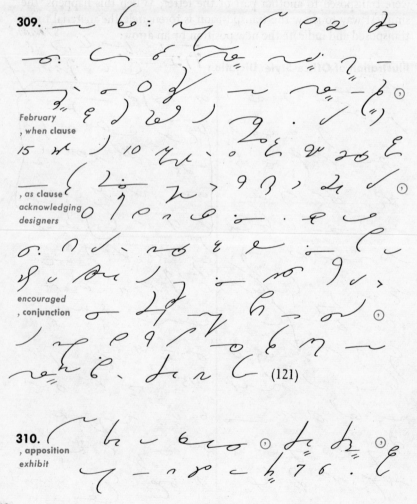

February

, when clause

15 ... 10

, as clause

acknowledging

designers

encouraged

, conjunction

(121)

310.

, apposition

exhibit

; no conjunction
attractive
comfortable

, *and* omitted
fast-selling
hyphenated
before noun

furthermore
, introductory

(135)

311.

, introducing
short quote
, introductory

. inside quote
, conjunction
especially

, parenthetical
, apposition
assistant

Smith's
, parenthetical

theater
, when clause

; illustrative ,
Men's
schedule

(170)

312.

; because of comma
, introductory

policy

, nonrestrictive

, introductory

Transcribe:

C.O.D.

, introductory

(137)

313.

clothing

, introductory

: enumeration

first-rate

hyphenated

before noun

, when clause

quality

, when clause

(109)

Transcription Quiz. In this quiz you are to do two things: (1) you are to supply the punctuation that is missing; (2) you are to supply the words that have been omitted from the shorthand.

As you read the Transcription Quiz letter, decide what punctuation should be used and what words have been omitted from the shorthand. Then make a shorthand copy of the letter, inserting in your notes the correct punctuation and the missing words.

Do not make any marks in the book itself. If you do, you will destroy the value of these quizzes to anyone else who may use the book.

314.

(125)

Lesson 44

315. Shorthand Spelling Drill

Words Ending in -cede, -ceed, -sede: *There is only one word with the spelling* -SEDE – SUPERSEDE. *There are three words with the spelling* -CEED – EXCEED, PROCEED, *and* SUCCEED. *All other words in this family are spelled* -CEDE.

-cede

Cede, precede, recede, concede, intercede, accede.

-sede, -ceed

Supersede; exceed, proceed, succeed.

Reading and Writing Practice

316. Transcription Word Study

reluctant Unwilling.

mother-daughter dresses Dresses of similar style and material for a mother and her daughter.

designate Name.

317

influence
; illustrative ,

; no conjunction
, introductory
instructions

, introductory
well-known
hyphenated
before noun

grateful
available

children's

, and omitted
self-addressed

(211)

318.

matching
ideal

colors
choose
, if clause

Children's

(104)

319.

infants'

LETTER PLACEMENT

Long Letters

In this lesson you will take up the placement of long letters (those containing more than 200 words).

On page 269 you will find letter No. 317, which contains 211 words, as Mary Brown wrote it in her notebook and as she transcribed it on her typewriter, which has pica type. You will notice that it took Mary about a column and a quarter in her notebook.

Whenever a letter requires a column and a quarter up to a column and a half in her notebook, Mary starts the inside address a little less than an inch below the date line and sets her margin stops for 1-inch margins at the left and at the right.

If she is typing on a typewriter that has elite type, she maintains the same margins but starts the inside address about an inch and a quarter below the date line.

Copy letter No. 317 in your notebook and notice how much space this long letter requires. Then, if possible, transcribe the letter on the typewriter from your notes, placing it by judgment.

Whenever a letter requires more than a column and a half in her notebook, Mary considers very carefully whether she should type it as a one-page letter or as a two-page letter. On one occasion she decided to type a letter on one page, only to find, when she completed the body of the letter, that she had no room for the closing—and she had to retype the letter.

If there is any doubt in your mind whether a letter will fit on one page, play safe; widen your margins and make it a two-page letter.

REGAL SERVICE CORPORATION

C. R. MARTIN
PRESIDENT
M. J. QUINETTE
VICE-PRESIDENT
W. C. WILLIAMSON
SEC'Y AND TREAS.

249 MONTGOMERY STREET • SAN FRANCISCO 4

January 12, 195-

The Wilson Shoe Store
13 West 77 Street
New York 27, New York

Gentlemen:

We realize that at t
That is why we are reluct
that may seem small to yo
your spring shoe business
"Styles in Shoes for Chil

These booklets are a
the name of your store; c
you give us mailing instr

The booklet contains
shoes that children will
addition, it contains a n
known doctors on what par
shoes for their children.

We have had many let
country telling us how gr
booklet available. It sh
children's shoes.

All you have to do i
the date on which you wis
office and return the let
velope that is enclosed.

ABC/BC

, introducing short quote

? inside quote

consequently

, introductory

, *when clause*

preschool

; because of comma

, nonrestrictive

(118)

320.

: enumeration

equipped

well-known hyphenated before noun

, *if clause*

designate
, introductory

(118)

321.

14

especially

, if clause
purchases

(102)

322.

, conjunction
exhausted

(47)

Lesson 45

323. Brief Forms and Derivatives

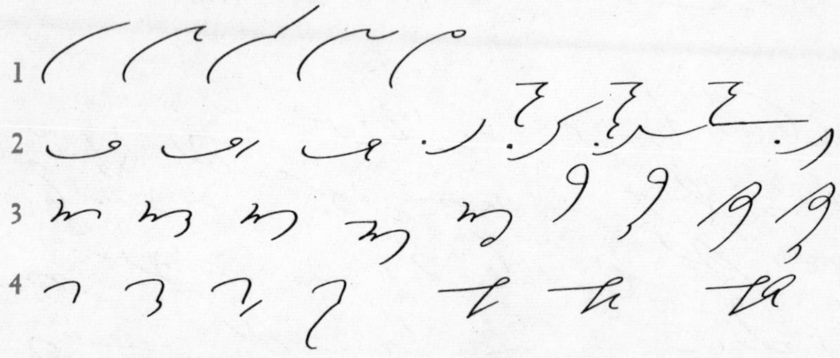

1. Time, times, timed, timer, timely; newspaper, newspapers, newspapermen.
2. Letter-let, lettered, letters; hand, handed, handle, handful.
3. Success, successes, successful, unsuccessful, successfully; advantage, advantages, disadvantage, disadvantageous.
4. Question, questions, questioned, questionable; merchant, merchants, merchandise.

Reading and Writing Practice

324. Transcription Word Study

ready-made suit A suit made for general sale.

custom-made suit A suit made for a specific individual, according to his measurements.

fanfare A showy, outward display.

clearance sale A sale at which odds and ends of stock are sold at low prices.

325.

, as clause
Clothing

; illustrative ,
Transcribe:
9 a.m.

, conjunction
morale

30

, introductory
local

, introductory
charge-account
hyphenated
before noun

(132)

326.
ever-increasing
hyphenated
before noun
, introductory

416 33

; because of comma
, parenthetical

; because of comma
, *and* omitted
competent

; no conjunction
, introductory
across

(135)

327.

Men's
material

, when clause
delighted

perfect
tailoring

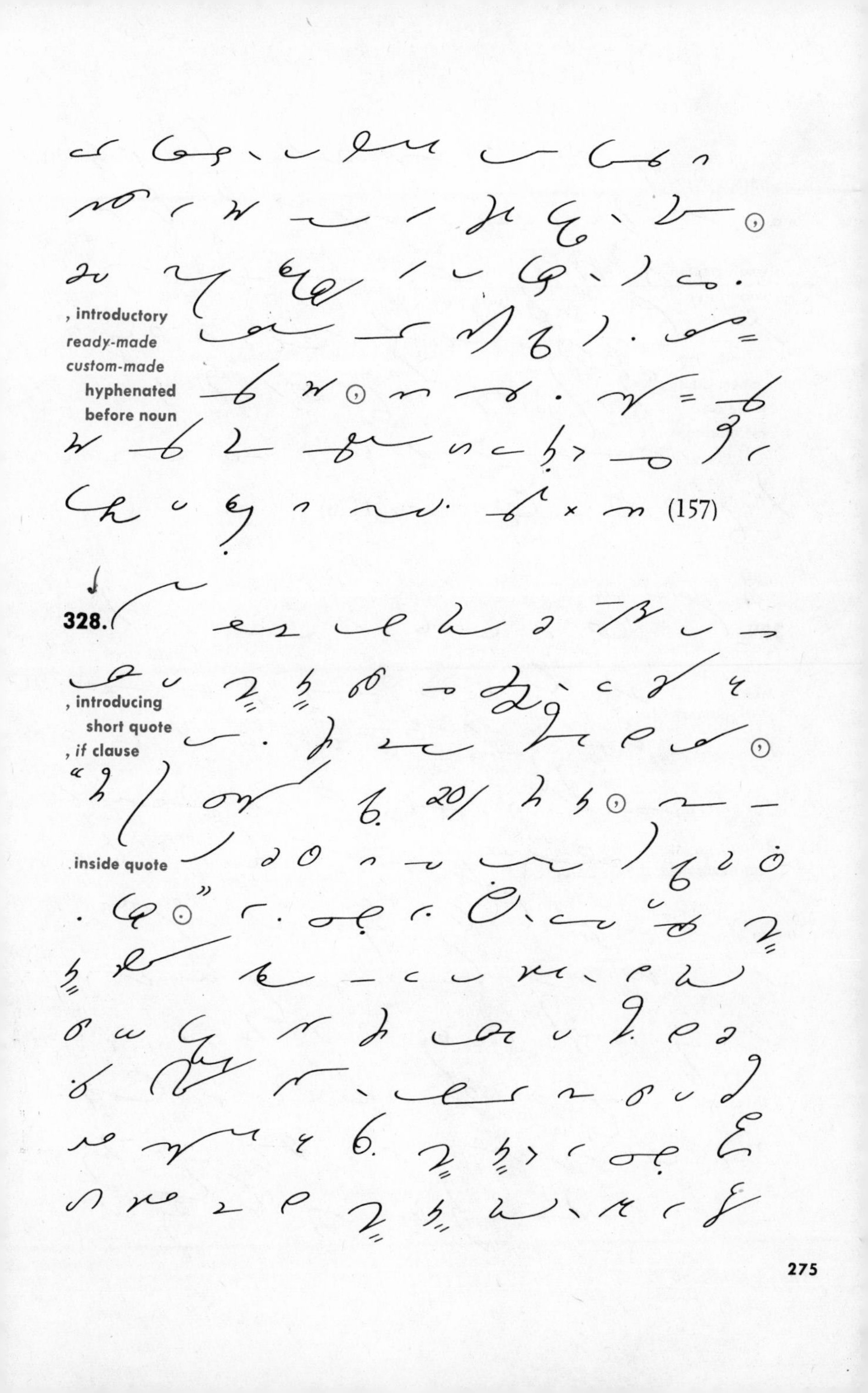

, introductory

ready-made

custom-made

hyphenated before noun

(157)

328.

, introducing short quote

, if clause

. inside quote

Obviously
, introductory

: enumeration
comparative

, introducing
short quote
, if clause
. inside quote

"20/"

(178)

329.

Men's
, introductory

Bureau
, nonrestrictive

150

Transcribe:
$150

, *if clause*

(144)

330.

pair

wear

, apposition

(93)

Punctuation Tip

If you have been paying careful attention to the marginal reminders in the Reading and Writing Practice exercises, you should be a fairly good "punctuator" by this time.

It is not enough, however, to think about correct punctuation only when you are transcribing business letters in class; you should be thinking about correct punctuation in all the writing you do, whether you are preparing a paper for the history class, corresponding with a friend, or making notes for yourself.

EBERHARD FABER
U.S.A.
6580

Erasing

Mary Brown is a good typist, but she is only human. She occasionally makes a mistake in the typing of her letters. Mary realizes, however, that the next best thing to *not* making a mistake is to correct it neatly and *rapidly*, with emphasis on *rapidly*. Here is the technique that Mary follows:

1. As soon as she realizes that her fingers have struck the wrong key, she immediately moves the carriage either to the right or to the left (so that the crumbs will not fall into the typing basket) and rolls the pack forward a number of lines so that she can erase conveniently.

2. She then places a metal eraser guard behind the original copy. (A 5 x 3 card may be used instead of a metal eraser guard. Be sure, however, that it is removed when the erasure has been completed.)

3. She reaches for her sand eraser, which she always keeps in the same place so that she can find it without any loss of time, and completely erases the incorrect letter on the original copy. She is careful (1) not to press too hard and thus damage the paper, and (2) not to smudge any other characters.

4. She then removes the guard, reaches for the soft eraser, which she also always keeps in the same place, and erases the carbon copy.

5. Her next step is to roll the paper back to the printing point and check to see that the pack has not slipped.

6. Finally, she types the correct letter over the erased point, using the pressure that matches the rest of her typing. She is careful not to hit the letter too hard, so that it will stand out like a sore thumb, a mistake that beginning typists sometimes make.

Through practice, Mary can now execute these six steps so quickly that she has the mistake corrected and is ready to resume trancribing in a matter of seconds after she makes it.

Why not try Mary's erasing procedure? Practice it until you can make an acceptable erasure on an original and a carbon in less than one minute.

Lesson 46

331. Shorthand Language Study

Un-: *Not.* UNPAID, *not paid.*

Unpaid, unfair, unfinished, unwritten, uncommon, unlucky, uncovered.

Non-: *Not.* NONPRODUCTIVE, *not productive.*

Nonproductive, nonresident, nonsense, nonstop, nonskid, noncoin.

Reading and Writing Practice

332. Transcription Word Study

noncoin telephone A telephone in which it is not necessary to deposit a coin in order to make a call.

sick-leave allowance The number of days in a year that an employee may be absent from work because of illness without losing any pay.

utilities Organizations that perform some public service, such as supplying gas, electricity, or water.

forfeit Lose the right to.

Chapter 10 Utilities

333.

telephone
, parenthetical

long-distance
station-to-station
hyphenated
before noun

, parenthetical
, introducing
short quote

10,

. inside quote
noncoin

: enumeration
, series

18

20'

, nonrestrictive
, *when* clause

60'

(138)

334.
principal
, introductory

excellent
possibilities
advancement

sick-leave
hyphenated
before noun
; illustrative ,

pamphlets
describing

. courteous
request

(160)

335.
overdue
; because of comma
, series

customer
, introductory

, parenthetical
discontinue

, introductory
disconnected
forfeit
, parenthetical
installation
; no conjunction
, introductory

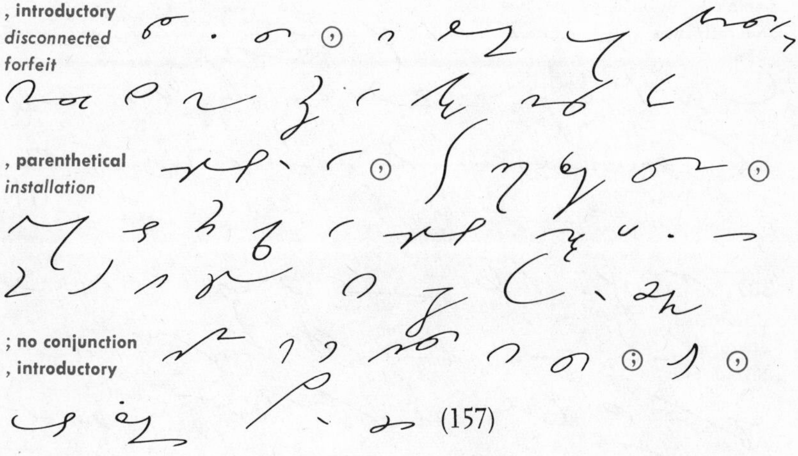

(157)

336.

Transcribe:
3 per cent
, and omitted
, if clause
, introductory
consumer
everyday
, series
equipment
; because of comma

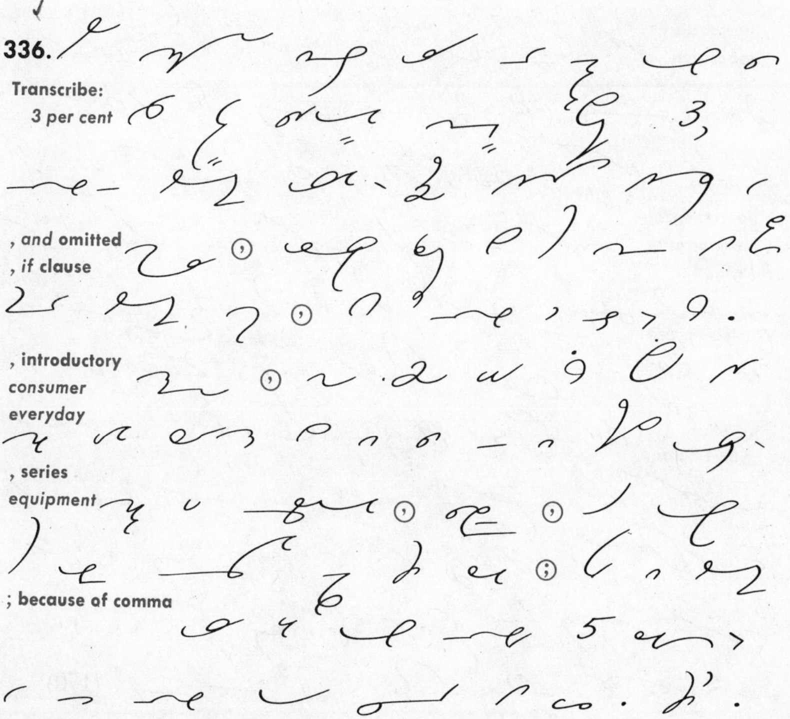

month's

, nonrestrictive

(149)

337.

dissatisfied

operators

discourteous

, introductory

, apposition

, parenthetical

, introductory

inflection

, introducing short quote

(170)

Lesson 47

338. Accuracy Practice. Follow the practice procedure outlined on page 138.

Group 1	Group 2	Group 3
affect	object	retain
effect	subject	redeem

Practice Drill

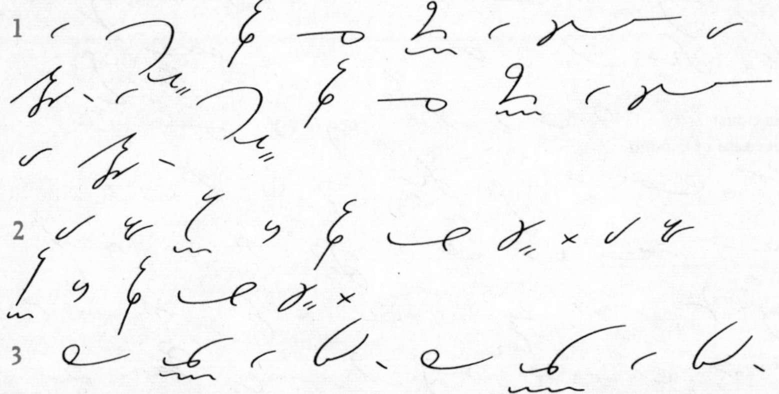

1. The Governor's speech may effect the settlement of the dispute. The Governor's speech may affect the settlement of the dispute.
2. What was the object of his speech last Saturday? What was the subject of his speech last Saturday?
3. I will retain the bond. I will redeem the bond.

Reading and Writing Practice

339. Transcription Word Study

contact To get in touch with.

considerate Thoughtful.

340.

, parenthetical

, as clause

; because of comma

(136)

341.

repairman
, parenthetical

, as clause
forward
accidentally

damage
, introductory
, parenthetical

3-4445

, if clause
arrangements

, conjunction

, introducing
short quote
; no conjunction

considerate
. inside quote

(178)

342.

electrical

, as clause

, apposition

, apposition

; because of comma

secretary

, apposition

, if clause

Thursday

, if clause

' Anderson's

, when clause

(142)

343.

punch-card

hyphenated before noun

schedule

customer's

: enumeration

; illustrative ,

adopted

(142)

344.

, introductory

repairing

appliances

12-month

hyphenated before noun

, if clause

, if clause

(74)

Lesson 48

345. Office-Style Dictation. One of the most common changes that a businessman makes in his dictation is the insertion of a word or a phrase in a sentence that has already been dictated. The dictator may say:

> Our representative will call on you on Friday, June 16–make that *our Chicago representative.*

Or the dictator may repeat the expression with the new word or phrase added, leaving it to you to notice which words have been added and to place them in your notes. For example, he may say:

> Our representative will call on you on Friday, June 16–no, *Our Chicago representative will call on you on Friday, June 16.*

You must be on the alert so that you can quickly find the point at which the addition is to be made. When you find the point, you insert the added word or phrase with a caret, just as you would in longhand.

Illustration of Office-Style Dictation

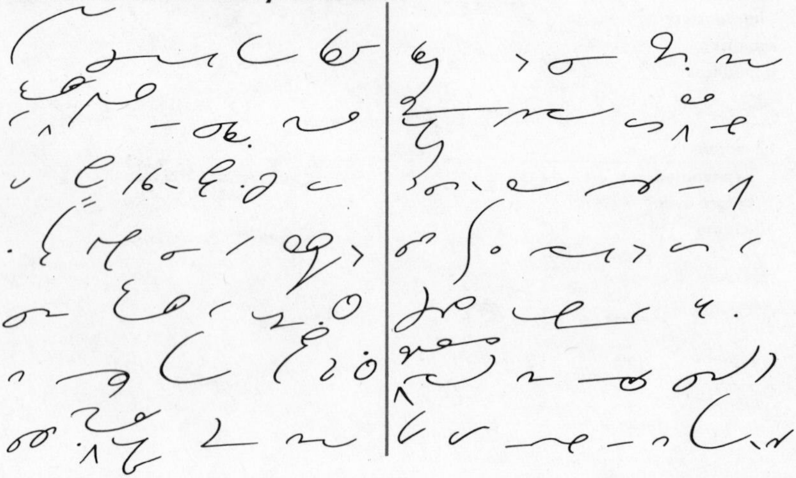

Reading and Writing Practice

346. Transcription Word Study

housing development A group of houses built in a particular area.

commitment A promise or pledge to do something.

347.

, apposition
, inside quote
response

, conjunction
distribution

, conjunction
nothing

, introducing short quote
. inside quote
son's

, introductory

; because of comma
, parenthetical
bear

(137)

348.

installing
development

, *if clause*
appreciate

, *as clause*
impossible

, *conjunction*
commitment

(116)

349.

appliances
somewhere
, *conjunction*

previous
assumed

(127)

350.

pressing
, introductory

, and omitted
comfortable
fortunate

, nonrestrictive

4-6201

; no conjunction

ideal

. courteous request

(150)

351.

sponsoring

5

5

110

(77)

Transcription Quiz. Supply all the missing punctuation and the words that have been omitted from the shorthand. Be sure that you do not overlook one colon and one semicolon that are necessary to punctuate the letter correctly.

352.

(153)

Typewriter Tip

In school you will no doubt do most of your typing on one make of machine. When you have completed your training, you will be thoroughly familiar with its operation.

Keep in mind, however, that you may not find that make of typewriter in the business office. There, you may have to type on any one of the various leading brands of standard, noiseless, and electric typewriters. Unless you have some familiarity with the machine on which you will have to type, you may find yourself at a disadvantage until you become accustomed to your machine.

You can make things easier for yourself if you will try to do a little typing on as many different makes of typewriters as possible while you are still in school.

Lesson 49

353. Shorthand Spelling Drill

Words Ending in -able, -ible: *By far the greatest number of words belonging in the* -BLE *family are spelled* -ABLE. *There is, however, no rule that will help you to decide whether to use* -IBLE *or* -ABLE. *It will be helpful to you, however, to study these words in family groups as they are given here.*

-able

Notable, probable, liable, obtainable, reasonable, honorable, comfortable, taxable, portable.

-ible

Terrible, sensible, possible, responsible, feasible, horrible, legible, illegible, intelligible.

Reading and Writing Practice

354. Transcription Word Study

relieved Helped, eased.

water main A large pipe through which water is taken from a reservoir.

conserve To save.

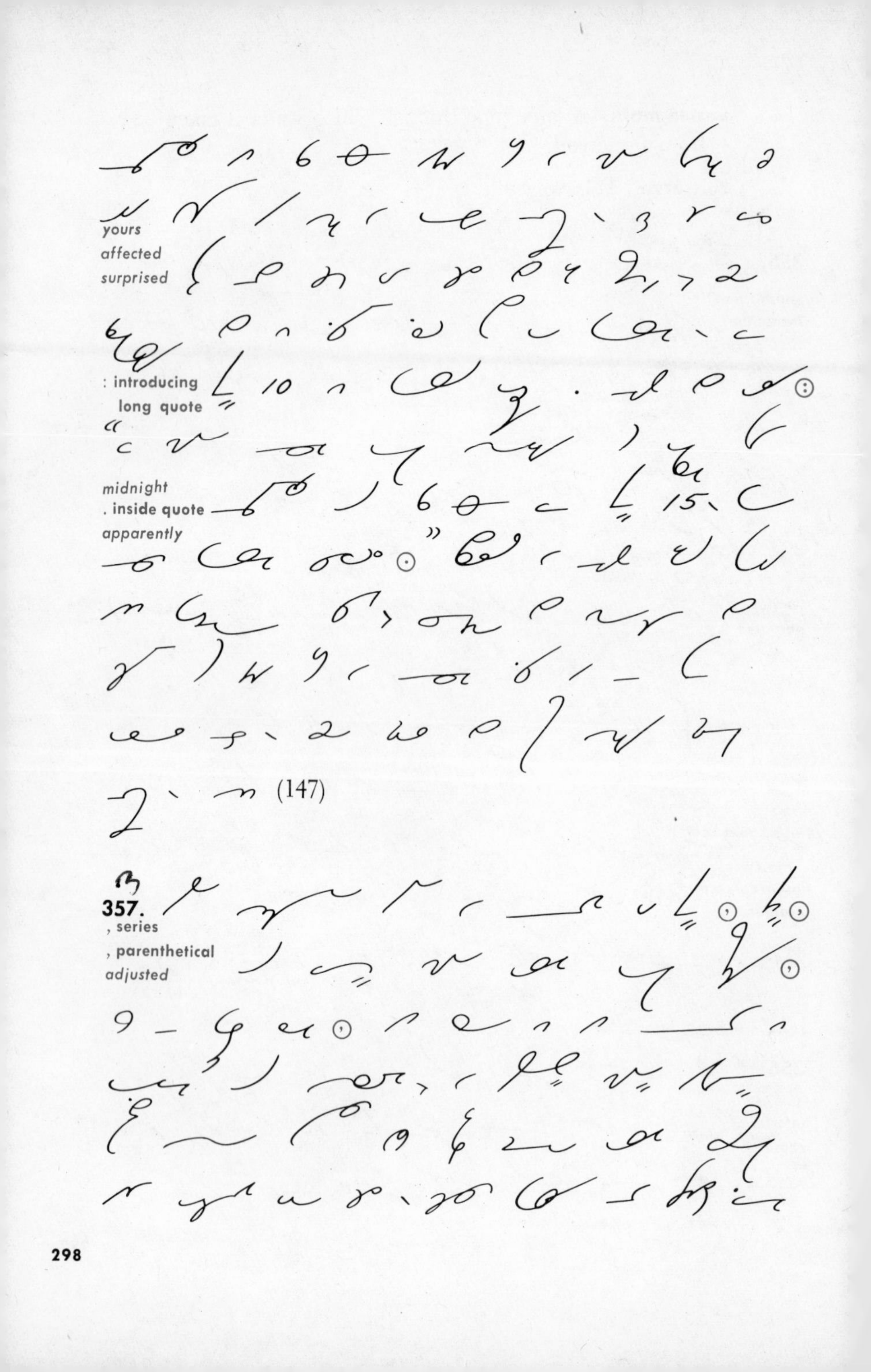

yours
affected
surprised

: introducing long quote

midnight
. inside quote
apparently

(147)

357.
, series
, parenthetical
adjusted

, introductory

. inside quote
, parenthetical
co-operation

. inside quote
, series

, conjunction

(148)

358.
Citizens
, nonrestrictive

, as clause
; because of comma

, *and* omitted
long-range
hyphenated
before noun

, as clause

(153)

359.

, as clause

; because of comma

city's

; no conjunction

, introductory

: enumeration

, series

, series
relieved

(130)

Lesson 50

360. Brief Forms and Derivatives

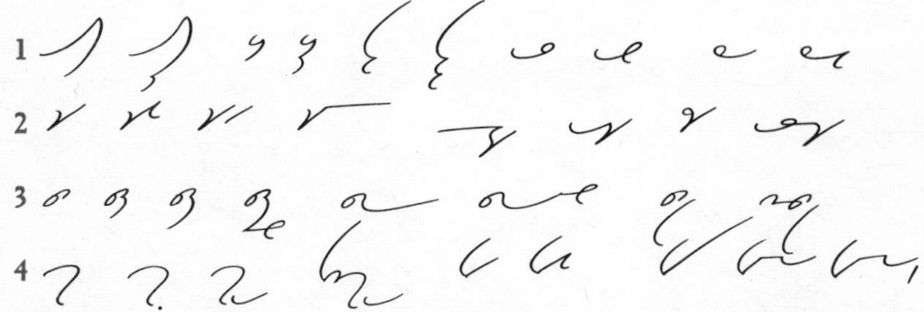

1. Individual, individuals; office, offices; business, businesses; regard, regards; were-year, years.
2. State, states, stated, statement, misstate, restate, estate, reinstate.
3. Use, uses, useful, usefulness, useless, uselessness, usable, unusable.
4. Company-keep, keeping, keeper, bookkeeper; part, parts, parted, partner, partnership.

Reading and Writing Practice

361. Transcription Word Study

consultant One who gives professional advice.

classified telephone directory The telephone book in which names are listed according to lines of businesses, such as plumbing, publishing, printing, and so on.

362.
offices
, as clause

; illustrative ,

, nonrestrictive
experience

advantage
, *if* clause

(164)

363.
, apposition
telephone

, conjunction

company's
, if clause

, parenthetical

, and omitted
self-addressed

(169)

364.

companies
connection
Safety

, series
danger
areas

, *if* clause
copies

, parenthetical
; no conjunction
public-service
hyphenated
before noun

(133)

365.

217

, introducing
short quote
. inside quote
, *when* clause

, *if* clause
local

(127)

366.

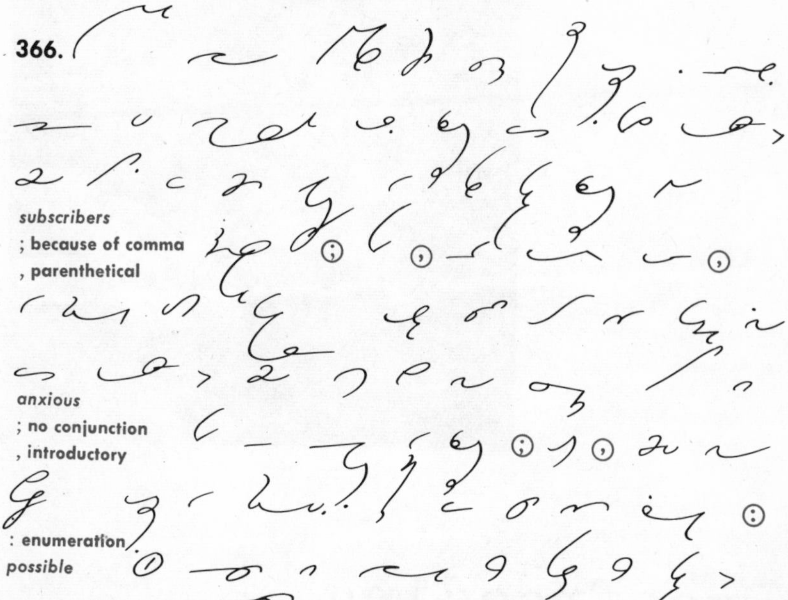

subscribers

; because of comma

, parenthetical

anxious

; no conjunction

, introductory

: enumeration

possible

interrupt

neighbor's

co-operation

(171)

Proofreading

Mary learned early in her career that it was no disgrace to make an error; the disgrace was in not catching and correcting the error. One of the reasons why Mary is a secretary is the fact that she never submits anything for Mr. Baker's signature until she has proofread it and corrected any mistakes.

Mary always proofreads her transcripts while they are still in the machine. It is then a simple matter to correct any errors that she finds. She knows from experience that making corrections after a letter is removed from the machine is a much more difficult and time-consuming process.

Mary learned that she cannot proofread her transcripts in the same way that she reads ordinary print, where her only purpose is to grasp the writer's meaning. Of course, she is interested in the meaning of the transcript; but, in addition, she is interested in the correctness of every stroke she types.

In her early days as a stenographer, Mary found that she had to proofread her transcripts almost *letter* by *letter*. Later, she found that she could proofread word by word, reverting to letter-by-letter reading only when she came to long and unusual words. She is also

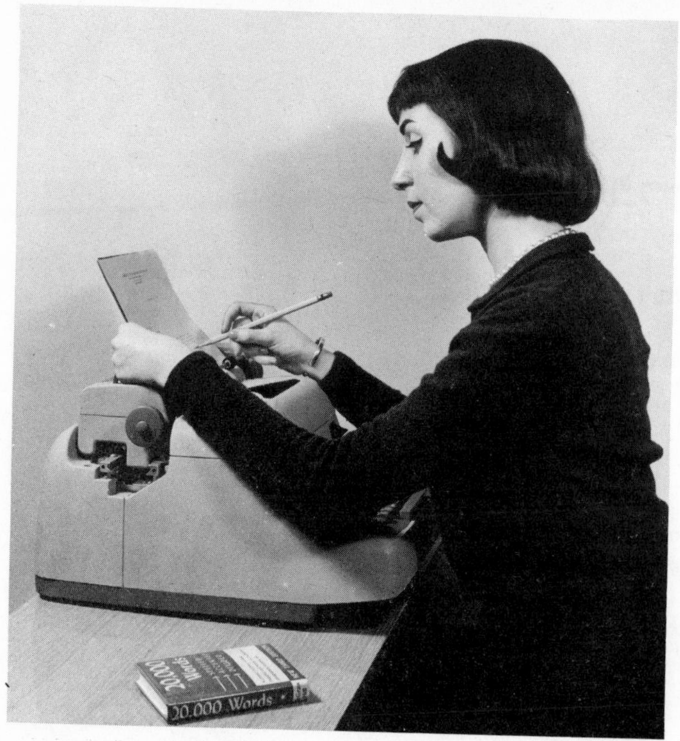

doubly cautious where numbers are involved; she always checks numbers with her notes.

Mary found that most of her errors fall in four classes:

1. Transpositions–typing *recieve* for *receive; conveneince* for *convenience,* etc.

2. Similar words – typing *to* rather than *too; fair* rather than *fare; though* rather than *thought; sale* rather than *sail.* She found that she had a tendency to type the more frequently used member of the pair; that is, instead of *too,* she would type *to;* instead of *sail,* she would type *sale.*

3. Words in which letters are doubled–typing *seel* for *sell; feel* for *fell.*

4. Numbers, especially those involving a 9 or a 0; a 4 or a 5.

By thus analyzing the types of errors she made–without realizing that she made them while she was typing–she was able to watch for them as she proofread.

You, too, will be able to make yourself a more efficient proofreader if you try to determine the types of errors that you make most frequently and then watch for them.

Lesson 51

367. Shorthand Language Study

Trans-: *Across, beyond, through.* TRANSCONTINENTAL, *across the continent.*

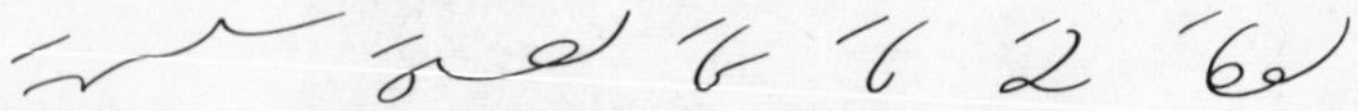

Transcontinental, transatlantic, transport, transpose, transfer, transparent.

-hood: *The state or condition of.* MANHOOD, *the state of being a man.*

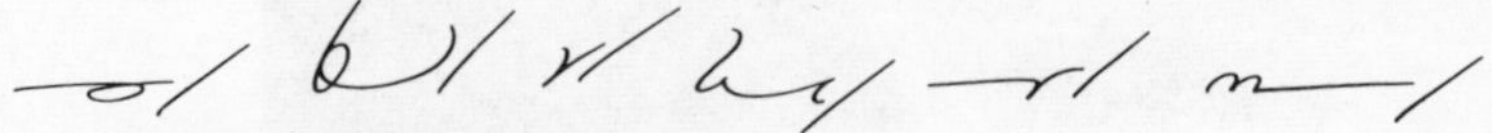

Manhood, childhood, statehood, falsehood, motherhood, womanhood.

Reading and Writing Practice

368. Transcription Word Study

posture chair A chair that may be adjusted to enable a person to sit in the most comfortable position.

duplicator A copying machine; a machine that turns out multiple copies.

radically Extremely; drastically.

369.

Chapter 11 Office equipment

except

, introductory

: enumeration

drawers

, parenthetical

, introductory

typewriter

up-to-date hyphenated before noun

, if clause

(147)

370.

company's

, conjunction

impressed

immediately

secretary

transferring

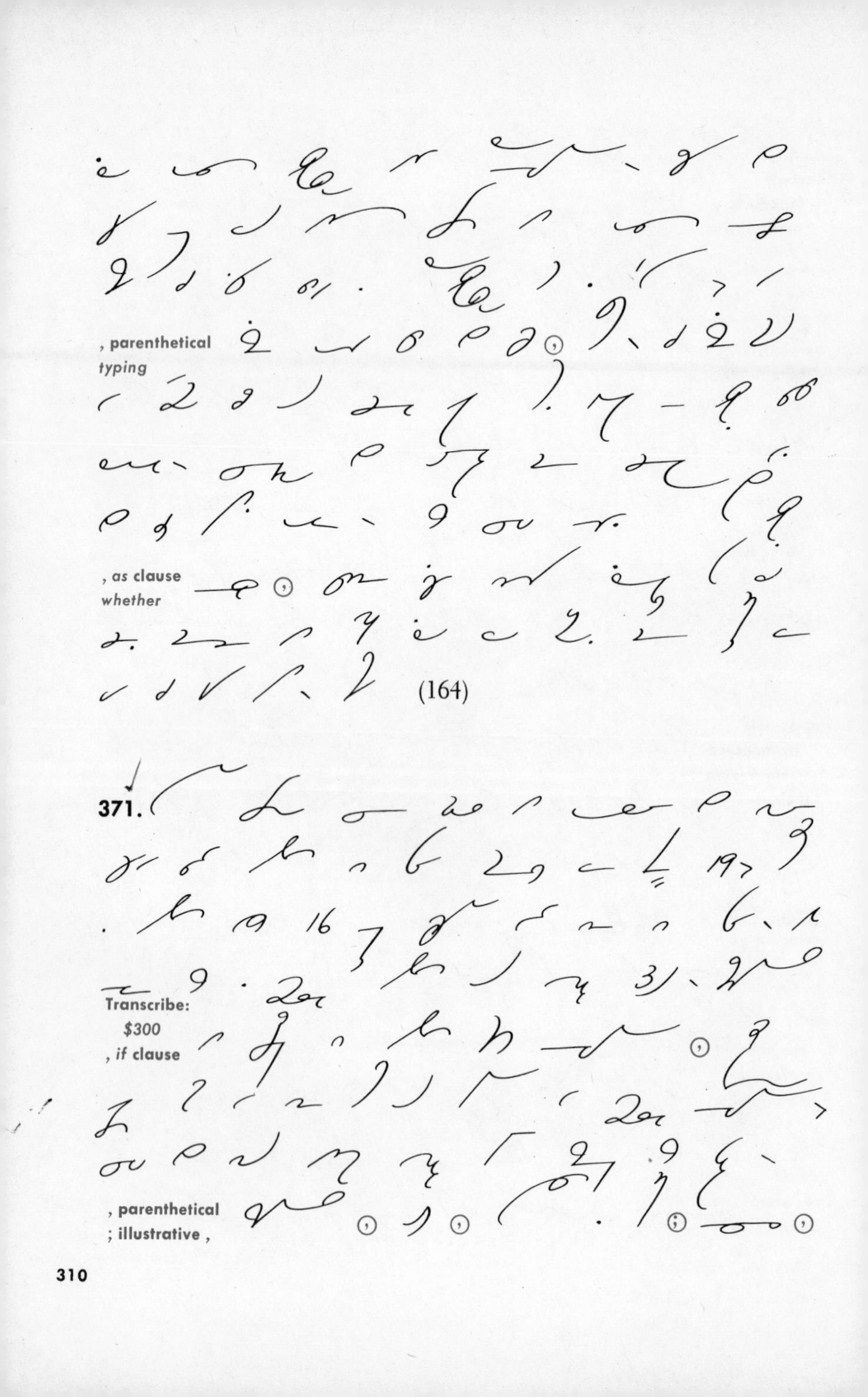

, parenthetical
typing

, as clause
whether

(164)

371.

Transcribe:
$300
, if clause

, parenthetical
; illustrative ,

; because of comma

, if clause

handle

(144)

372.

, nonrestrictive

: introducing long quote

duplicator

, conjunction

radically

. inside quote

, and omitted

, as clause

, introductory

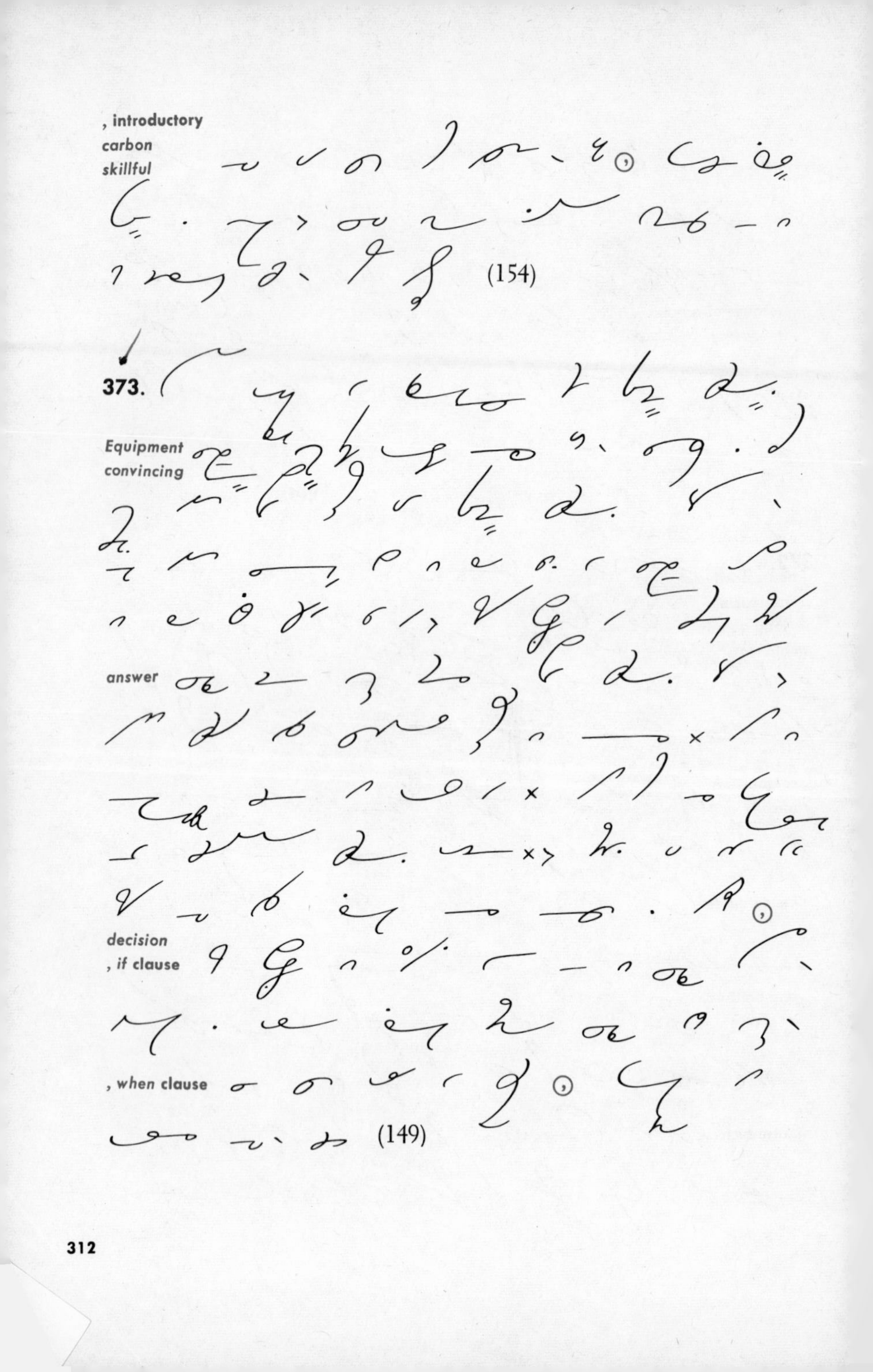

, introductory
carbon
skillful

(154)

373.

Equipment
convincing

answer

decision
, if clause

, when clause

(149)

Lesson 52

374. Accuracy Practice. Follow the practice procedure outlined on page 138.

Group 1	**Group 2**	**Group 3**
red	organizer	past
lead	worker	best

Practice Drill

1. Mark the paper with red pencil. Mark the paper with lead pencil.
2. He is the best organizer in the company. He is the best worker in the company.
3. The past month was the best month. The best month was the past month.

Reading and Writing Practice

375. Transcription Word Study

capacity Position.

waterproof Capable of resisting or shedding water.

fireproof Capable of resisting fire or heat.

376.

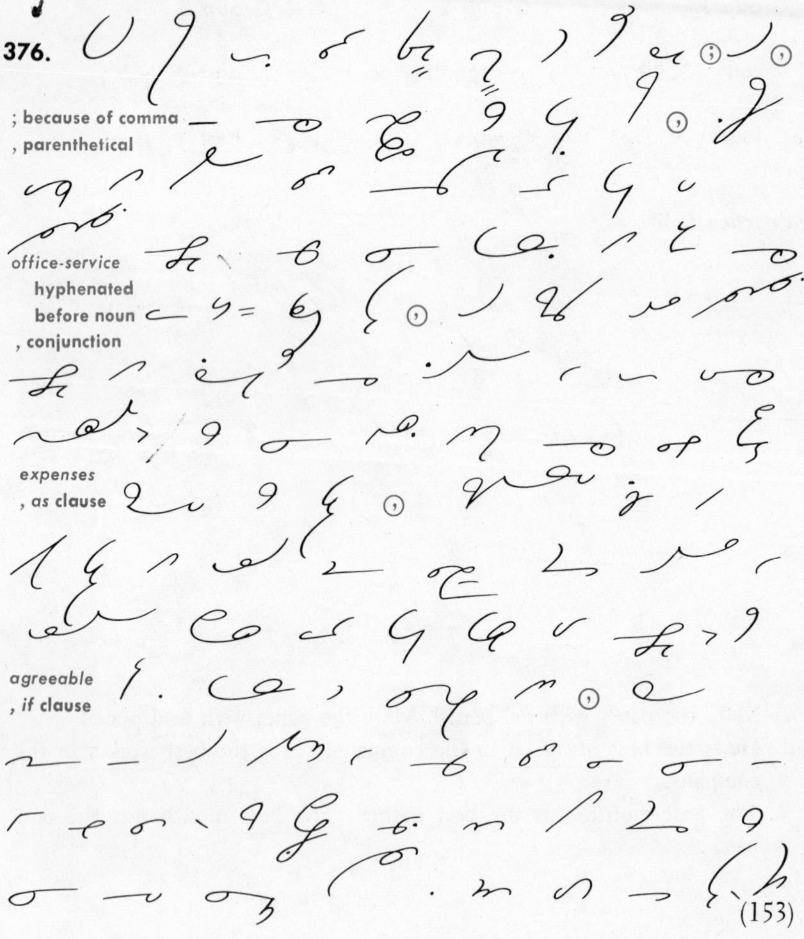

377.

, introductory
complaints

, nonrestrictive
requires

, introductory
tired

customer's
, when clause

drawers
Transcribe:
2 feet

, conjunction
buy

fatigue
, if clause

(160)

378.

: enumeration
waterproof

all-steel
hyphenated
before noun
, nonrestrictive
, introducing
short quote

features
; no conjunction
. inside quote

, parenthetical
proper

, if clause

(141)

379.
coolers
factories
, series

Association
, nonrestrictive

furniture

; illustrative ,

, and omitted

self-addressed

(134)

380.

arrangement

, introductory

, conjunction

possible

, as clause

, introductory

, if clause

(138)

Lesson 53

381. Office-Style Dictation. A dictator may sometimes wish to make a long insertion. He may, for example, interrupt his dictation and say, "Go back and insert a sentence after the first one in the letter." When this happens, you should:

1. Write a large A in a circle at the point where the new material is to be inserted.

2. Then draw two heavy lines after the last sentence that you have taken from dictation, to separate the insert from the rest of your dictation.

3. Under the two heavy lines, write "*Insert A*," encircled, and write the insert.

4. Draw two heavy lines to indicate the end of the insert.

Illustration of Office-Style Dictation

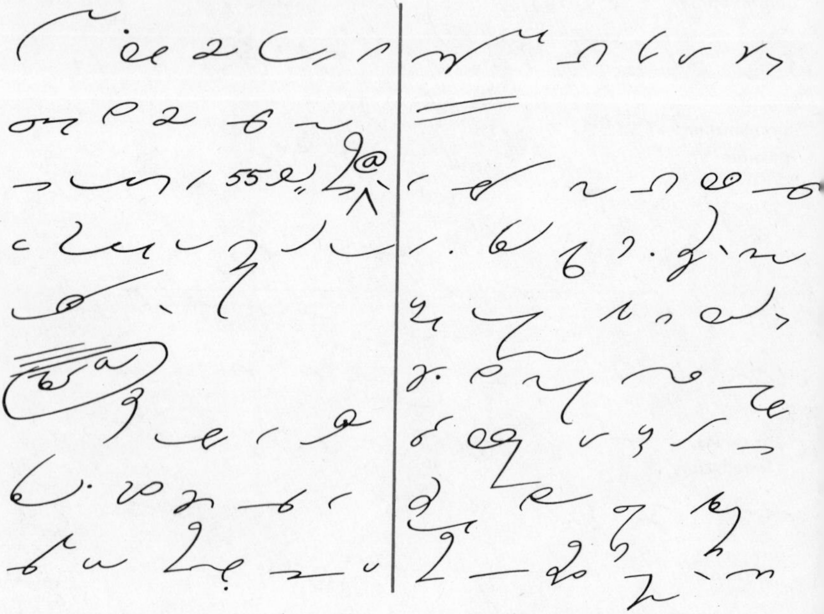

Reading and Writing Practice

382. Transcription Word Study

adjoining Next to. (Do not confuse with *adjourning*, which means "suspending or putting off till another time.")

justify To prove or show to be just.

383.

384.

adjoining
typewriter

; because of comma
, nonrestrictive
reasons

justify
appreciate
available

(130)

385.

well-known
hyphenated
before noun
lose

, introductory
firm's

, *when* clause

: enumeration

recommend

requirements

(150)

386.

, *as* clause

duplicating

afraid

, parenthetical

supervisor

, introducing short quote

. inside quote

, parenthetical

, *and* omitted

(110)

387.

various
except
, conjunction

; no conjunction
accept

, parenthetical
slight

, introductory

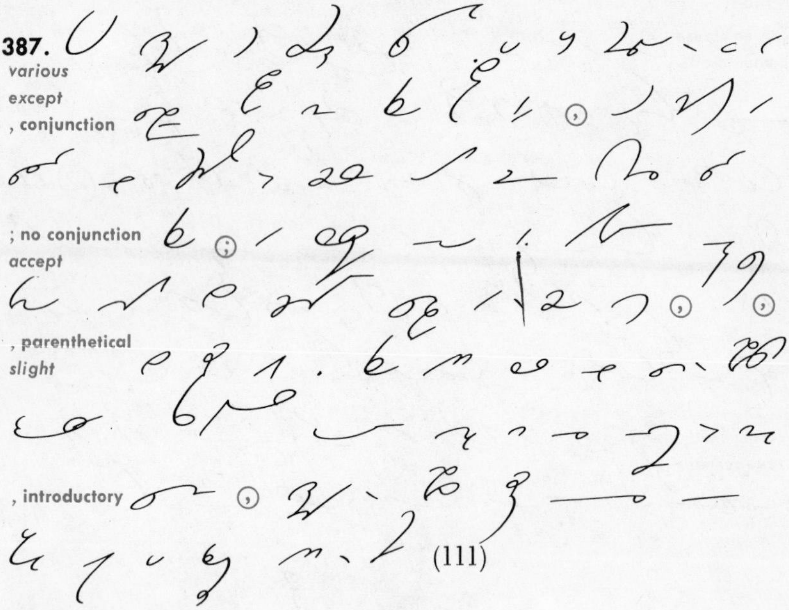

(111)

388.

copyholder
burdened
gadgets

; illustrative ,
, series
levers

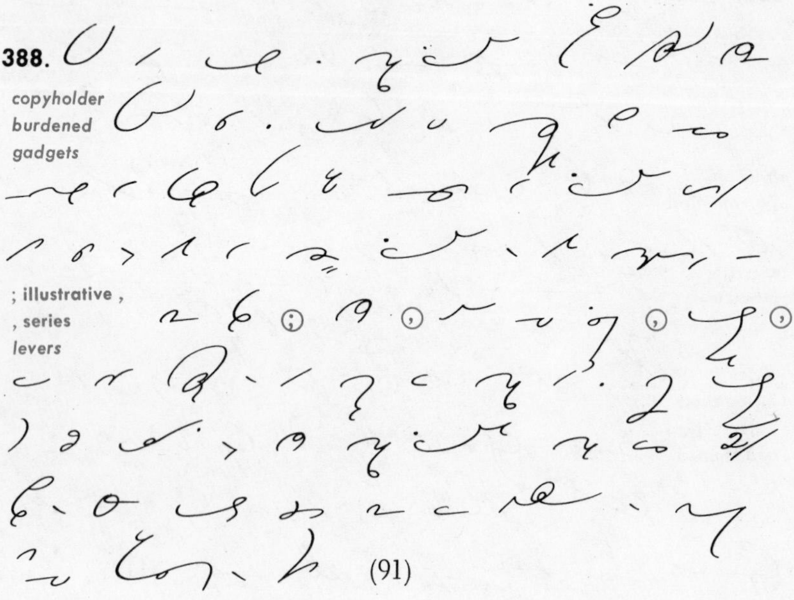

(91)

Transcription Quiz. Supply all missing punctuation and words omitted from the shorthand. This quiz calls for lots of commas as well as one semicolon. If you can correctly supply all the missing punctuation, it will be a real feather in your cap!

389. (144)

Lesson 54

390. Shorthand Spelling Drill

Words Ending in -ant, -ent: *Once again, there is no rule that will help you to decide whether to use* -ANT *or* -ENT. *Studying the word family groups, however, will help you master them.*

-ant

1. Applicant, defendant, triumphant, tenant, tolerant, warrant.
2. Ignorant, pleasant, expectant, servant, observant, relevant.

-ent

1. Innocent, independent, dependent, superintendent, correspondent, apparent, opponent.
2. Proponent, consistent, persistent, permanent, prominent, eminent.

Reading and Writing Practice

391. Transcription Word Study

wholesale house A company that sells only to retailers; it does not sell to the general public.

annual Yearly. (Do not confuse with *annul,* which means "to make void.")

complimentary Free.

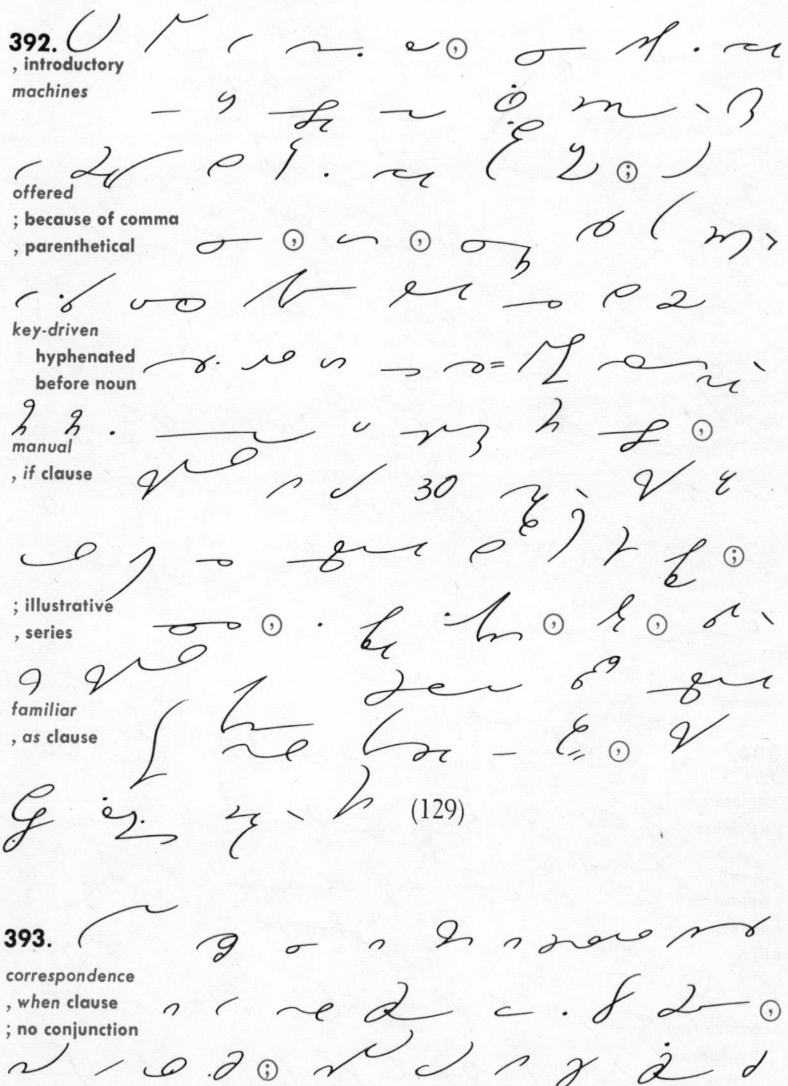

, series

quantity

(150)

394. *inquiry*

wholesale

, as clause

, appositio*n*

believe

differs

executive-type

hyphenated before noun

, introductory
comfortable
, and omitted
good-looking
hyphenated before noun
, if clause
delivery
(148)

395.
, as clause
annual
: enumeration
, series
21, 22, 23
, apposition
history
, nonrestrictive
championships
, introductory
, introducing short quote
. inside quote

guest
, *if* clause
; no conjunction

(140)

396.
trade-in
hyphenated
before noun

allowance
, introductory

, parenthetical
liberal

, *if* clause
appraise

; no conjunction
Engineering

, introductory
thousands

, *if* clause (154)

Lesson 55

397. Brief Forms and Derivatives

1. Week, weeks, weekly, week end, weekday; correct, corrected, correction.
2. Side, sided, sides, beside, inside, outside, decide, coincide, sideline.
3. Got, forgot, forgotten; recognize, recognizes, recognition.
4. Want, wanted, wants, wanting; conclude, concluding, conclusion, conclusive.

Reading and Writing Practice

398. Transcription Word Study

decorator One who advises on the proper furnishing of homes, offices, and other rooms.

internal On the inside.

constitute Make up.

399.

, as clause

survey

company's

some time
, conjunction
, nonrestrictive
accepting
, apposition
; because of comma
central
, introductory
correspondence

(146)

400.
; because of comma
, parenthetical
model
, *if clause*
, nonrestrictive
drawers

; no conjunction
fairness

best-run
hyphenated
before noun
, introductory

(140)

401.

executives
; illustrative ,

, parenthetical

modern
, and omitted

, *if* clause

(128)

402.

, conjunction

mechanics

: introducing long quote

, conjunction

. inside quote

, introductory

150/

50/

, nonrestrictive

16

350/

(147)

403.

ten-year-old
hyphenated
before noun

duplicator
, apposition

, as clause
operator's

; no conjunction
, introductory
portable

(161)

404.

, series
available

(50)

The letter is transcribed

After transcribing and proofreading a letter, the first thing that Mary does is to draw a line through her shorthand notes for that letter. She is very careful to draw that line *only* through that transcribed letter. She once had a sad experience when she drew a line through the shorthand notes for a short letter that followed the longer letter she had finished transcribing. The result was that the short letter never was transcribed—and Mr. Baker was caused considerable embarrassment.

Then:

1. She picks up the piece of correspondence that has been answered.

2. Over that correspondence she clips (some companies prefer to staple) the carbon of the letter she has just typed. Thus the latest communication is always *on top.*

3. Finally, over all she places the letter to be signed, with the envelope attached.

4. If a letter is urgent, she immediately takes it to Mr. Baker for his signature. If not, she places it, face down, in the box that she keeps for completed work. Why face down? To protect its contents from the eyes of curious passers-by!

Mary makes it a point to deliver the letters she has transcribed several times a day rather than all at once toward the end of the workday. In this way, her employer can sign them at his convenience and not have to do so in a hurry at the last minute. In addition, Mary thus protects herself against having to stay after five o'clock to retype a letter on which she has made a mistake (which very, very seldom happens) or on which Mr. Baker wishes to make changes.

Mr. Baker paid Mary the finest tribute that an employer can pay to his secretary or stenographer; he often signs routine letters without reading them. But Mary had to earn that tribute!

Lesson 56

405. Shorthand Language Study

-en: *Forms adjectives meaning made of.* WOODEN, *made of wood. It also forms verbs meaning to make.* WHITEN *means to make white. It is also the past-participle ending of many irregular verbs, as* BREAK, BROKEN.

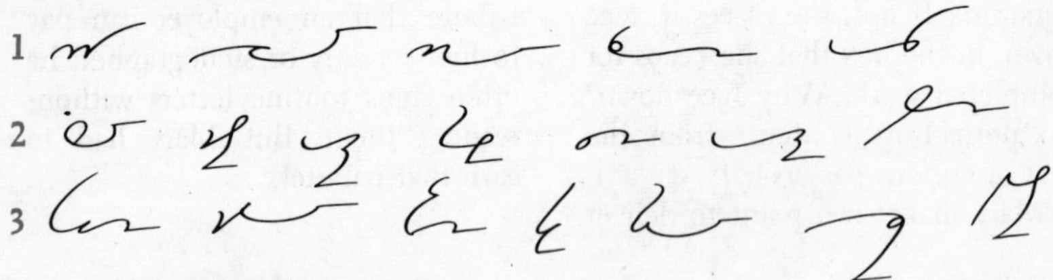

1. **Wooden, golden, woolen, silken, leaden.**
2. **Harden, stiffen, roughen, freshen, weaken, loosen, darken.**
3. **Broken, stolen, spoken, chosen, fallen, given, driven.**

-ish: *Forms adjectives for names of peoples.* DANE, DANISH. *It is added to other words to form adjectives meaning resembling or suggesting.* CHILDISH, *resembling or suggesting a child.*

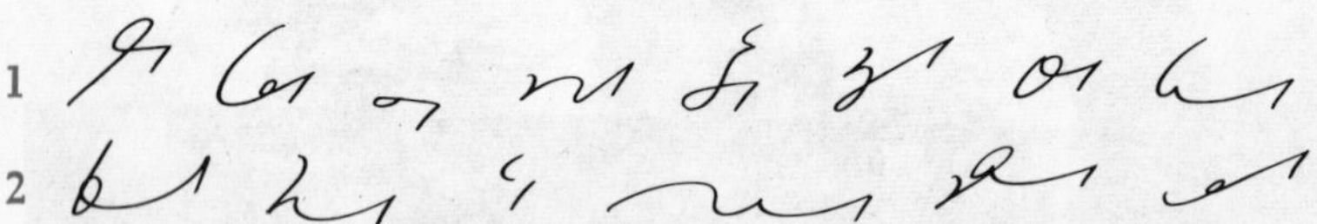

1. **Danish, British, English, Scottish, Spanish, Swedish, Irish, Polish.**
2. **Childish, foolish, selfish, girlish, stylish, reddish.**

Reading and Writing Practice

406. Transcription Word Study

rag content Most paper is made from wood pulp. Better grades of paper, however, also contain some linen. The greater the linen (rag) content, the better the paper.

inventory form The form on which the amount of stock on hand is recorded.

spoilage That which has been marred or ruined.

407.

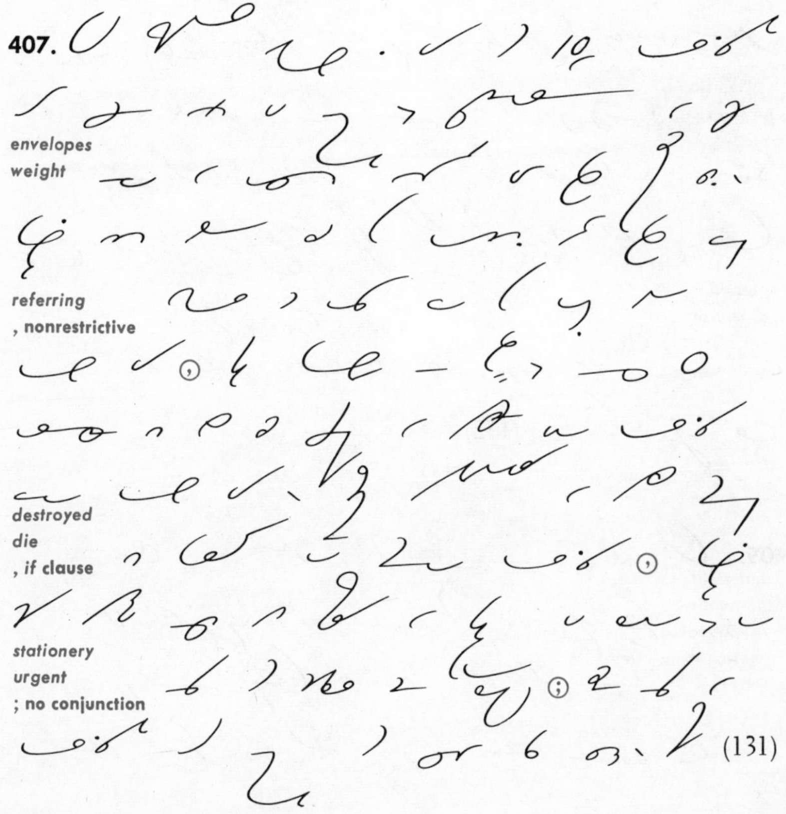

408.

president's
distribute

, **introducing**
short quote
purchasing

. **inside quote**
, **parenthetical**
responsible

, **when clause**
inventory

operation
, **as clause**

(152)

409.
, **and omitted**
high-quality
hyphenated
before noun
, **series**

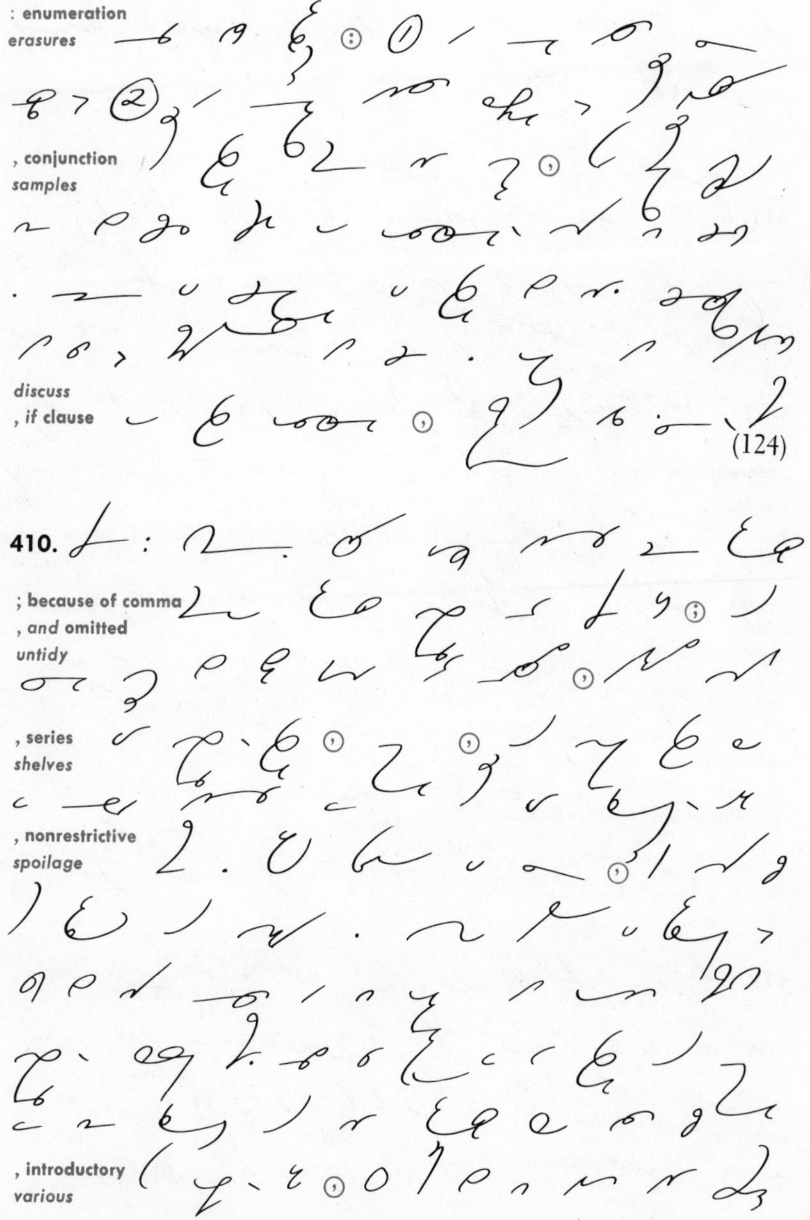

: enumeration
erasures
, conjunction
samples
discuss
, if clause
(124)
410.
; because of comma
, and omitted
untidy
, series
shelves
, nonrestrictive
spoilage
, introductory
various

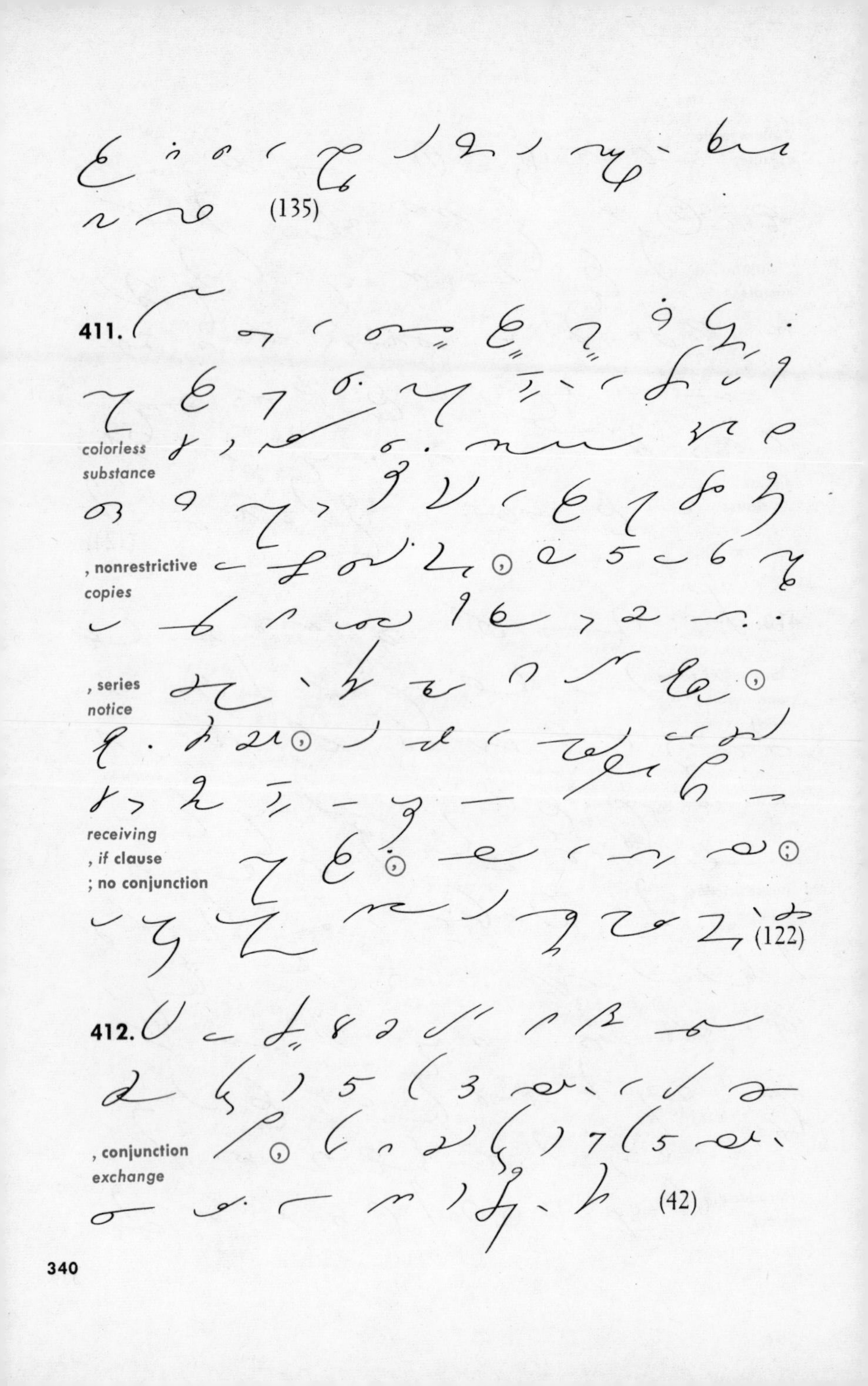

(135)

411.

colorless
substance

, nonrestrictive
copies

, series
notice

receiving
, if clause
; no conjunction

(122)

412.

, conjunction
exchange

(42)

Lesson 57

413. Accuracy Practice. Follow the practice procedure outlined on page 138.

Group 1	Group 2	Group 3
thick	ought	pass
thin	should	base

Practice Drill

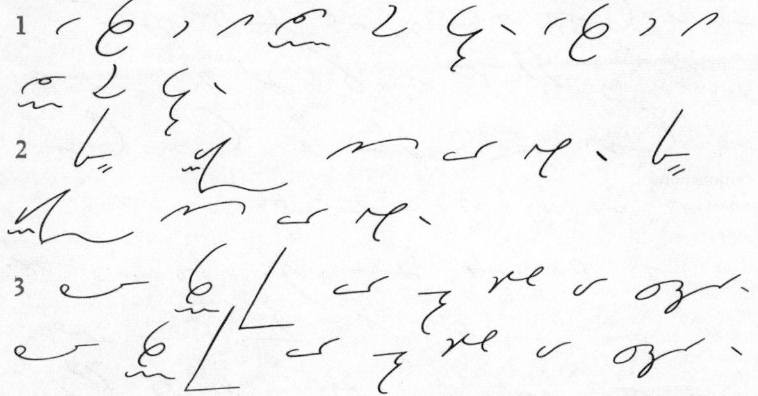

1. The paper is too thick for our purposes. The paper is too thin for our purposes.
2. John ought to be glad to go on the trip. John should be glad to go on the trip.
3. He will not base judgment on the newspaper stories of the accident. He will not pass judgment on the newspaper stories of the accident.

Reading and Writing Practice

414. Transcription Word Study

stationery Such items as paper, clips, pens, notebooks, cards, etc. (Do not confuse with *stationary*, which means "fixed, not changing.")

bristles Short, stiff hairs.

monetary Pertaining to money.

415.

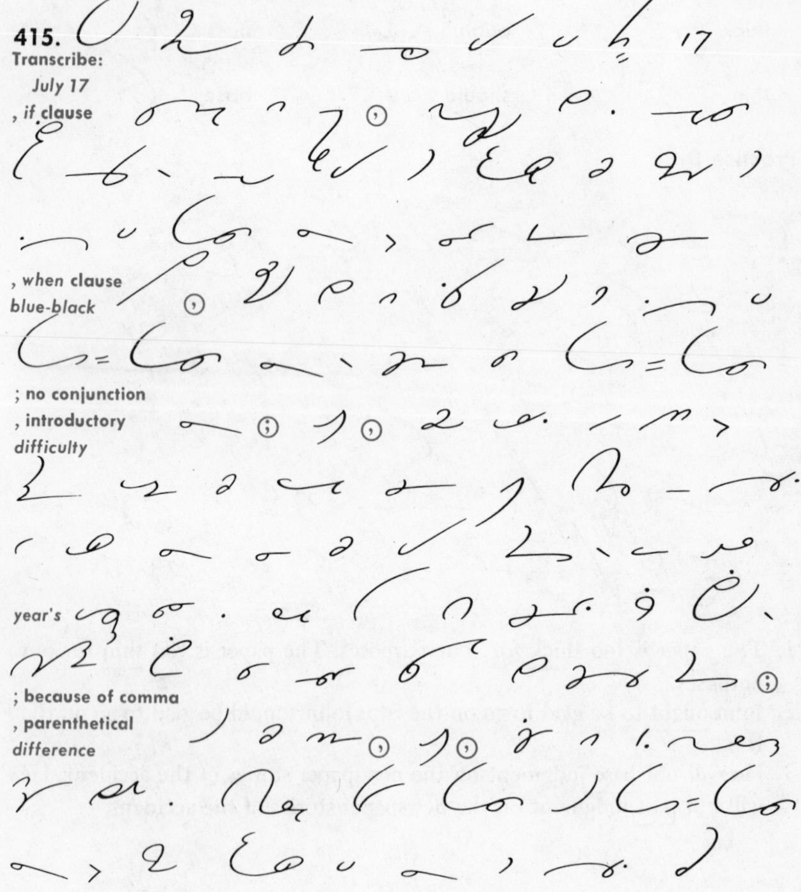

, as clause
appreciate

(153)

416.

secretary's
supplies

, parenthetical

: enumeration
, series
stapler

(111)

417.

, apposition
, when clause

15

; illustrative ,
, series
, introductory

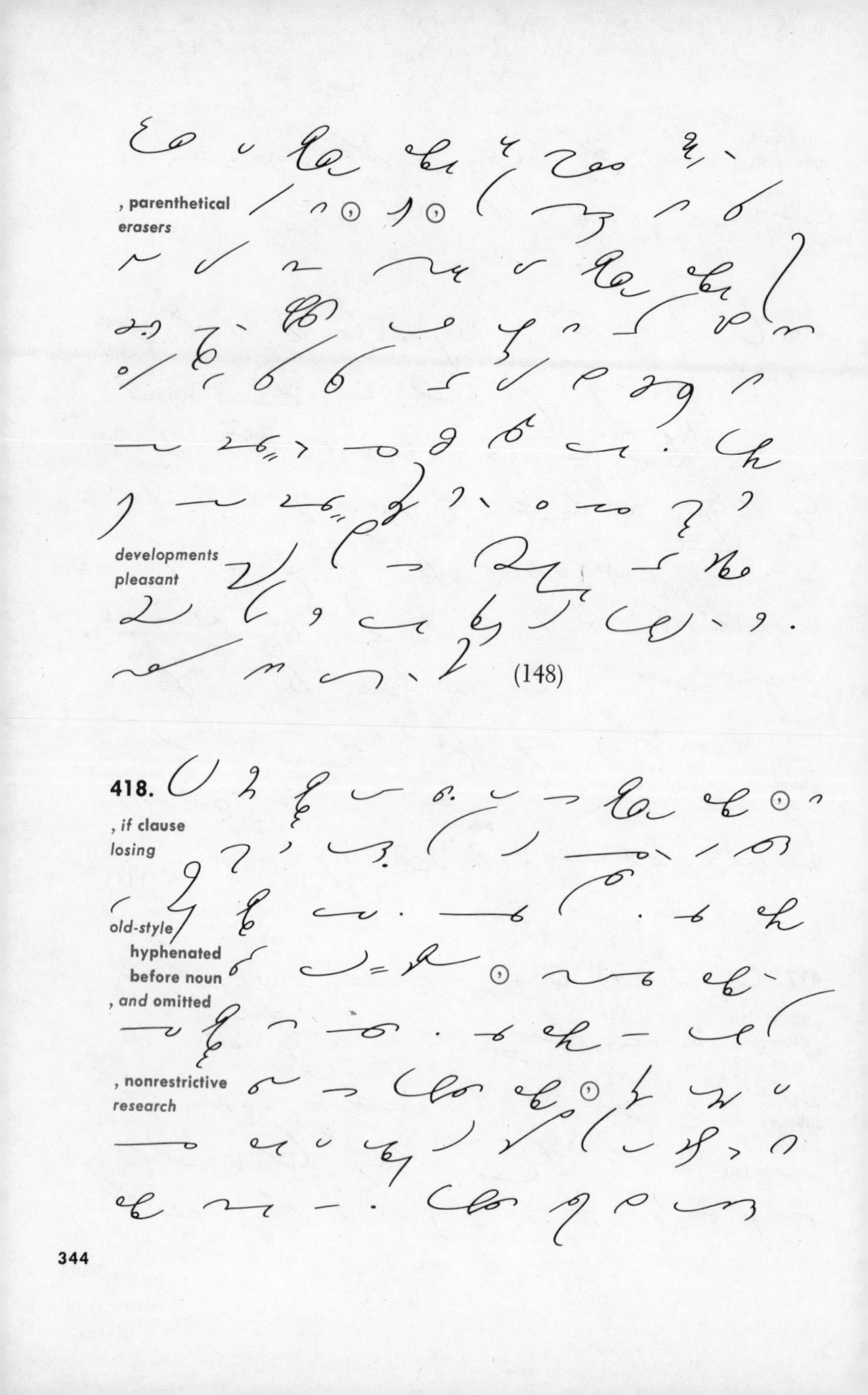

, parenthetical
erasers

developments
pleasant

(148)

418.

, if clause
losing

old-style
hyphenated
before noun
, and omitted

, nonrestrictive
research

bristles

50

, introductory

, introducing short quote

. inside quote

(136)

419.

, introductory

ribbons

nylon

slightly

; no conjunction

10

, introductory

guaranteed

, introductory

whether

(130)

Lesson 58

420. Office-Style Dictation. Indention is one of the best ways for emphasizing a few lines of typewritten copy. If, for example, the letter is typed with a 50-space line, indented material might be typed on a 40-space line, so that it stands out from the rest of the letter.

If your dictator, *before* he dictates, mentions that the material is to be indented, the shorthand notes can be indented slightly and a large square bracket can be placed on each side of the material to be indented. If he decides on the indention *after* he has dictated the material, you can place the bracket on each side of the section to be indented. That will remind you, when transcribing, to make the necessary change in the margin.

Illustration of Office-Style Dictation

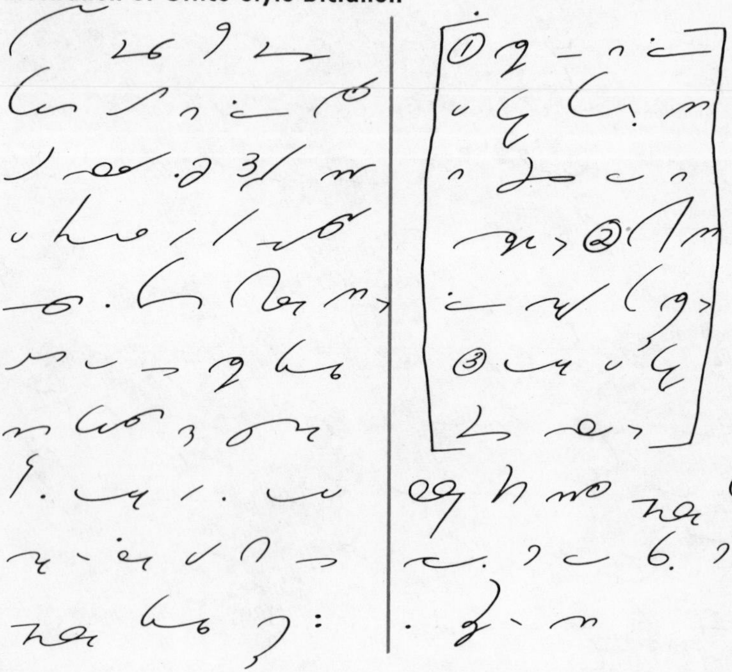

Reading and Writing Practice

421. Transcription Word Study

assumption Act of taking for granted.

manila folder A folder made from a strong brown paper made of hemp grown in the Philippines.

422.

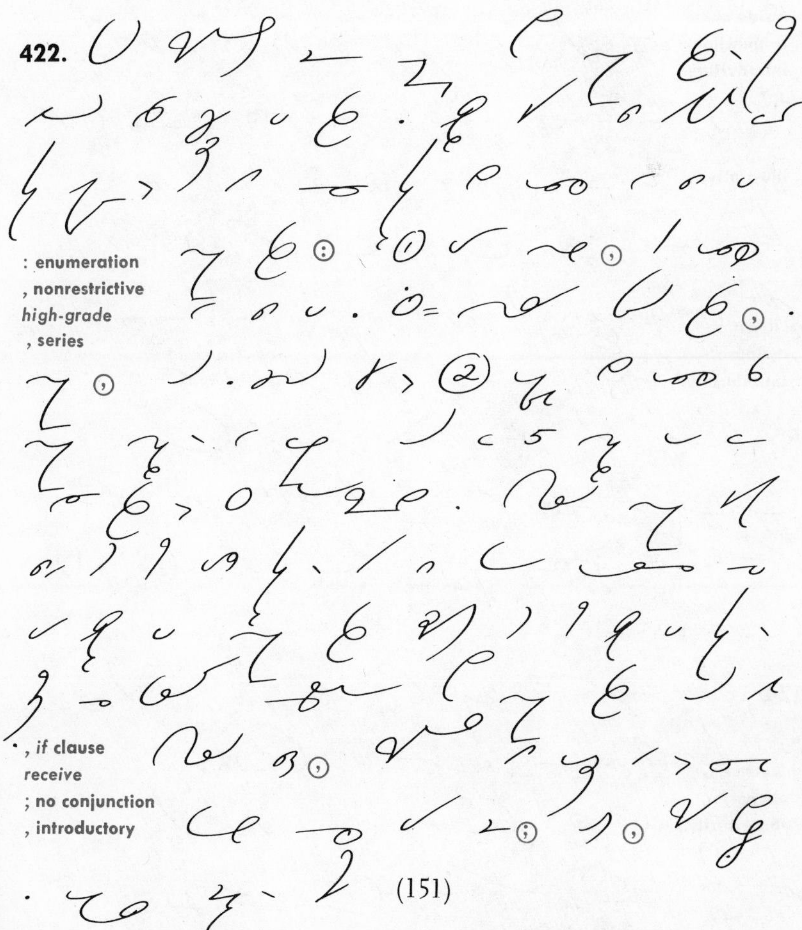

423.

, introducing short quote

, inside quote

, conjunction

, introductory

; illustrative ,

assumption

, *if* clause

, introductory

(130)

424.

announce

stationery

, nonrestrictive

, *and* omitted
texture
erasures

, introductory
ream

(145)

425.
company's
manila

stationery
, conjunction

, series
; because of comma
quotations

, apposition
Director

, as clause
won't

(138)

426.
stationery
Smith's
, introductory

colors
quality

, when clause
matching

, series
children

, when clause
. courteous
request

(138)

Transcription Quiz. Supply the missing punctuation and the words that have been omitted from the shorthand. Watch carefully for the two semicolons that are necessary to punctuate this letter correctly.

427. [shorthand] (144)

Lesson 59

428. Shorthand Spelling Drill

Words Ending in -ize, -yze, -ise: *Most of the words in this group are spelled* IZE. *Try to remember these words in their own family groupings.*

-ize

Realize, authorize, emphasize, criticize, economize, equalize, recognize.

-yze

Analyze, paralyze.

-ise

Exercise, surprise, surmise, revise, compromise, supervise, merchandise, enterprise.

Reading and Writing Practice

429. Transcription Word Study

supplements Additions to.

public address system Transmitting equipment that enables a speaker to be heard in a large area or in many different places.

430.

envelopes
legal

respectively
weight
completely

(91)

431.
supplies
Transcribe:
52 Street

52

, and omitted
up-to-the-minute
hyphenated
before noun

Transcribe:
$50
, introductory

50/

10,

catalogue

, nonrestrictive

, as clause

(160)

432.

employees'

bulletin

, nonrestrictive

, parenthetical

; because of comma

announced

, parenthetical

, if clause

(122)

433.

, introducing short quote

? inside quote

stationery

recommend

apt

; no conjunction

, if clause

; illustrative ,

, nonrestrictive

likely

(155)

434.

ball-point hyphenated before noun

: enumeration

enclosed

(2)

, introductory
recommend

, introductory

; because of comma
, *if* clause
quantities

, conjunction

(136)

435.
dictionaries
; no conjunction
, introductory

volumes
, conjunction

advice

(77)

Lesson 60

436. Brief Forms and Derivatives

1. Probable, probably, improbable; cover, covered, discover, recover, uncover.
2. Ship, shipping, shipper, shipment; out, outing, outside, outline, output.
3. Order, orders, ordered, orderly, disorder; suggest, suggested, suggests, suggestive.
4. Decide, decided, decidedly, undecided; most, almost, foremost.

Reading and Writing Practice

437. Transcription Word Study

desperately Frantically.

recipient One who receives.

438.

, introductory
Society
Fiftieth

, and omitted occasion

, introducing short quote

, inside quote

(137)

439.

twenty-fifth anniversary misfortune

barrel

, introductory

, if clause

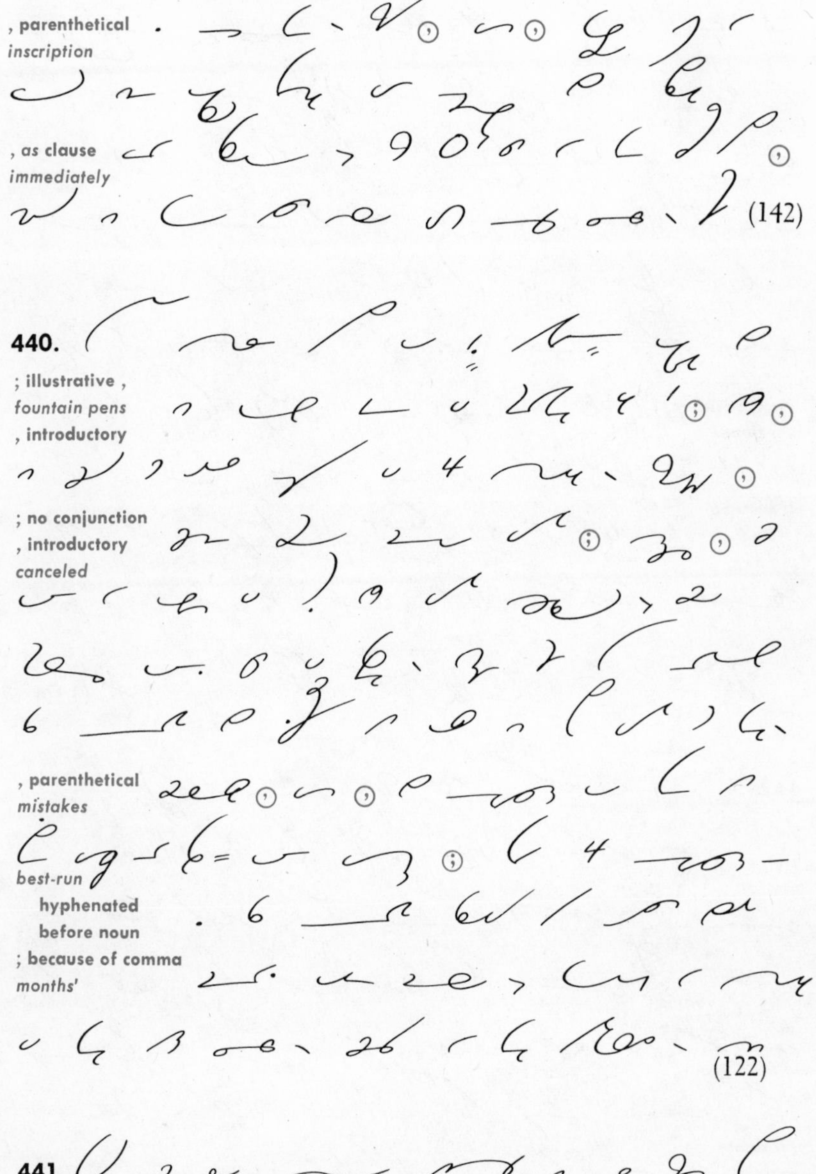

, parenthetical
inscription

, as clause
immediately

(142)

440.

; illustrative ,
fountain pens
, introductory

; no conjunction
, introductory
canceled

, parenthetical
mistakes

best-run
hyphenated
before noun
; because of comma
months'

(122)

441.

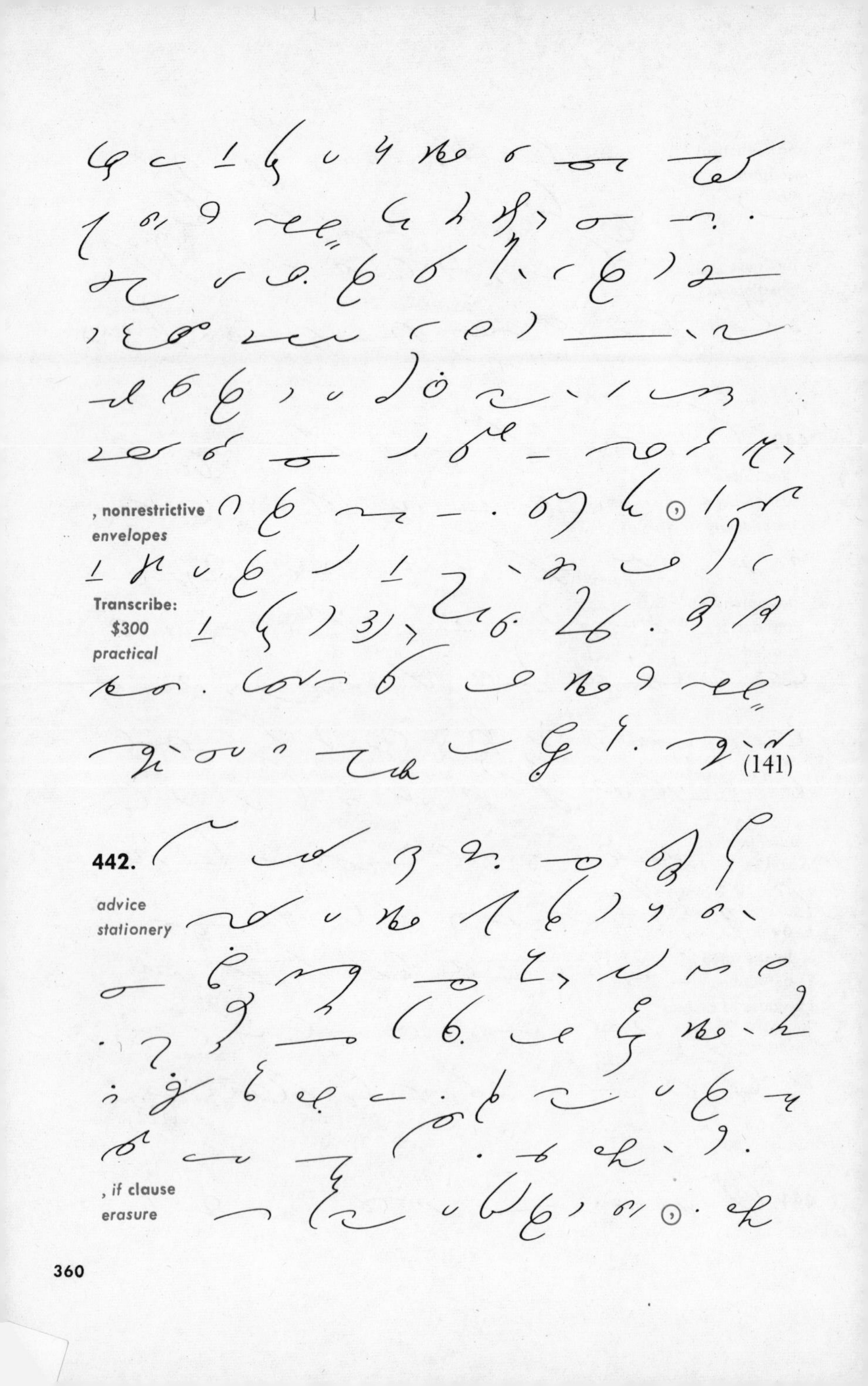

, nonrestrictive

envelopes

Transcribe:

$300

practical

(141)

442.

advice

stationery

, if clause

erasure

high-quality

hyphenated before noun

, introductory

(146)

443.

old-fashioned

favorable

, conjunction

recipient

assignment
, if clause

(198)

444.

stapler
featuring

, introductory
plastic

, introductory

Transcribe:
$3
, conjunction

(86)

Part IV

Transcription Alertness

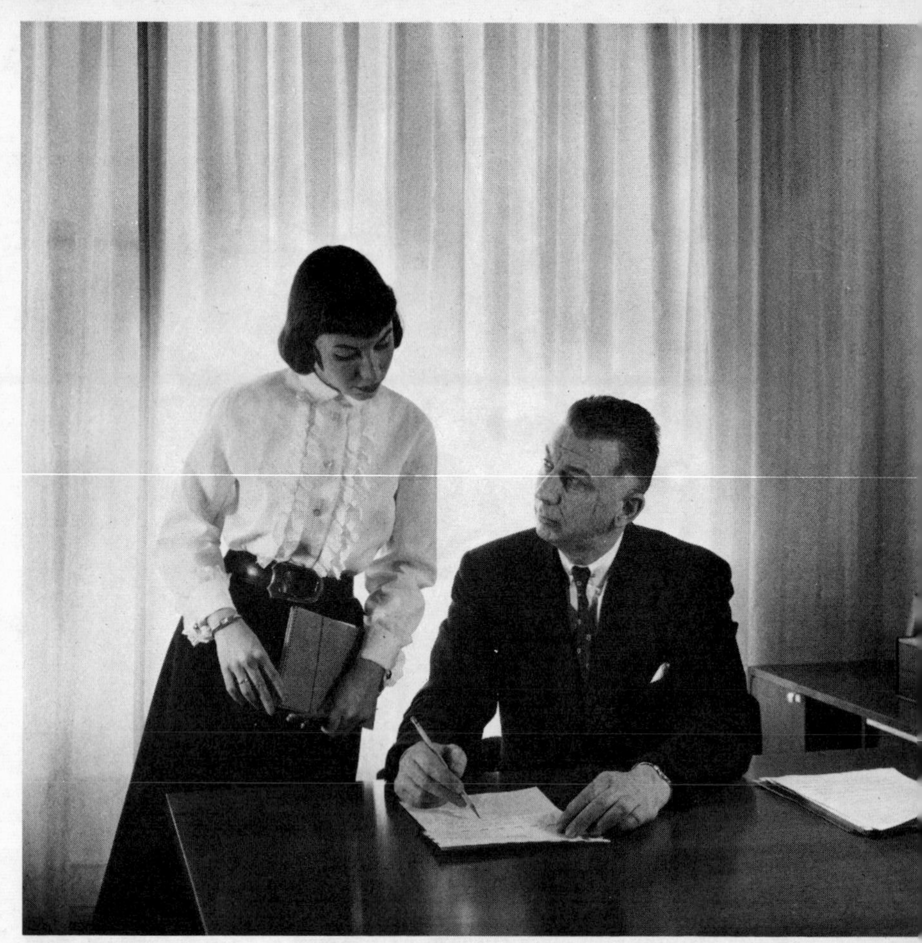

Mary Brown, watchdog

Mr. Baker expects Mary to do more than take down and transcribe mechanically the material that he dictates. He realizes that occasionally, as he dictates, he makes errors in grammar, and even errors in fact. Because he often concentrates so hard on the thought he is trying to express, his subject does not always agree with his verb; he sometimes uses a plural pronoun intead of a singular pronoun; he sometimes makes errors in dates, names, amounts, and other important facts.

But he does not worry because he knows that Mary is his watchdog for mistakes of that type and that she will correct obvious mistakes automatically, but ask him when there is a question in her mind about anything.

He knows that Mary will not simply transcribe a letter as it was dictated and then, when he finds an error, try to excuse herself by saying, "But that's what you said."

Here are some of the types of dictator's errors that Mary would change without asking Mr. Baker.

If he should dictate: "Who did you see when you called at the office?" she would transcribe: "Whom did you see when you called at the office?"

If he should dictate: "Not one of the men are capable," she would transcribe: "Not one of the men is capable."

If he should dictate: "Of the two books, I can't decide which is best," she would transcribe: "Of the two books, I can't decide which is better."

Most dictators would not make mistakes of this type if their minds were not occupied with more important details than grammar.

Here are some of the types of dictator's errors that Mary would take up with Mr. Baker, tactfully, of course:

"I will see you on Friday, April 16." (April 16 is a Thursday. Therefore, there is some question whether Mr. Baker means Thursday, April 16, or Friday, April 17.)

In one paragraph Mr. Baker says: "I am sending two cases today and another two on Wednesday." Later he says, "These five cases should meet your requirements for the entire year." (If he sent two cases on one day and two on another, that would make a total of four. Did he mean to send three cases on one of the days, or should he have said "these four cases"?)

In one paragraph he says; "Mr. Frank Smith was here to see me today." In a later paragraph he says, "Harry Smith impressed me as a good salesman." (Was the man's name Harry or Frank Smith?)

When Mary Brown discovers errors of this type, she goes to Mr. Baker and says something like this: "Mr. Baker, in my notes I have the statement that you will see Mr. Green on Friday, April 16. I wonder whether it should be Thursday, April 16, or Friday, April 17."

"Mr. Baker, I want to be sure that I have these figures right. Are you sending two cases today and two on Wednesday?"

Your employer will also expect you to be his watchdog for mistakes.

Lesson 61

445. Shorthand Language Study

Fore-: *Before, ahead, in front.* FORECAST, *to plan ahead.*

Forecast, foresee, foresighted, foregoing, foreground, foretell.

-claim: *To speak.* EXCLAIM, *to speak out.*

Exclaim, declaim, proclaim, disclaim, acclaim.

Reading and Writing Practice

446. Transcription Word Study

distressed Bothered; worried.

inferior Of poor quality.

concession A grant or lease of a portion of premises for some definite purpose.

447.

Chapter 13 Food

, *and omitted*
ever-present
hyphenated
before noun

: *enumeration*
storeroom

, *series*
employees'
storage

, *if clause*
estimates

(133)

448.

, *as clause*

; because of comma
, introductory
affects

, conjunction
demand

(137)

449.

seniors

part-time hyphenated before noun

, if clause
appreciate

, introductory

, nonrestrictive
except
busiest

(125)

STEPHEN SAMPSON & SONS 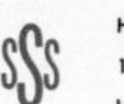 HUMBLE BUILDING
1216 MAIN STREET
HOUSTON 1, TEXAS

February 22, 19--

Mr. Perry R. Strong, President
Harrison Manufacturing Company
4125 North Fifth Avenue
Denver 8, Colorado

Dear Mr. Strong:

Subject: Employees' Handbooks

We are sending you today by express all the material that we have available on how to prepare an employees' handbook.

You will be interested, I think, in our experience in helping the Martin Miller Company prepare its latest handbook. When we were called in, that company already had a handbook; but it was out of date. The organization had grown considerably since that handbook was prepared; consequently, the book had to be completely rewritten. The new handbook was ready at the end of last year. It benefited by many lessons that had been learned during the work on the first handbook.

While working with Martin Miller Company, we learned that the following three points are important in preparing a handbook:

1. It should not be a rule book listing things that should and should not be done by employees.

2. It should take advantage of the pleasant feeling of satisfaction with which an employee starts a new job. The handbook should play a definite part in maintaining that feeling of satisfaction.

3. It should set down facts that will make employees feel that they are important parts of the company. It should give them information on every phase of the company's organization and activities.

In the first edition of t
devoted to the history of
felt, had been accomplish
the handbook was prepared

Mr. Perry R. Strong 2 February 22, 19--

These are just a few thoughts that come to me at this time. I am sure that the Martin Miller Company would be glad to send you a copy of their new handbook. I believe that you may find many suggestions in it that you would be able to use when you prepare your handbook.

Needless to say, we are at your service. If you think that a visit with one of our men would be helpful, call us and we will arrange an appointment.

Cordially yours,

R. L. Kane, Vice-President

RLK:IRT

P. S. I have just learned that Fred Hopkins, the member of our staff who worked with Martin Miller Company, will be in Denver all next week. Would you like to meet him and talk with him?

Two-Page Letter
Blocked Style, with Subject Line and Postscript
Standard Punctuation

450.

accede

; because of comma

, parenthetical

, introductory

severe

, conjunction

, conjunction

likely

(115)

451.

, introducing short quote

. inside quote

, nonrestrictive

concession

, parenthetical

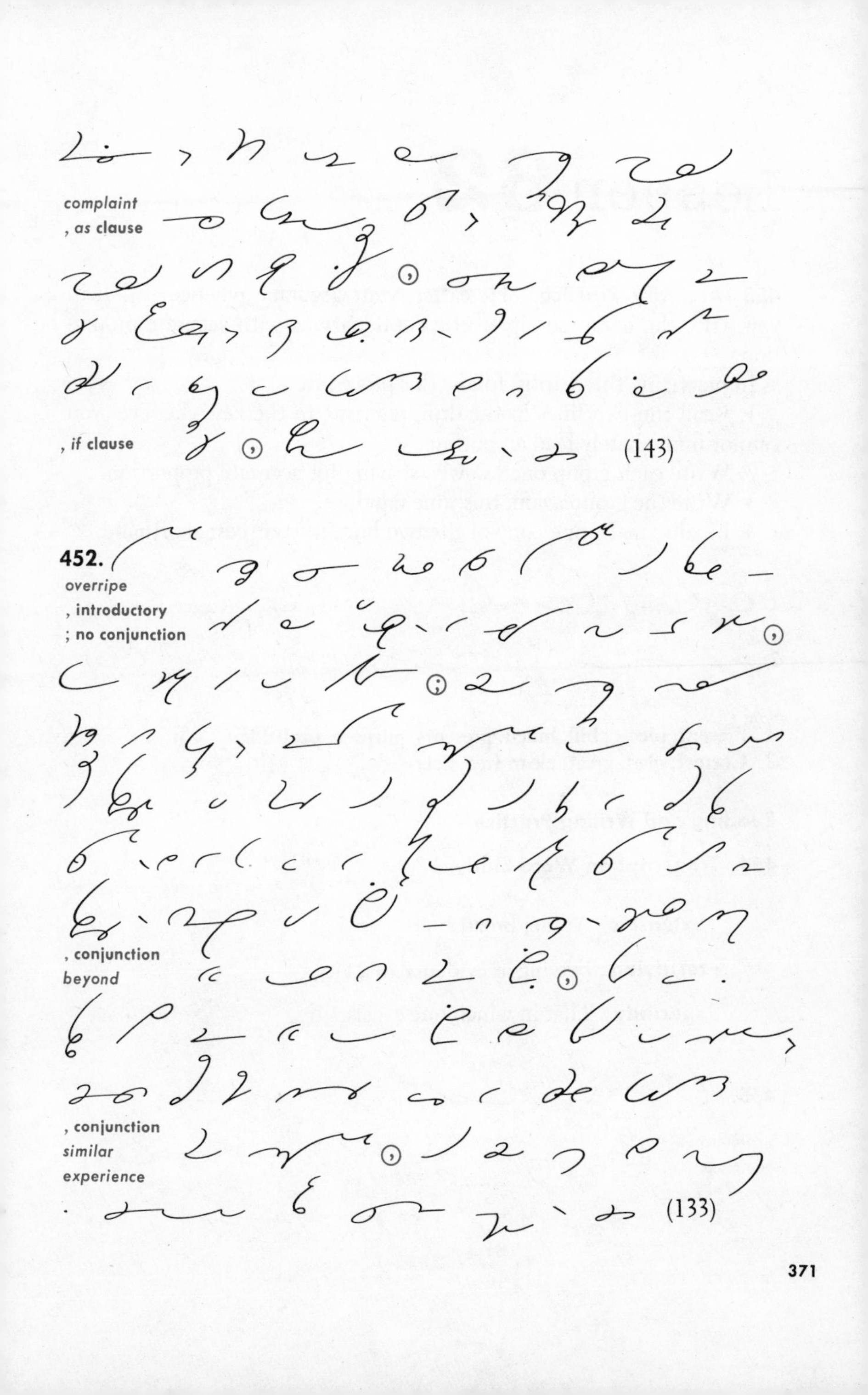

complaint
, as clause

, if clause

(143)

452.
overripe
, introductory
; no conjunction

, conjunction
beyond

, conjunction
similar
experience

(133)

Lesson 62

453. Accuracy Practice. Hereafter, your accuracy practice will help you write the common alphabetic combinations with accurate proportion.

In practicing these drills, follow this procedure:

1. Read the two lines in the drill, referring to the key whenever you cannot immediately read an outline.
2. Write each group once slowly, striving for accurate proportion.
3. Write the group again, this time rapidly.
4. Finally, make one copy of the two lines in your best shorthand.

1. Present, please; bill, billed; presents, purpose, probable.
2. Correct, glad; great, clear; free, flee.

Reading and Writing Practice

454. Transcription Word Study

extensive Wide; broad.

testifying Serving as evidence to a fact.

specialty That in which one excels.

455.

, conjunction
numerous

, introductory
extensive

color
, parenthetical

(110)

456.
, nonrestrictive
formerly

recommendation
testifying
, series

, and omitted
hard-working
hyphenated
before noun

, introducing
short quote
. inside quote

, *if clause*

(169)

457.

fulfilled

; **no conjunction**

, **nonrestrictive**

Steak

Bell's

, **parenthetical**

; **because of comma**

(102)

458.

: **enumeration**

, **series**

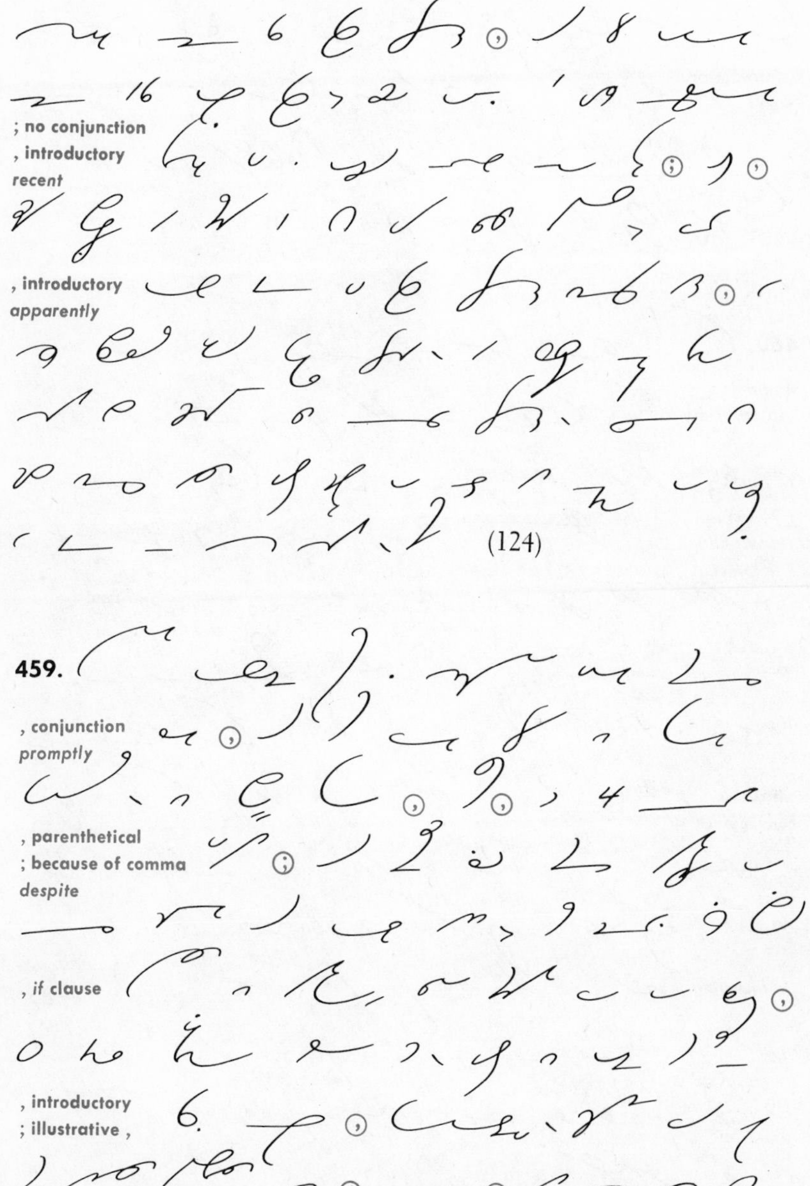

; no conjunction
, introductory
recent
, introductory
apparently
(124)
459.
, conjunction
promptly
, parenthetical
; because of comma
despite
, if clause
, introductory
; illustrative ,

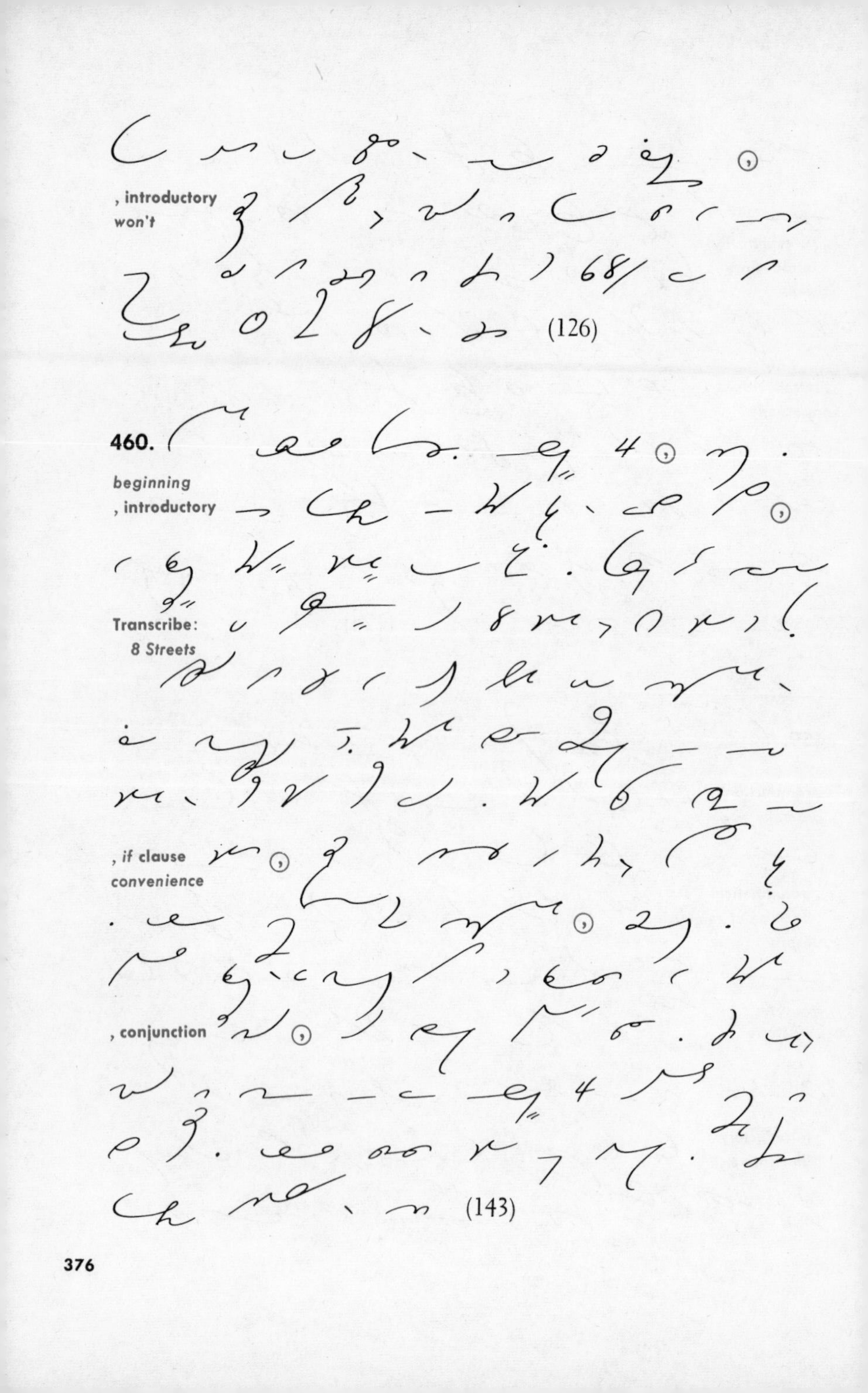

, introductory
won't

(126)

460.

beginning
, introductory

Transcribe:
8 Streets

, *if clause*
convenience

, conjunction

(143)

Lesson 63

461. Office-Style Dictation. Some dictators interrupt their dictation to give instructions about spelling, punctuation, and other details of transcription. Always record these instructions, no matter how elementary they may seem to you.

If your dictator spells a proper name or a word, record the spelling in longhand immediately above your shorthand outline.

If he dictates punctuation, place the marks in your notes, encircling them so that you do not try to read them as shorthand outlines.

Illustration of Office-Style Dictation

Reading and Writing Practice

462. Transcription Word Study

soft drinks Sodas.

periodically At regular times or intervals.

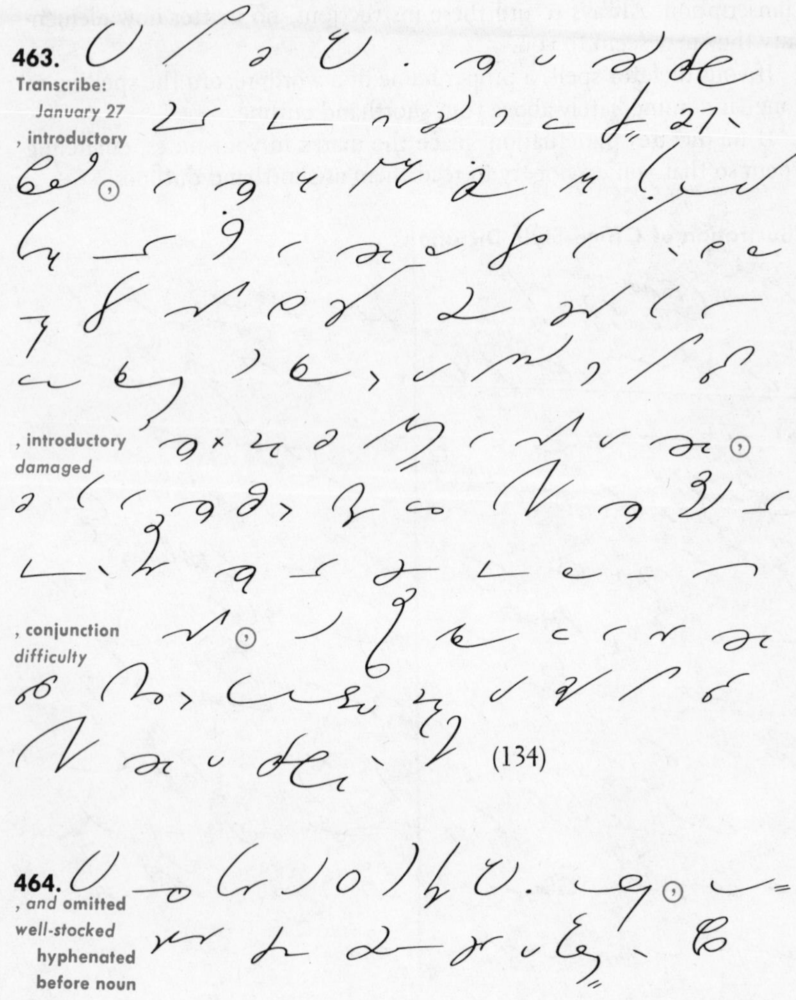

, introductory

; illustrative ,
tender

, if clause
personally

. courteous
request

(151)

465.
privilege
, as clause
, parenthetical

: enumeration
weather

, conjunction

top-quality

hyphenated

before noun

(104)

466.

, as clause

handled

; because of comma

, introductory

possibilities

company's

, apposition

: introducing

long quote

distributors

? inside quote

, introductory

co-operate

(140)

Transcription Quiz. Can you supply all the missing punctuation and the words that were omitted in the shorthand? In addition, can you find the mistake that the dictator made and that it would be your job to correct in your transcript?

467.

(145)

Lesson 64

468. Shorthand Spelling Drill

Words Ending in -ous, -us: *There is a fairly large group of words in which the ending is pronounced* us. *In most cases, it is spelled* -ous.

-ous

Tremendous, enormous, famous, numerous, generous, nervous.

-us

Stimulus, terminus, minus, surplus, bonus, focus.

Reading and Writing Practice

469. Transcription Word Study

menu A list of the items that will be served at a meal.

underprivileged Deprived of rights to which people as a whole are entitled.

donate Give.

470. Women's annual

, if clause
enough

Transcribe:
10 p.m.

menus
idea

(134)

471.

annual
, parenthetical

success
, if clause

; no conjunction
, introductory

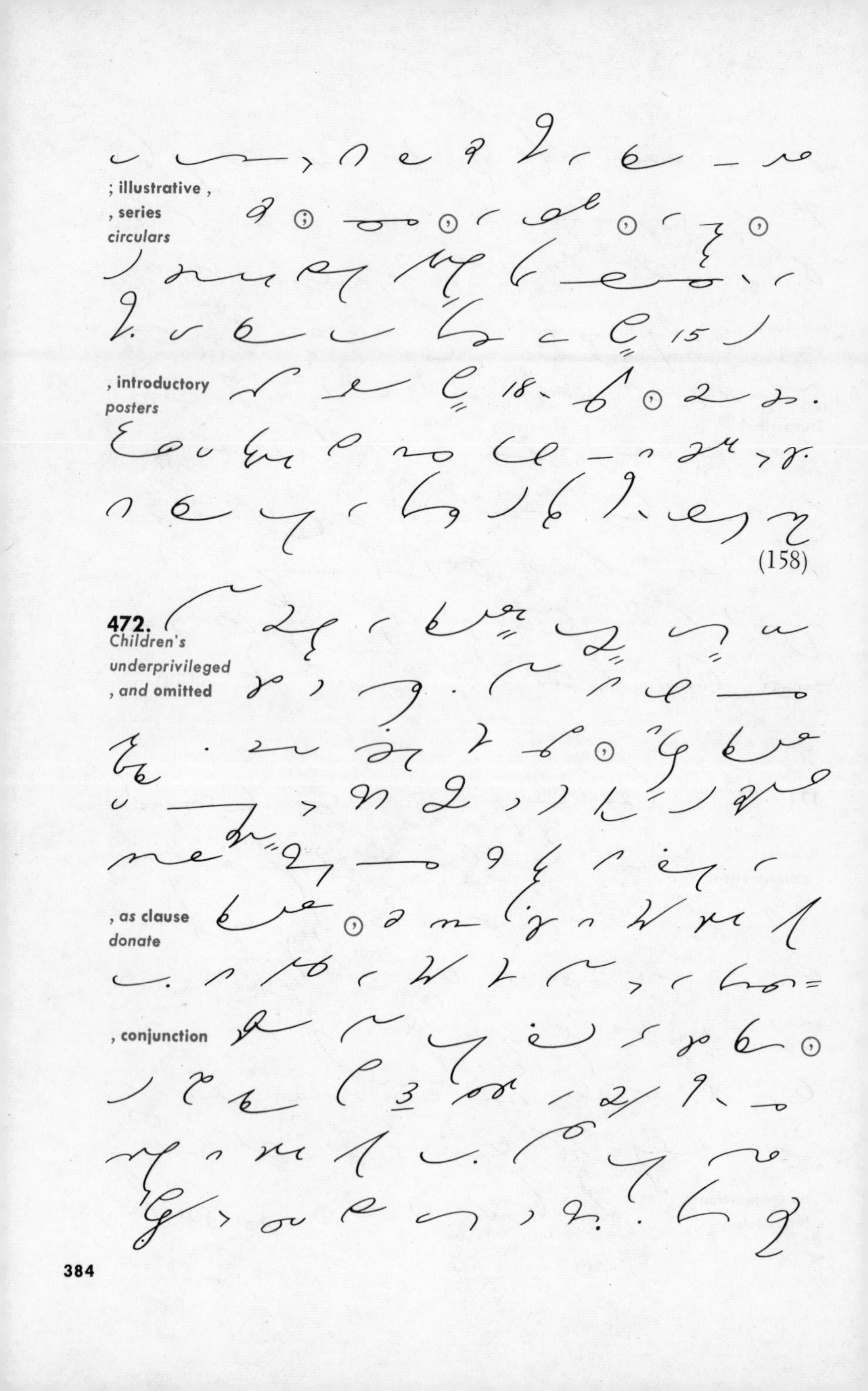

; illustrative ,

, series

circulars

, introductory

posters

(158)

472.

Children's

underprivileged

, and omitted

, as clause

donate

, conjunction

; because of comma
, parenthetical
worthy

(152)

473.

personally
, as clause

: enumeration
, series
, parenthetical

, series
daughter's

, nonrestrictive
pleasure

(154)

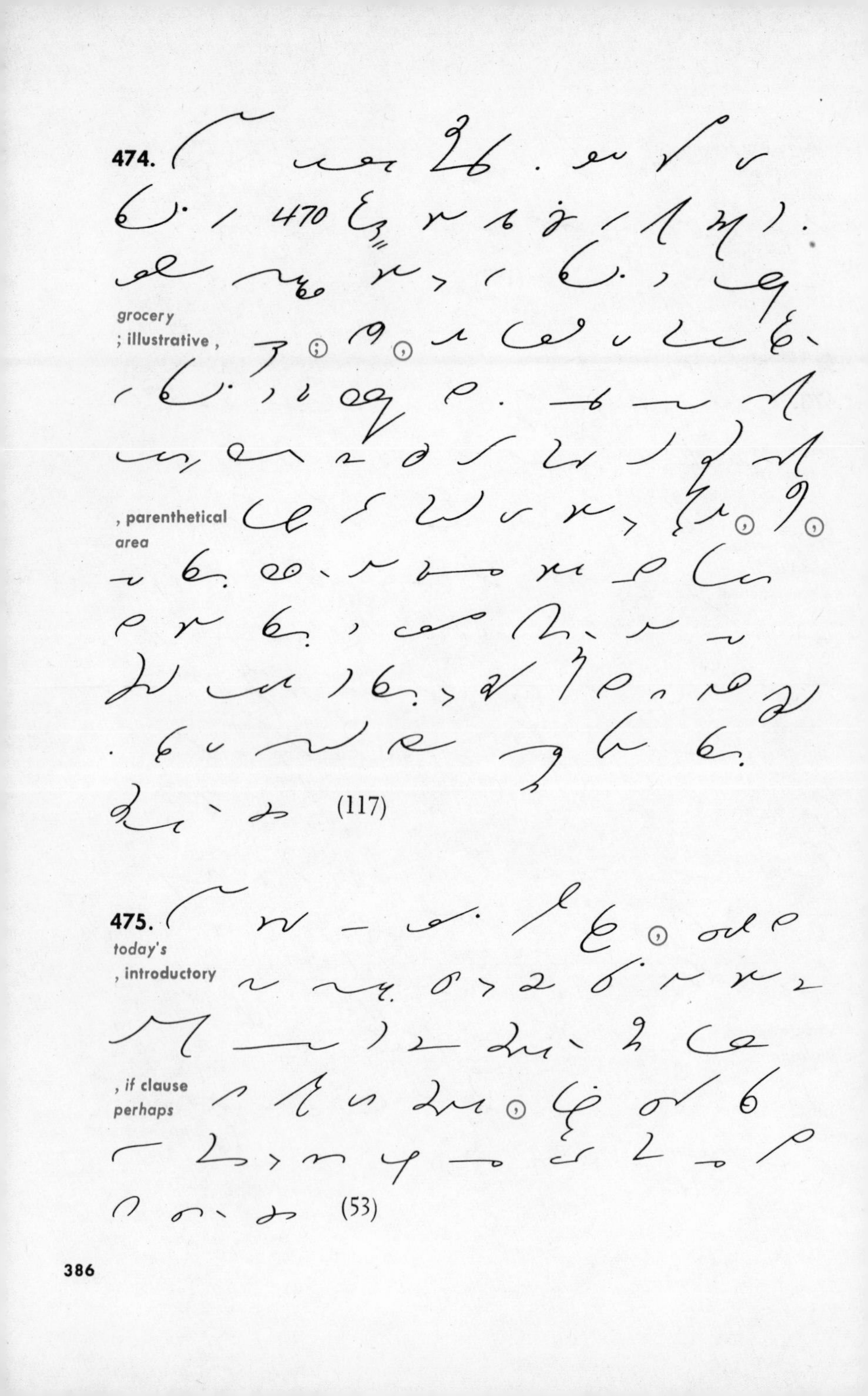

474.

grocery

; illustrative ,

, parenthetical

area

(117)

475.

today's

, introductory

, if clause

perhaps

(53)

Lesson 65

476. Brief Forms and Derivatives

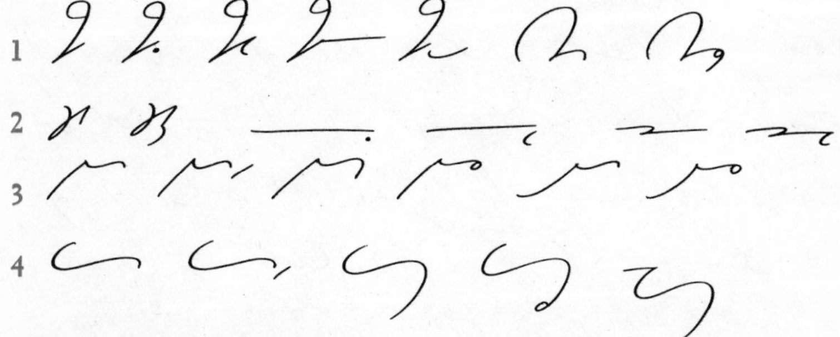

1. Advertise, advertising, advertises, advertisement, advertiser; difficult, difficulties.
2. Situation, situations; morning, mornings; number, numbers.
3. Direct, directed, direction, directly, indirect, indirectly.
4. Progress, progressed, progressive, progressively, unprogressive.

Reading and Writing Practice

477. Transcription Word Study

margin of profit The difference between the price a merchant pays for a product and the amount for which he sells it.

home economist One whose specialty is the thrifty and wise management of the home.

478.

local

, as clause

Johnson's

, introductory

well-known hyphenated before noun

, introductory

; no conjunction

woman

, and omitted

self-addressed

, parenthetical

(167)

479.

, apposition

submitted

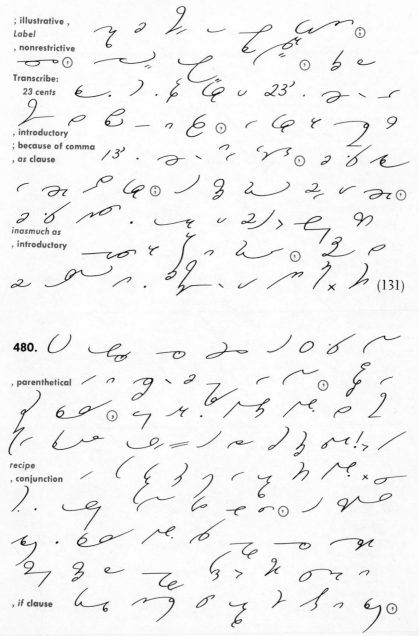

; illustrative ,
Label
, nonrestrictive

Transcribe:
23 cents

, introductory
; because of comma
, as clause

inasmuch as
, introductory

(131)

480.

, parenthetical

recipe
, conjunction

, if clause

; no conjunction

(109)

481.

, apposition

. inside quote

receive

economist

, apposition

; because of comma

ideas

results

, introductory

appreciate

, introductory

, *when* clause

specify

(135)

482.

, as clause

Christmas

; no conjunction

, introductory

suffered

dissatisfied

, parenthetical

, nonrestrictive

: enumeration

local

principal

employees

, introductory

, if clause

(173)

Implied instructions

In the very first letter that Mr. Baker dictated, he mentioned that he was enclosing a booklet that explained the company's products. Mary transcribed the letter accurately but did not enclose the booklet. Her employer signed and mailed the letter without noticing that the booklet had not been enclosed.

When the customer received the letter without the booklet, he was considerably annoyed. He had to take time to write another letter explaining that the booklet had not been enclosed. As the customer represented a very good account,

Mr. Baker, too, was considerably annoyed. The results of Mary's failure to make the enclosure might have been serious.

"When I say that I am enclosing something or going to do something, I don't mean literally that *I* am going to do it" he told her. "I mean that something is going to be done, and it is *your* job to do it or to see that it is done."

Thereafter, when her employer dictated:

"I am enclosing a booklet," she was sure it was in the envelope when she handed in the letter.

"I will see that each salesman gets a copy of the bulletin," she saw to it that the bulletin was duplicated and a copy sent to each salesman.

"I am making a reservation for April 10 at the Nelson Hotel," she either made the reservation herself or placed a memorandum on Mr. Baker's desk reminding him to do so.

"I will meet you at the airport when your plane arrives," she noted the fact on his calendar pad and then reminded him of his engagement in plenty of time for him to meet the plane.

After she had carried out the instructions implied in the dictation, she always noted on the carbon the action she took, together with the date.

Some stenographers make doubly sure that they do not forget to take care of implied instructions; they make some indication at the end of the dictated letter to remind them, such as, "send catalogue"; "send salesmen bulletins"; or "make hotel reservations."

Lesson 66

483. Shorthand Language Study

-scribe: *To write.* SUBSCRIBE, *to write below* (SUB); *therefore, to sign. Subscribing to a magazine refers to subscribing, or signing, your name below the formal agreement to pay for the magazine.*

Subscribe, inscribe, describe, transcribe, prescribe, ascribe, circumscribe.

-scription: *The writing; the noun ending for verbs ending in* -SCRIBE. SUBSCRIPTION, *the actual writing that results when you subscribe your name.*

Subscription, inscription, description, transcription, prescription, conscription.

Reading and Writing Practice

484. Transcription Word Study

unfurnished Without any furniture.

prestige Power to command admiration or esteem.

retreat A place of privacy.

Real estate

485.

two-bedroom hyphenated before noun

, *and* omitted

, *as* clause

, series

prestige

terrace

absolutely

settle

, *as* clause

, parenthetical

mind

(144)

486.

grocery-store hyphenated before noun

already

, conjunction

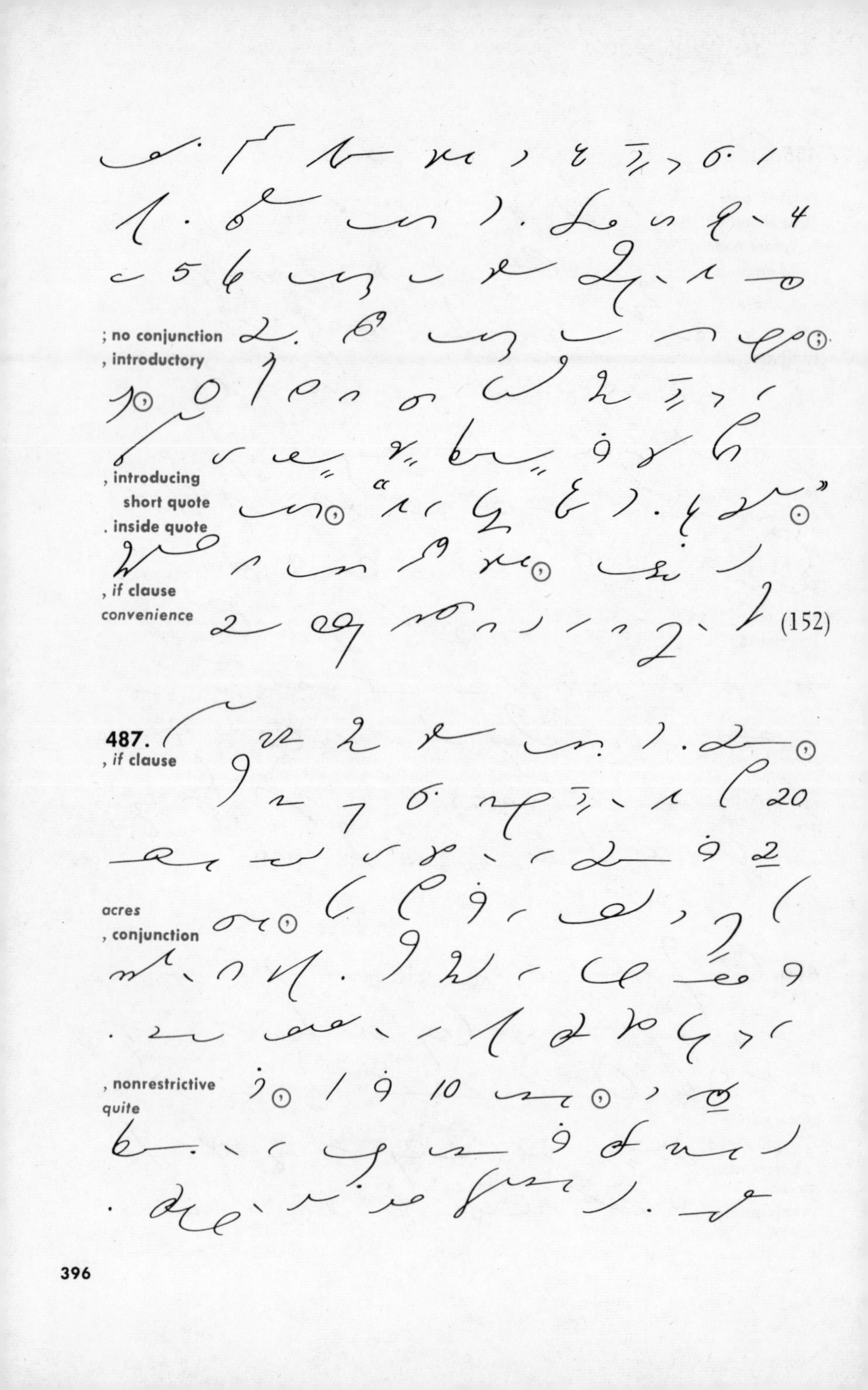

; no conjunction

, introductory

, introducing short quote

. inside quote

, if clause

convenience

(152)

487.

, *if clause*

acres

, conjunction

, nonrestrictive

quite

, conjunction

75

, if clause
, conjunction
appointment

(138)

488.

; because of comma
, when clause
announced

development
, conjunction

: enumeration
acres

45

piece
, conjunction

, if clause
company's

(158)

489.

occupies
raised

, introductory

San Francisco
; illustrative ,
30

reasonable
, if clause

(120)

490.

(53)

Lesson 67

491. Accuracy Practice. Follow the practice procedures outlined on page 372.

1. **Keys, guess; case, gas; late, laid.**
2. **Return, rate; cash, catch, gauge; take, deck.**

Reading and Writing Practice

492. Transcription Word Study

slogan A brief phrase adopted for use in advertising a product.

site Seat or location. (Do not confuse with *cite,* which means "to quote"; and *sight,* which refers to vision.)

tract An area or region or stretch of land. (Do not confuse with *track,* which means "the path along which something moves.")

493.

; no conjunction
, introductory
bargain

, conjunction
modern

; no conjunction
pictured

; illustrative ,
, *when* clause

, introducing
short quote
. inside quote
, *if* clause

(146)

494.

slogan
adopted
. inside quote

½-acre hyphenated before noun

site

, conjunction

talked-about hyphenated before noun

, conjunction

lovely

(138)

495.

son's

, conjunction

: enumeration

, series

acres

, parenthetical

, and omitted

, if clause

(89)

496. 142

tract

, nonrestrictive

motel

; because of comma

, *when* clause

(96)

497. 15

San Francisco

; illustrative ,

25 30

two-story

hyphenated before noun

five-year

hyphenated before noun

5

, conjunction

(133)

Transcription Quiz. Supply the missing punctuation and the words omitted from the shorthand. Also, correct the mistake that the dictator made in the second paragraph.

498.

(135)

Lesson 68

499. Office-Style Dictation. The types of instructions to which you should pay very close attention are those that require you to do something *before* you transcribe. In the middle of a letter, for example, the businessman may say, "Send a carbon of this letter to Jones." You must have this information *before* you start transcribing the letter; therefore, when this happens, you must record the fact that you are to send Jones a carbon *at the beginning of your notes for that letter.*

You can see the importance of leaving a few blank lines at the head of each letter.

Illustration of Office-Style Dictation

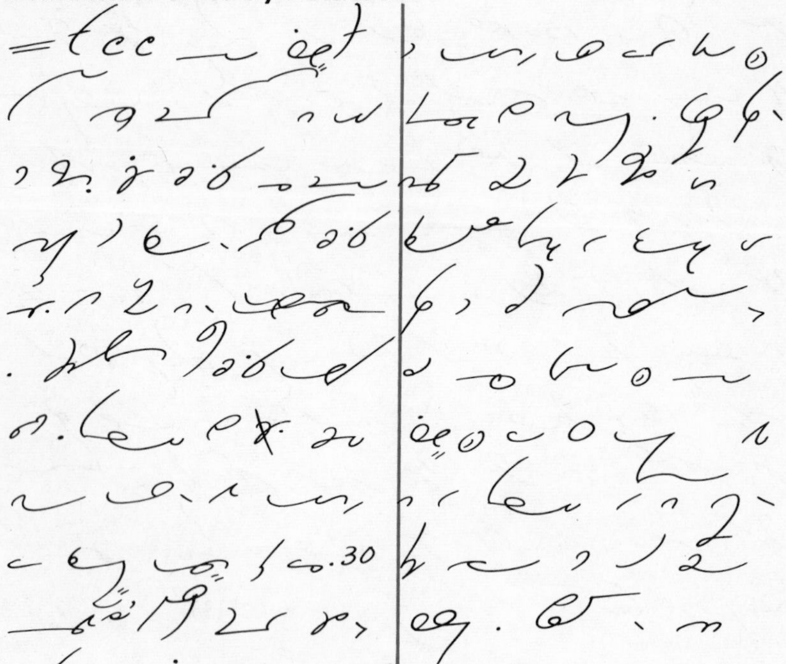

Reading and Writing Practice

500. Transcription Word Study

alternative A choice of two things.

trend General direction.

layout The arrangement of something planned.

501.

, *as clause*
: *enumeration*
alternatives

, *if clause*
demand

, *parenthetical*
whether

, *introductory*
; *because of comma*

, parenthetical

(161)

502.

, conjunction
applications

centrally
, introductory

; illustrative ,
air-conditioned

, conjunction
available

, and omitted
practical

(136)

503.

; no conjunction

, introductory

three-room
hyphenated
before noun

, *if* clause

appreciate

, introductory

, introductory

Transcribe:
$150

150

(151)

504.

annual

8

13

, apposition

, nonrestrictive

, introductory
discussions

year's
, when clause

, introducing
short quote
. inside quote

(141)

505.

leasing
area

, parenthetical

250

, conjunction
profit

, if clause

(117)

Lesson 69

506. Shorthand Spelling Drill

Words Ending in -ious, -eous, -ius: There is no rule to guide you in the spelling of these endings; you must memorize the correct spelling of each word. These groupings, however, will help you to master the spelling of these words.

-ious

Various, serious, curious, studious, tedious, ingenious, previous, obvious.

-eous

Courteous, discourteous, erroneous, hideous, advantageous, gorgeous, disadvantageous.

-ius

Radius, genius.

Reading and Writing Practice

507. Transcription Word Study

option The privilege of buying or selling a property within a stated time and at a specified price.

heavily wooded Containing many trees.

disturbed Bothered.

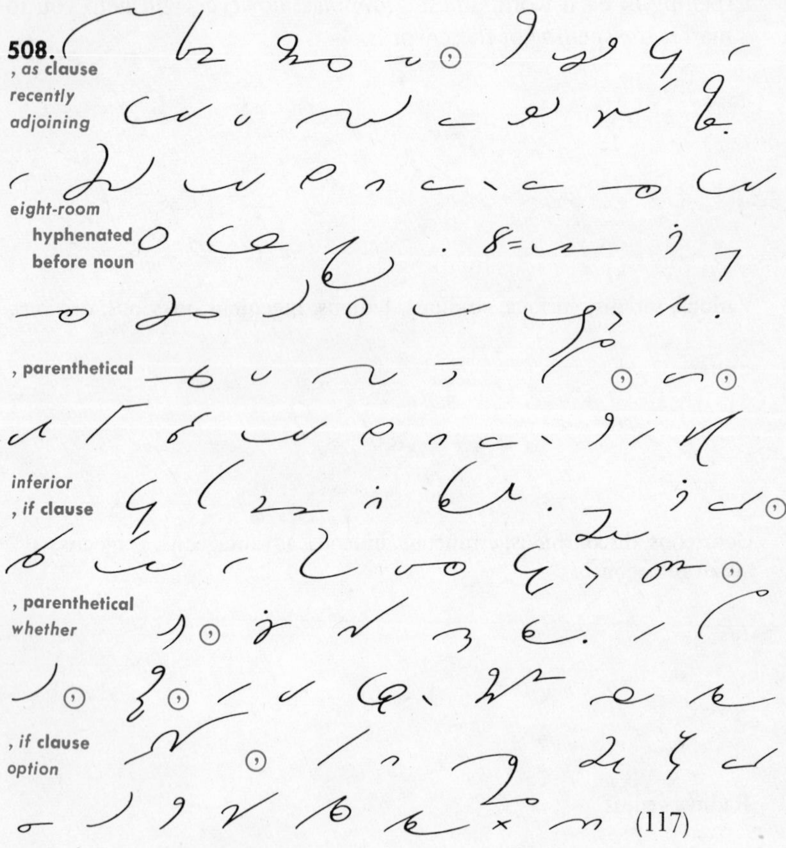

509.

choose

, *if* clause

: enumeration

cottages

; no conjunction

heavily wooded
no hyphen
after *ly*

, *and* omitted

, series

kitchen

, introductory

, introducing
short quote

. inside quote

(148)

510.

site

, conjunction
really
160
acres
, parenthetical
, series
first-class
hyphenated
before noun
, parenthetical
4
, apposition
; because of comma
50
, parenthetical
location
45
(163)

511.
30
pieces
; illustrative ,
, nonrestrictive
, as clause

, parenthetical

(127)

512.

Broadway

, introductory

, introductory

; no conjunction

, parenthetical

; because of comma

, introductory

; because of comma

further

(133)

Lesson 70

513. Brief Forms and Derivatives

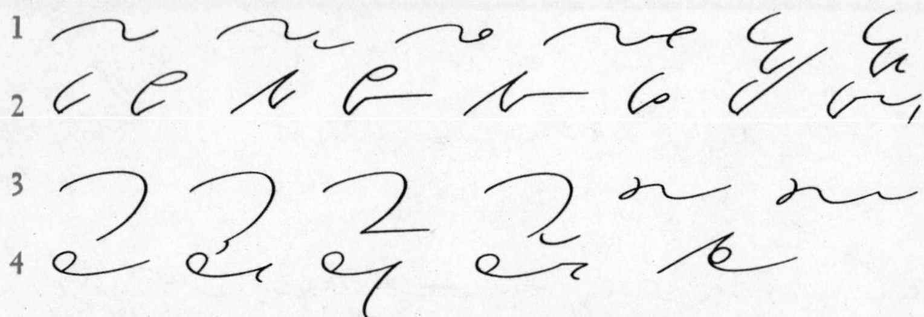

1. Great, greater, greatly, greatness; property, properties.
2. Part, apart, depart, apartment, department, partly, parted, partnership.
3. Govern, governs, government, governor; circle, circular.
4. Allow, allows, allowable, allowance, disallow.

Reading and Writing Practice

514. Transcription Word Study

de luxe Specially fine or elegant.

alterations Changes.

515.

, conjunction

two-room

hyphenated before noun

, as clause

area

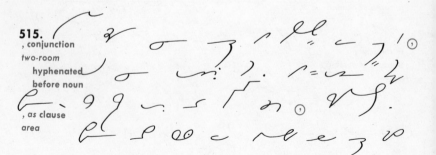

single
, conjunction

reasonable
; illustrative ,

; no conjunction
, introductory

(147)

516.

income-producing
hyphenated
before noun
, as clause

de luxe
, conjunction

125

, introductory
difficulty

, introductory
usually

, if clause
appointment

(163)

517.

expires
, apposition
; because of comma

, nonrestrictive

, introductory
ample

, introductory
; because of comma
, if clause

; because of comma

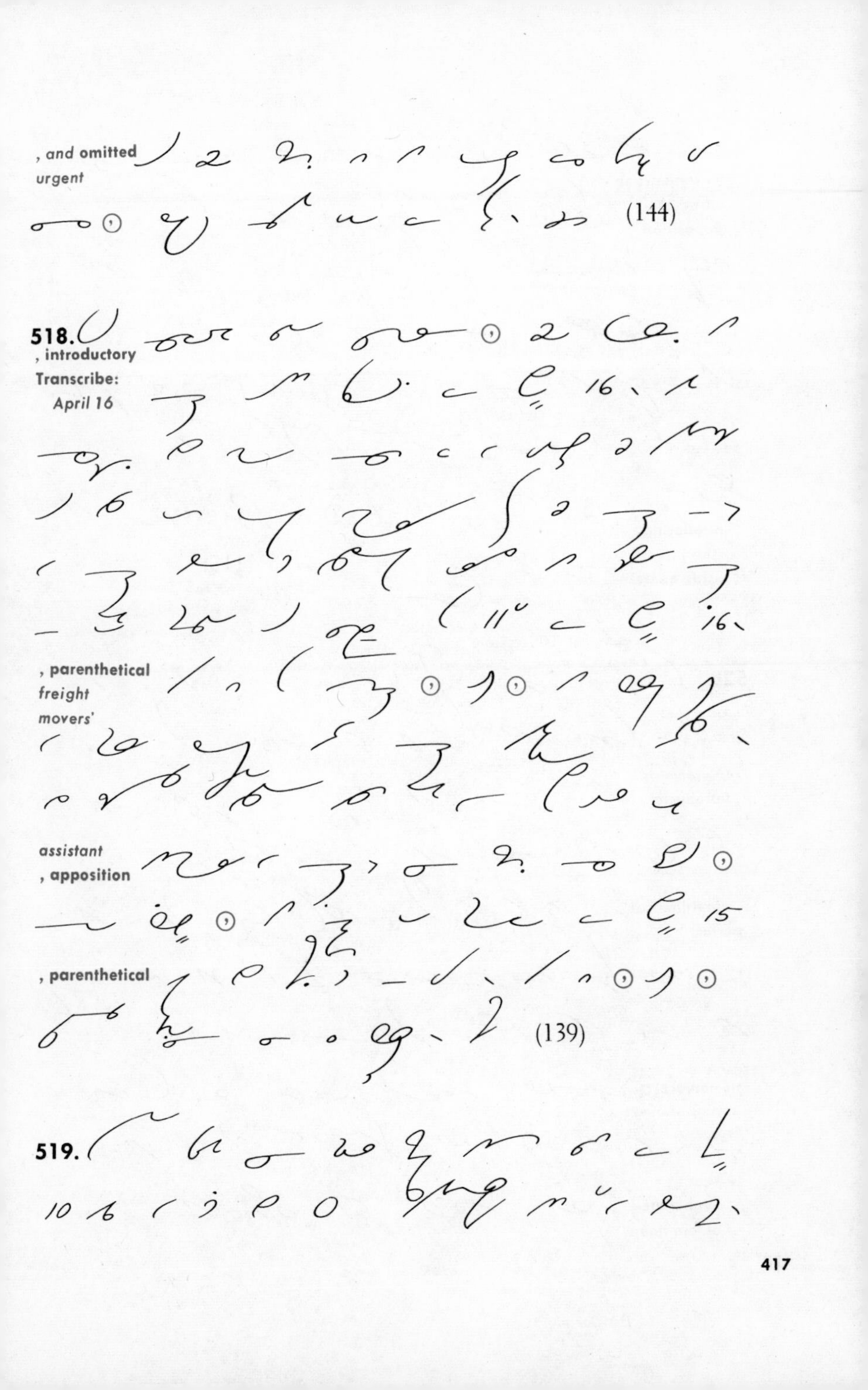

, *and omitted*
urgent

(144)

518.
, **introductory**
Transcribe:
April 16

, **parenthetical**
freight
movers'

assistant
, **apposition**

, **parenthetical**

(139)

519.

; no conjunction
, introductory
, apposition

, introducing short quote
. inside quote

(115)

520.

requirements
, introductory

, parenthetical
perfect

elementary

two-car
hyphenated before noun

, parenthetical
, nonrestrictive

, introductory
bargain

, if clause
convenient

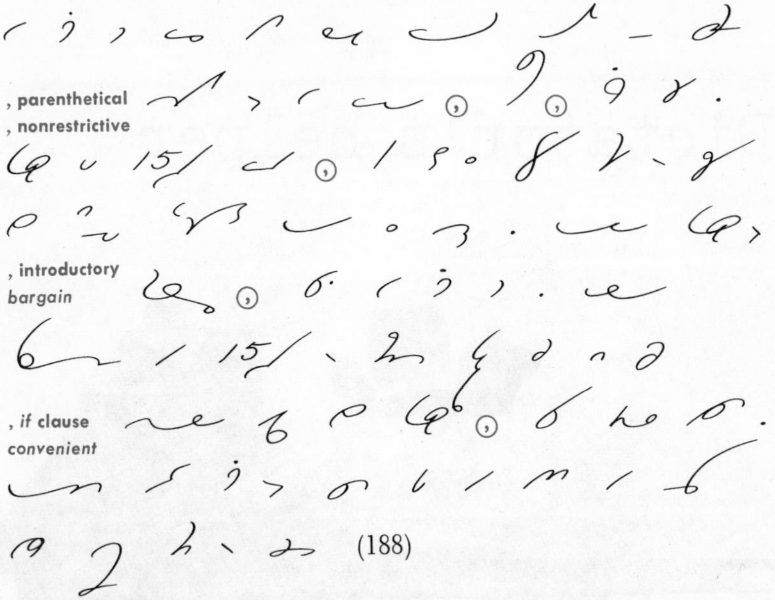

(188)

Vocabulary Tip

The more words with which you are familiar, the easier will your task of taking dictation and transcribing rapidly become. You will be wise, therefore, to take advantage of every opportunity to increase your command of words.

A good way to increase your vocabulary is to do a great deal of reading – of books, newspapers, and magazines. Whenever you come across a word in your reading with which you are not familiar, look it up in the dictionary. Some words have several meanings, and you must be careful to select the one that fits the context in which the word occurs.

After you have found the correct meaning of the unfamiliar word, reread the sentence in which you found it to see how the meaning fits the context.

Then, keep a list (in shorthand if you like) of all new words, together with their meanings.

Dictator's helper

Like many other girls in her position, Mary opens all Mr. Baker's mail each morning—all, that is, except the letters marked "Personal." She knows from experience that some of the mail will require immediate attention, some can wait a bit, and some can be read at Mr. Baker's leisure. Therefore, she arranges the mail in that order before she places it on his desk.

With some letters, she does more than place them on his desk: she gathers all the information that her employer needs before he can answer the letters.

For example, when a customer writes that he has not received a shipment of goods, she first finds out whether the goods have been shipped. If they have been, she finds out when and by what carrier. If they have not, she tries to learn the reason and get an approximate

date when they will be shipped. This information she then types on a sheet of paper and attaches it to the letter of complaint or jots it down at the foot of the letter. In some cases she even obtains all related correspondence from the file and attaches it to the incoming letter.

Thus, when her employer is ready to dictate the answer to that letter, he has all the information he needs.

By gathering all this information beforehand, Mary is, in addition, helping herself, because she then knows just about what the dictated letter will contain. This information, of course, will be of great help to her in transcribing the letter.

By gathering all the information necessary to answer certain types of letters and then learning, through Mr. Baker's dictation, how those letters are answered, Mary can look forward to the thrill one day of hearing her employer say, "You write the letter, Mary. You know what to tell them."

Lesson 71

521. Shorthand Language Study

Re-: *Again.* REINSERT, *to put in again.*

1. Reinsert, reinstate, reinstall, reinvest, reissue, reinsure.
2. Renew, repeat, replace, reply, reproduce, resell.

-let: *Small.* BOOKLET, *a small book.*

Booklet, pamphlet, leaflet, bracelet, ringlet.

Il-: *Not.* ILLEGAL, *not legal.*

Illegal, illegality, illegible, illiterate, illogical.

Reading and Writing Practice

522. Transcription Word Study

testimony A solemn statement made to establish a fact.

Chapter 15 Law

notary public An official who certifies deeds and other official papers to make them authentic.

523.

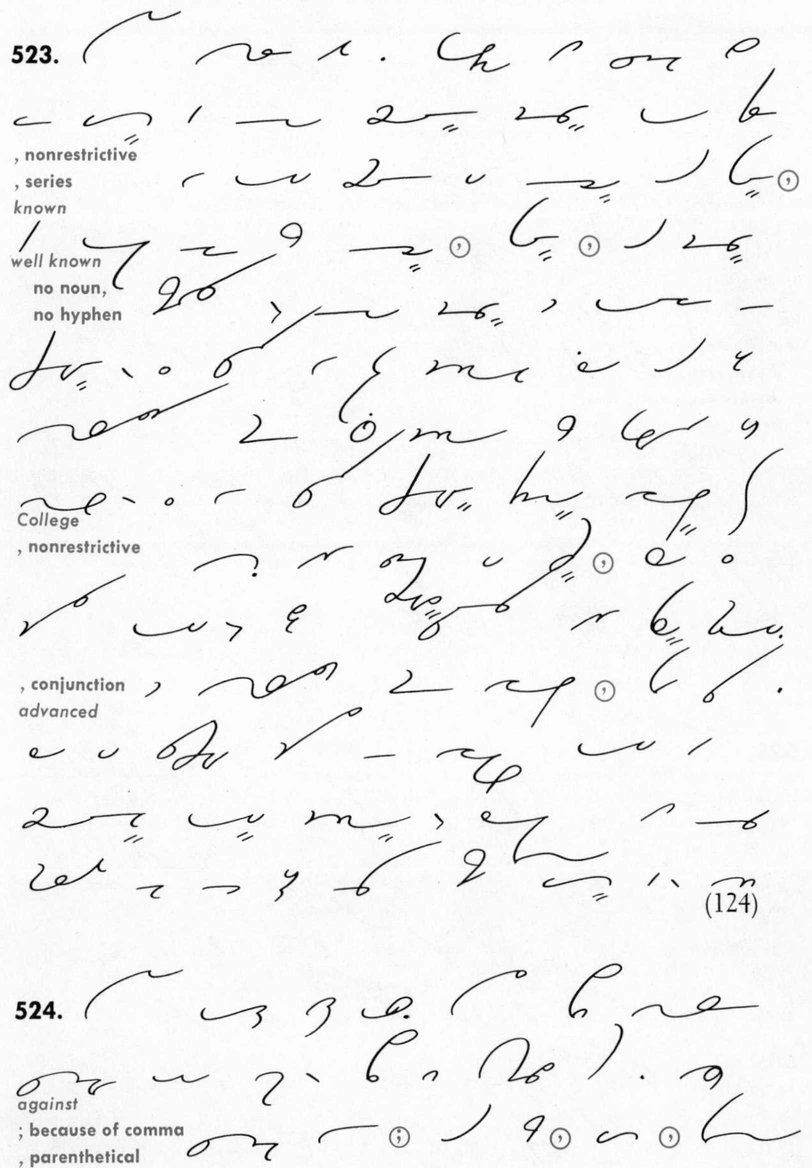

524.

, parenthetical

accident
, if clause
appointment

out-of-town
hyphenated
before noun
, if clause

(147)

525.

consultant
, apposition

, and omitted

testimony
, conjunction

, parenthetical
client
reporter's

, if clause
appointment

(115)

526.

client
, apposition

partnership
, conjunction

; because of comma
, introducing
short quote
. inside quote

, as clause
Florida

(138)

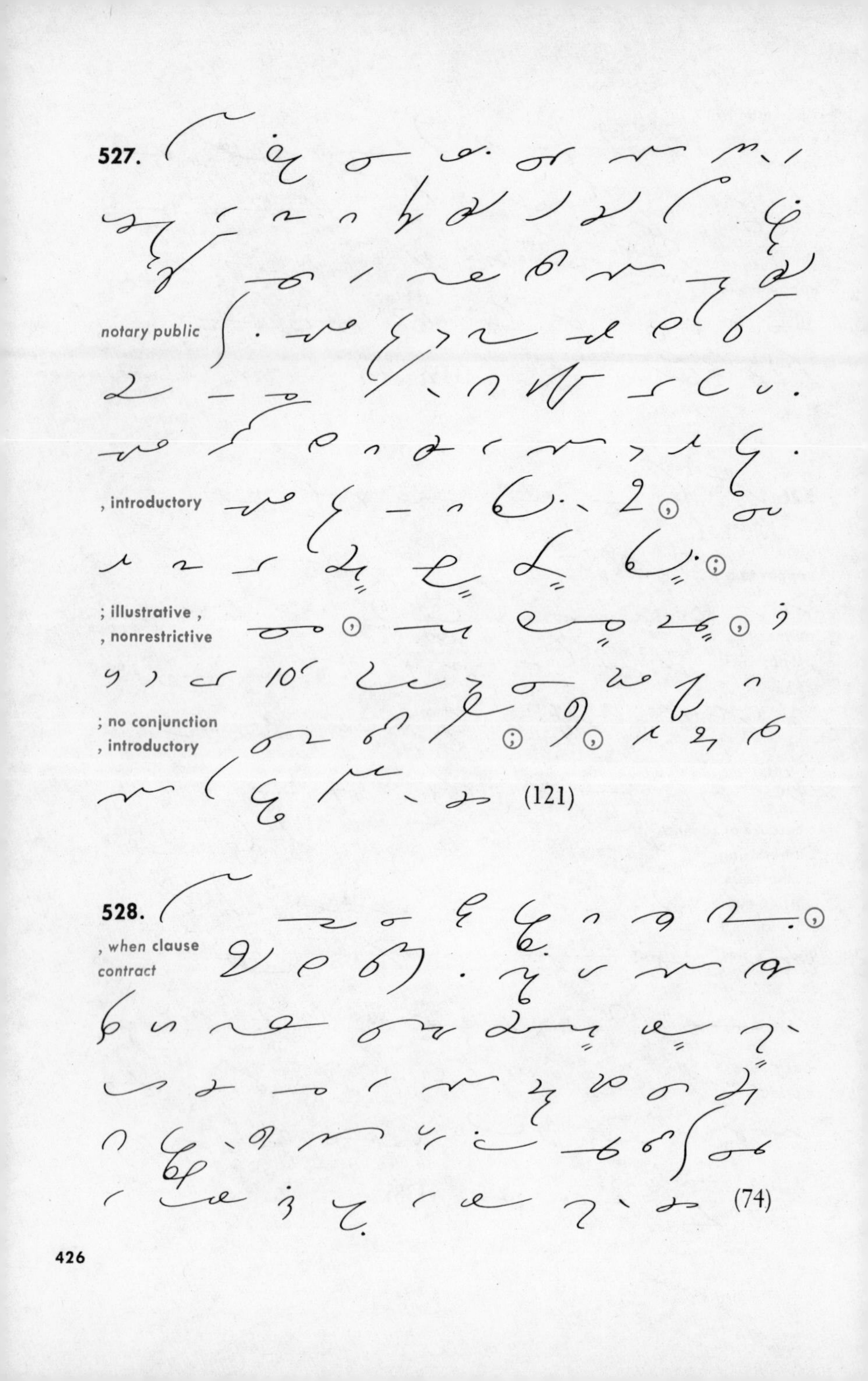

527.

notary public

, introductory

; illustrative ,
, nonrestrictive

; no conjunction
, introductory

(121)

528.

, when clause
contract

(74)

Lesson 72

529. Accuracy Practice. Follow the practice procedures outlined on page 372.

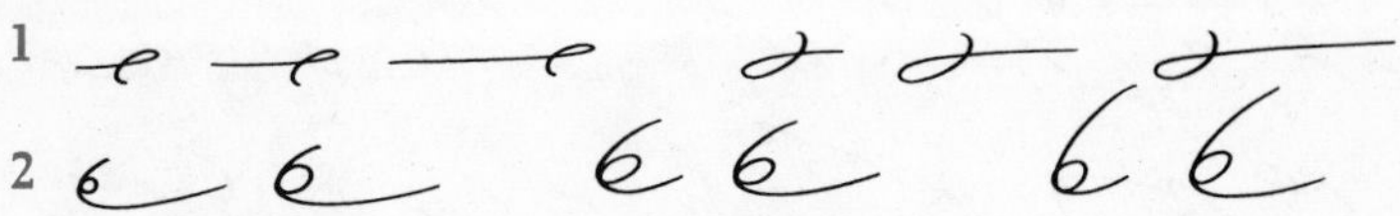

1. Next, miss, monies; sane, same, salmon.
2. Sell, sale; pair, pale; bear, bale.

Reading and Writing Practice

530. Transcription Word Study

allotted Assigned to.

settlement Payment in full.

531.

: enumeration
already

, *if clause*
picture

(144)

532.

, introductory
, parenthetical

, *as clause*
, nonrestrictive
X-rays

, *and* omitted

; no conjunction
, introductory

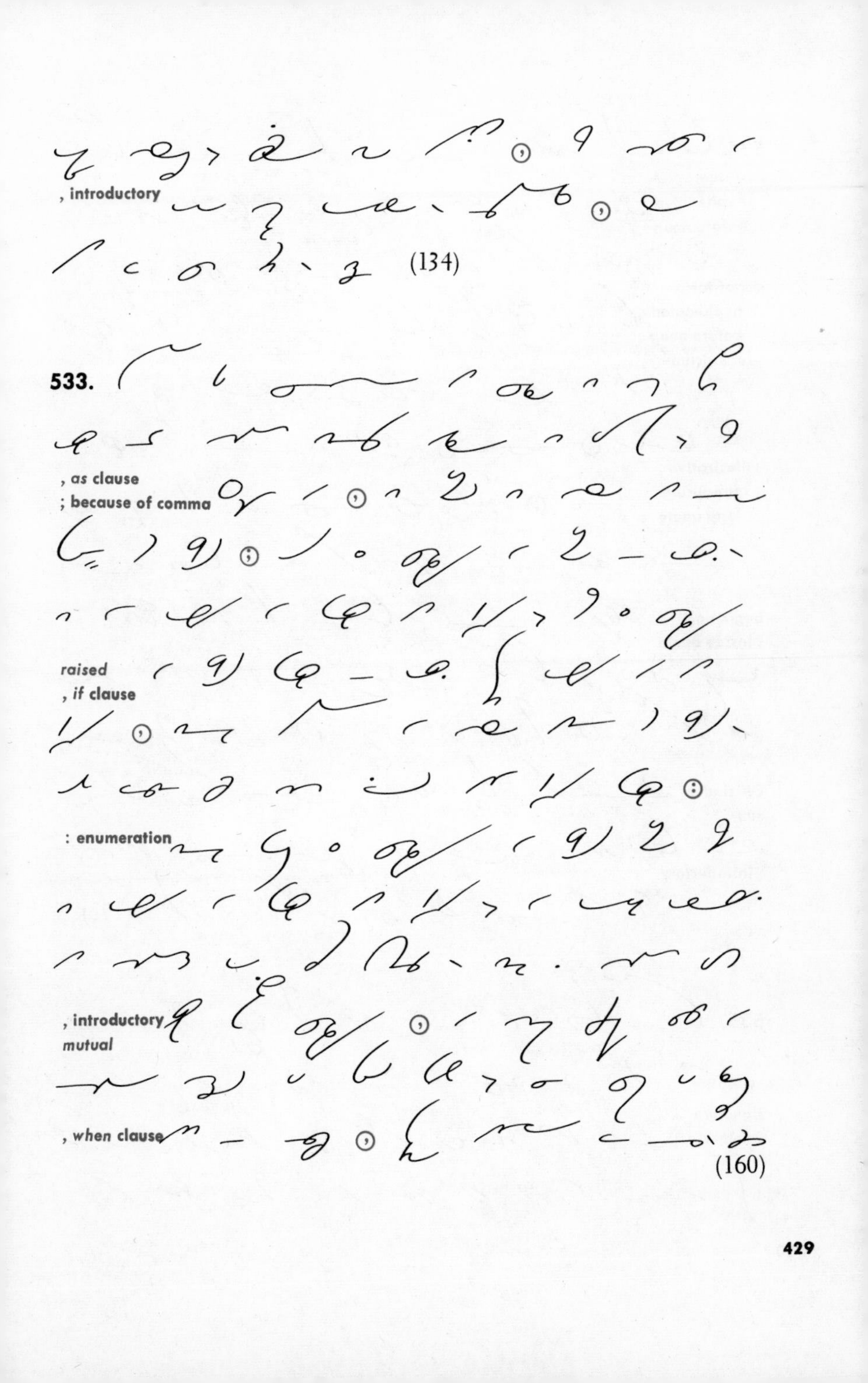

, introductory

(134)

533.

, *as* clause

; because of comma

raised

, *if* clause

: enumeration

, introductory

mutual

, *when* clause

(160)

534.

past-due
hyphenated before noun

out-of-town
hyphenated before noun

, conjunction

; illustrative ,
: introducing long quote

beginning
. inside quote

, if clause
suit

, introductory

(152)

535.

signature
whether

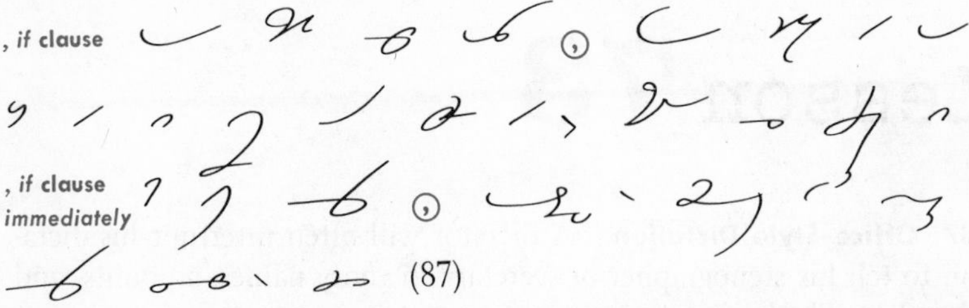

Transcription Quiz. Supply the missing punctuation and the words omitted from the shorthand. Also, be sure to catch the very serious error that the dictator made in the second paragraph.

536.

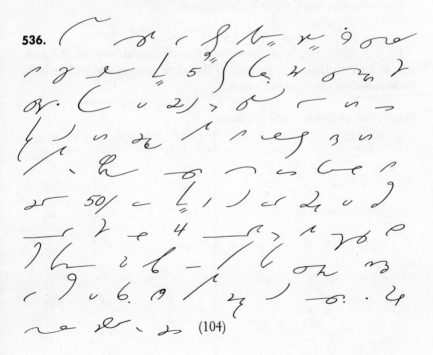

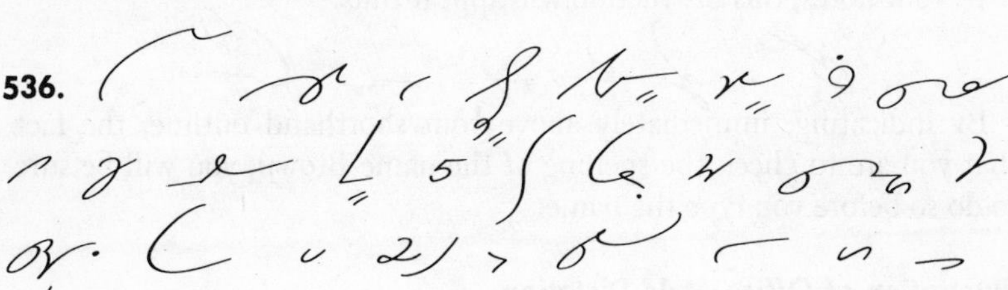

(104)

Lesson 73

537. Office-Style Dictation. A dictator will often interrupt his dictation to tell his stenographer or secretary to verify names, amounts, and other data. The businessman may say:

> I had a visit from your representative, Mr. Brown—I am not sure whether he spells it *Brown* or *Browne*. Check the spelling of the name.

In your notes, this instruction will appear thus:

By indicating, immediately above your shorthand outline, the fact that you are to check the spelling of the name *Brown*, you will be sure to do so *before* you type the name.

Illustration of Office-Style Dictation

Reading and Writing Practice

538. Transcription Word Study

conform Bring into agreement.

convene Get together.

liable Answerable.

539.

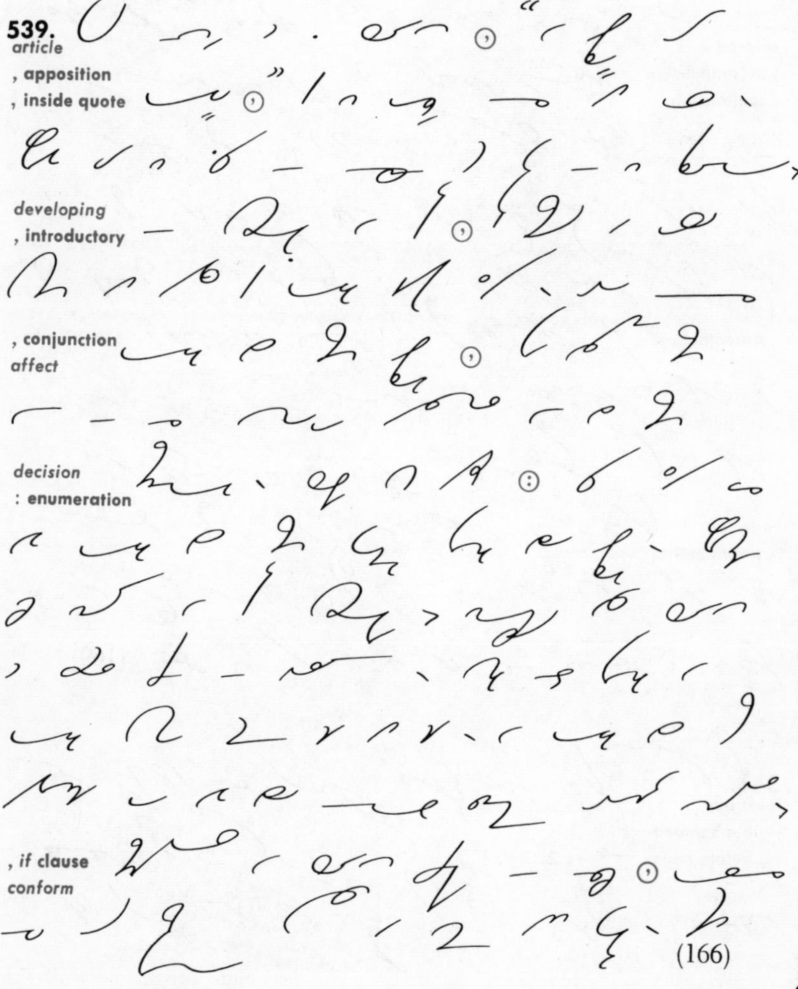

(166)

540.

, apposition
lawyer

offered
; no conjunction
, conjunction

belief
, parenthetical

advice
, parenthetical

(169)

541.
past-due
hyphenated
before noun

, parenthetical
retain

; because of comma
, parenthetical

, introductory
legal
rights

(149)

542.
son's
, nonrestrictive

testimony
, introductory

; because of comma
, parenthetical

last-minute
hyphenated before noun

, as clause
advance
, parenthetical

; no conjunction

(148)

543.

, and omitted
modern

library
excellent

hit-and-miss
hyphenated before noun

; illustrative ,
, series

10 15 21

(138)

Lesson 74

544. Shorthand Spelling Drill

Words Ending in -ment: *Words ending in* E *retain the* E *before the ending* -MENT. *Words ending in* -DGE, *however, drop the* E *before* -MENT.

Encouragement, engagement, announcement, statement, requirement, acquirement.

but

Judgment, acknowledgment, abridgment.

Reading and Writing Practice

545. Transcription Word Study

breach of contract Breaking of an agreement.

completion Finish.

witness One who gives evidence at a trial.

loophole An opening that provides a means of escape.

546.

Mississippi
, introducing short quote

. inside quote
, apposition

, parenthetical
refused

; because of comma
offered

breach
; illustrative ,

evidence
, introductory

(178)

547. *Congratulations*
completion

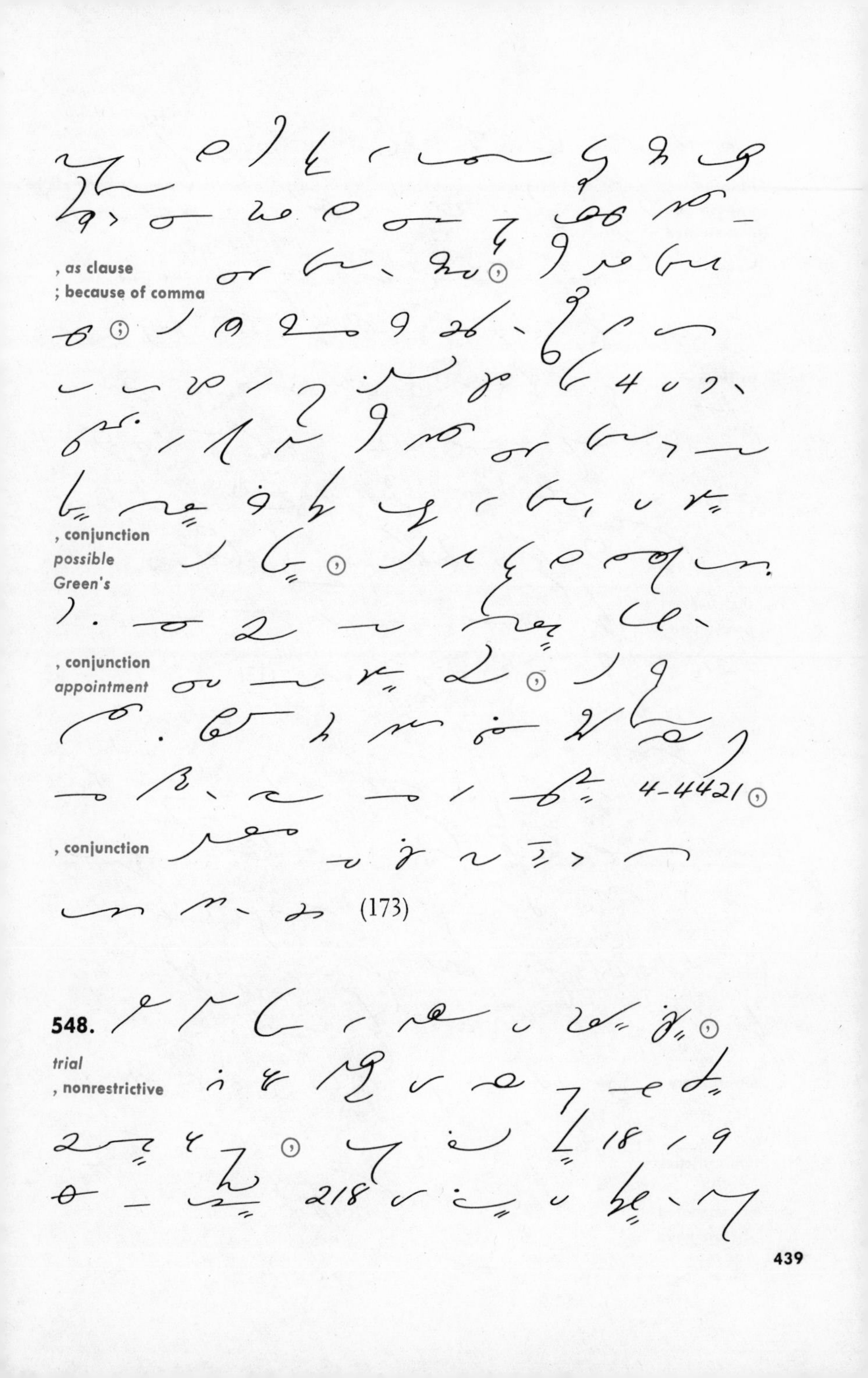

, as clause
; because of comma

, conjunction
possible
Green's

, conjunction
appointment

4-4421

, conjunction

(173)

548.

trial
, nonrestrictive

18

218

physician
, apposition
, and omitted

, as clause

, if clause
; no conjunction

0216

(138)

549.

: enumeration

unstable
employee

15

, introductory

4 10

, nonrestrictive
part-time
hyphenated
before noun

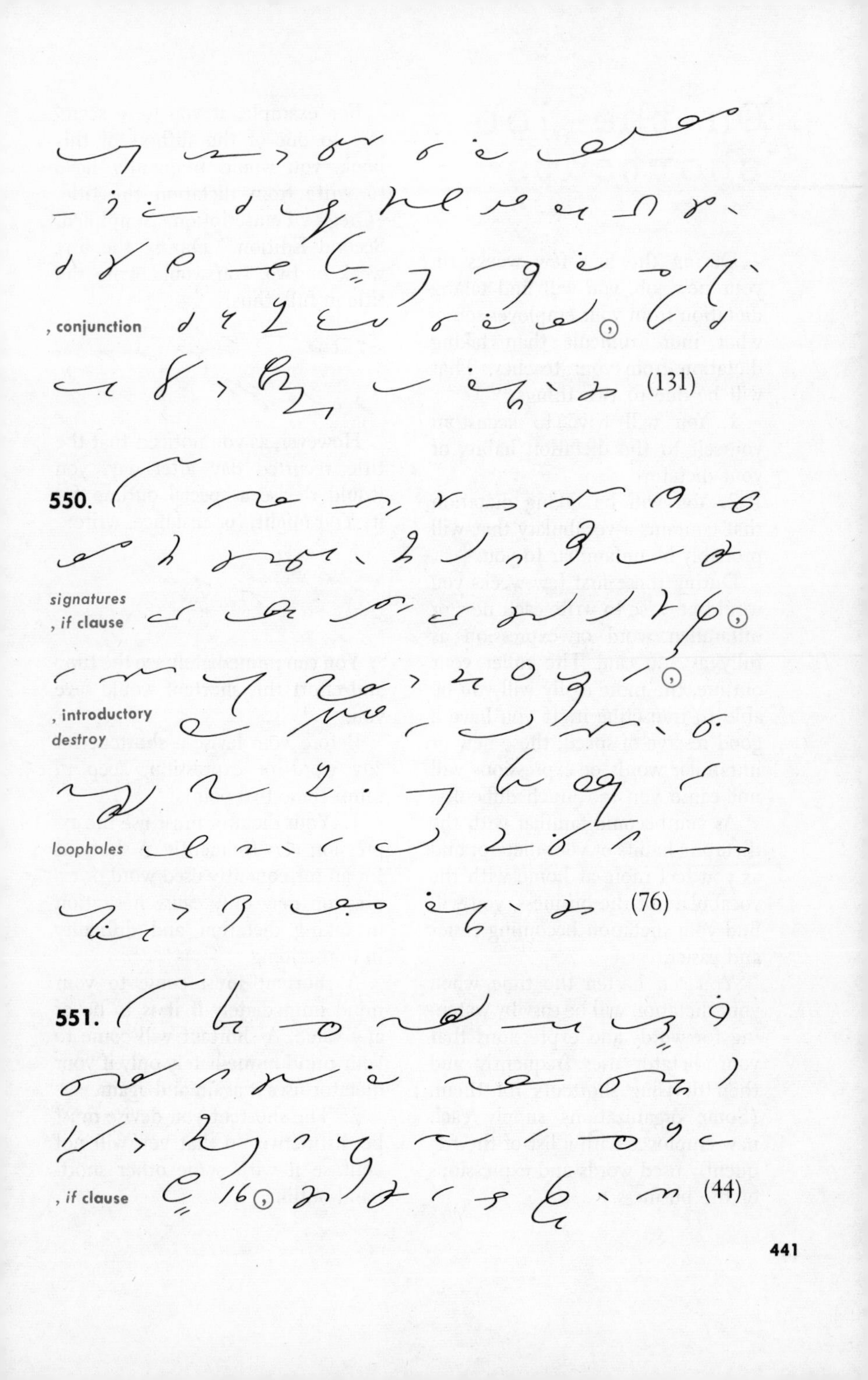

(131)

, conjunction

550.

signatures

, if clause

, introductory

destroy

loopholes

(76)

551.

, if clause

(44)

On-the-job shortcuts

During the first few weeks on your new job, you will find taking dictation from your employer somewhat more difficult than taking dictation from your teacher. That will be due to two things:

1. You will have to accustom yourself to the dictation habits of your dictator.

2. You will be taking dictation that contains a vocabulary that will probably be unfamiliar to you.

During these first few weeks you would be wise to write each new or unfamiliar word or expression as fully as you can. The fuller your outline, the more easily will you be able to transcribe it. If you have a good reserve of speed, these new or unfamilar words or expressions will not cause you too much difficulty.

As you become familiar with the dictating habits of your dictator and as you feel more at home with the vocabulary of the business, you will find your dictation becoming easier and easier.

You can hasten the time when your dictation will be easy by watching for words and expressions that your dictator uses frequently and then devising shortcuts for them. (Some organizations supply each new employee with a list of the frequently used words and expressions of the business.)

For example, if you were secretary to one of the authors of this book, you would frequently have to write from dictation the title, "Gregg Transcription Simplified, Second Edition." During the first week or two, you would write the title in full, thus:

However, as you noticed that the title recurred day after day, you would devise a special outline for it. You might, for instance, write:

You can immediately see the time and effort this shortcut would save you.

Before you devise a shortcut for any word or expression, keep in mind these two points:

1. Your dictator must use the expression *very* frequently. A shortcut for an infrequently used word or expression may only cause hesitation in taking dictation and difficulty in transcribing.

A shortcut must come to your mind immediately if it is to be of any value. A shortcut will come to your mind immediately only if your dictator uses it again and again.

2. The shortcut you devise must be distinctive, so that you will not confuse it with some other shorthand outline.

Guard against the temptation to devise too many shortcuts, especially in the early stages of your new job. Some beginners get the mistaken idea that, if a few shortcuts will save time and effort and enable them to write more easily, a great many shortcuts will simplify their task even more. That, unfortunately, is not the case.

Here are examples of the types of shortcuts you might devise if you work:

1. In a lawyer's office

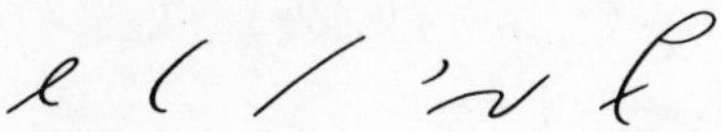

Testimony, plaintiff, defendant, Supreme Court, abstract of title.

2. In a bank

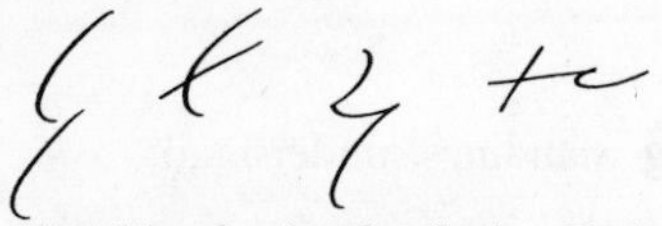

Bankbook, bank draft, Federal Reserve Bank, chattel mortgage.

3. In an insurance office

Insurance policy, endowment policy, cash value, policyholder.

4. In a railroad office

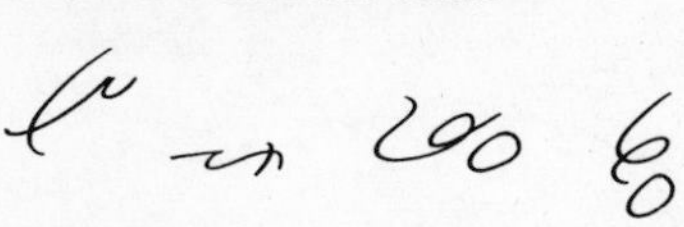

Baltimore and Ohio, New York Central, freight agent, passenger agent.

5. In an accountant's office

Accounts receivable, accounts payable, profit and loss.

6. In a publisher's office

Galley proof, page proof, original manuscript, editor-in-chief.

Final caution: Devise shortcuts *only* for words and expressions that occur over and over again!

Lesson 75

552. Brief Forms and Derivatives

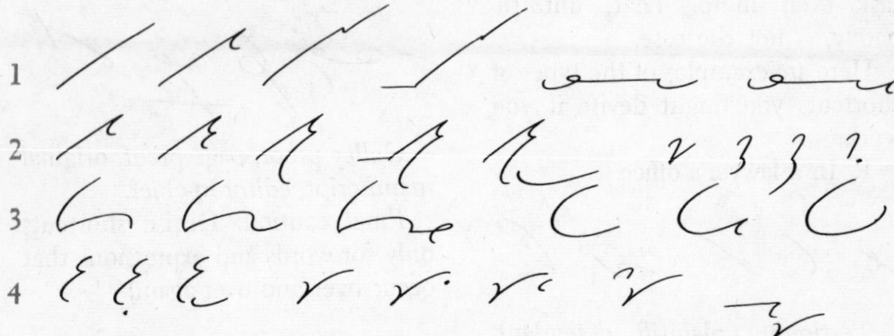

1. Date, dates, dated, undated; remainder, remainders.
2. Dear Sir–desire, desires, desirable, undesirable, desirability; wished, wishes, wishful, wishing.
3. Big, bigger, bigness; bill, bills, billed.
4. Speak, speaking, speaker; stand, standing, standings, understand, misunderstand.

Reading and Writing Practice

553. Transcription Word Study

legal secretary One who does secretarial work in a lawyer's office.

docket The list of cases to be tried by the court.

554.

, apposition

. inside quote

, conjunction
experiences

firm's
, as clause
; because of comma

, introductory
definite

accept
: enumeration

; because of comma
, if clause
days'

, conjunction

(174)

555.

long-awaited
hyphenated
before noun
, introductory

, if clause
partial
remainder

. courteous
request

(127)

556.

, and omitted
well-trained
hyphenated
before noun

legal
; illustrative ,

, conjunction
lawyer

secretaries
, if clause

142

; no conjunction
course

(118)

557.

especially
, as clause

, and omitted
modern

(119)

558.

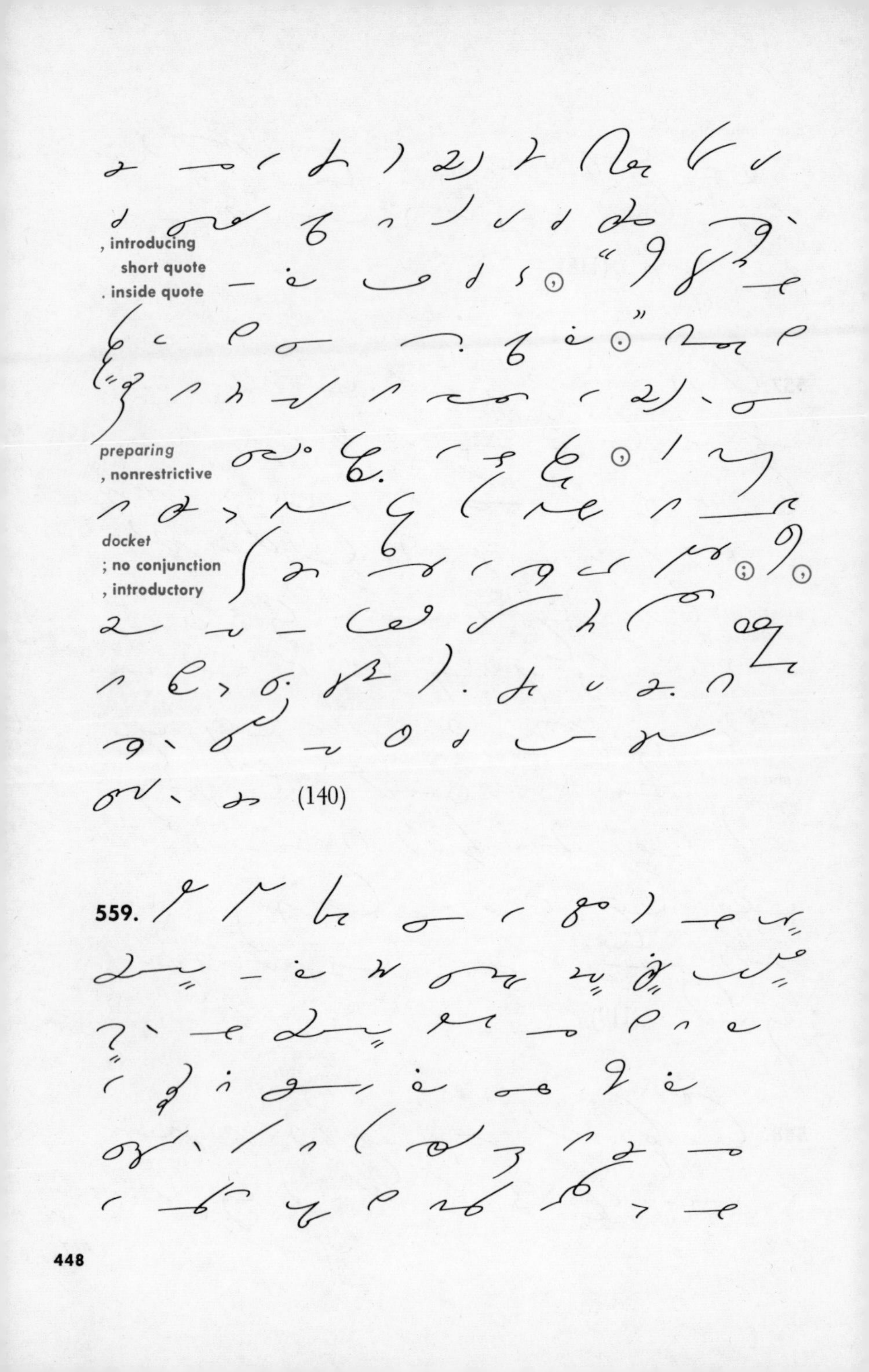

, introducing short quote

. inside quote

preparing

, nonrestrictive

docket

; no conjunction

, introductory

(140)

559.

, nonrestrictive
impossible

(117)

560.

determine
liable

, as clause
appointment

(102)

Mary Brown, letter writer

Mary Brown first entered Mr. Baker's employ as a stenographer. At the beginning, Mr. Baker dictated only his routine correspondence to her; and he supervised her work very closely.

After Mary had proved to Mr. Baker that she could transcribe rapidly and accurately and that she was "promotional material," Mr. Baker made her his secretary when the opening arose.

As Mary learned more and more about the business and its policies and procedures, Mr. Baker found that he could turn over to her the handling of routine correspondence. The important letters, of course, he continued to dictate. Others he dictated only partially—perhaps a paragraph or two—and Mary completed the letter from information that she had gathered. For most letters he simply told her what he wanted, and she wrote the entire letter for his signature. For example, he said: "Thank Smith for his order. Tell him we can't ship it for two weeks because we are out of stock. We should have stock by April 10 and will ship as soon as it comes in. Tell him that Jones will call on him soon to tell him about our new line."

In her book Mary wrote in shorthand:

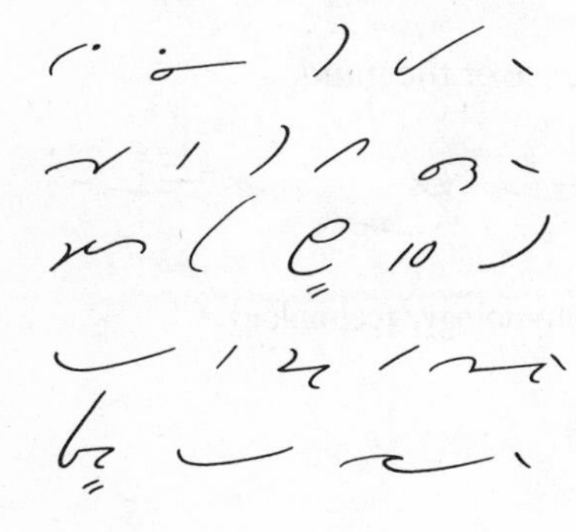

Here is the letter that Mary placed on Mr. Baker's desk for signature:

"Dear Mr. Smith: Thank you for your order for 12 gross of our No. 16 mechanical pencils. We wish we could give you our usual prompt service on this order, but unfortunately our supply of these pencils is temporarily exhausted. However, we expect a supply on April 10, and your order will be one of the first that we will ship.

As you may know, we recently placed on the market a new line of stationery items. Our representative, Mr. Jones, will be in to see you soon to tell you about them. Cordially yours,"

By relieving Mr. Baker of his routine correspondence in this way, Mary performs a real service to him; she releases his time for the more important duties of his position.

Lesson 76

561. Shorthand Language Study

-itis: *Inflamation of.* APPENDICITIS, *an inflamation of the appendix.*

Appendicitis, arthritis, bronchitis, neuritis, tonsillitis.

-logy: *A science.* PSYCHOLOGY, *the science of the mind.*

Psychology, mineralogy, terminology, physiology, technology.

Reading and Writing Practice

562. Transcription Word Study

general practitioner A doctor who does not confine his practice to one specialty.

accumulated Gathered, collected.

pneumonia Inflammation of the lungs.

563.

serious

, as clause

; because of comma

Chapter 16

Medicine

; no conjunction
gradually
exercises

, introductory

(145)

564.

Hospital
, nonrestrictive

advised
physical

, parenthetical
normal

, if clause
Temple's
hesitate

(146)

565.

, nonrestrictive
New Orleans

two-bedroom
hyphenated
before noun

, if clause

(101)

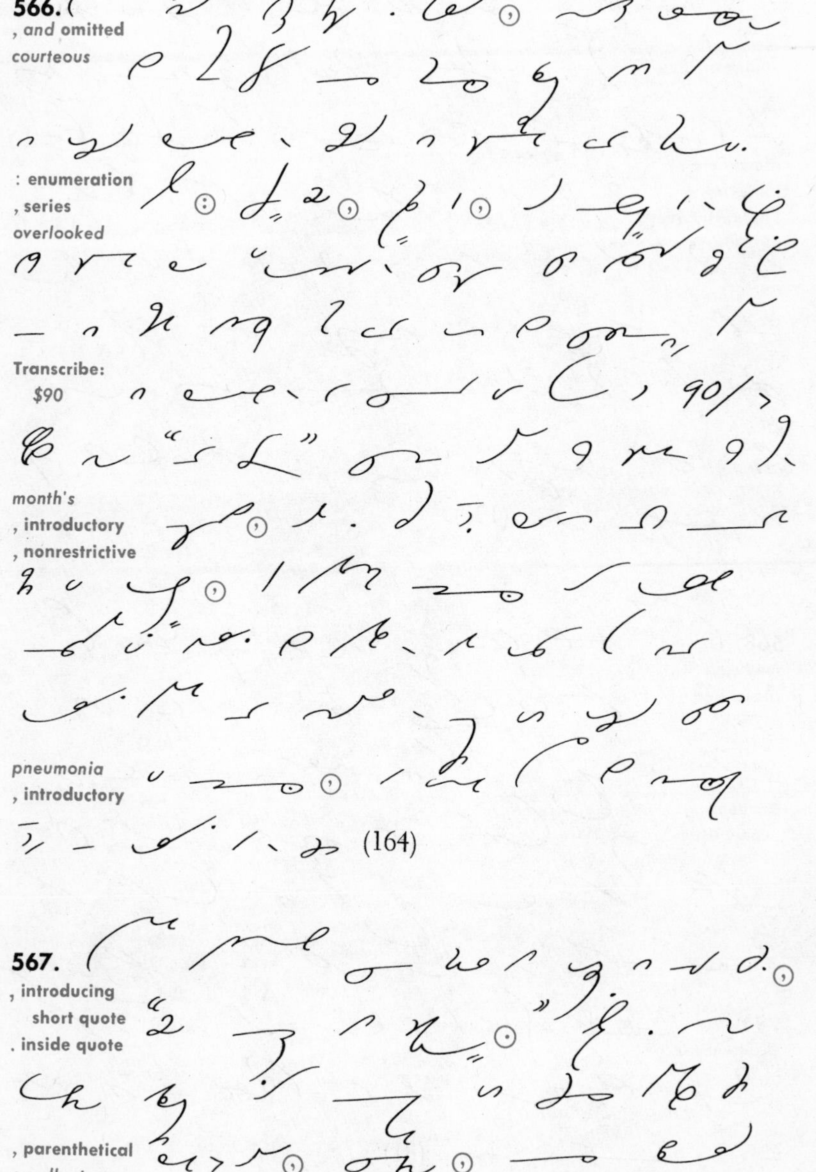
566.
, and omitted
courteous
: enumeration
, series
overlooked
Transcribe:
$90
month's
, introductory
, nonrestrictive
pneumonia
, introductory
(164)
567.
, introducing
short quote
. inside quote
, parenthetical
excellent

, nonrestrictive

practitioners

; illustrative ,

, nonrestrictive

(131)

568.

medicine

prescribed

accident

, conjunction

30

, if clause

difference

(81)

Lesson 77

569. Accuracy Practice. Follow the practice procedures outlined on page 372.

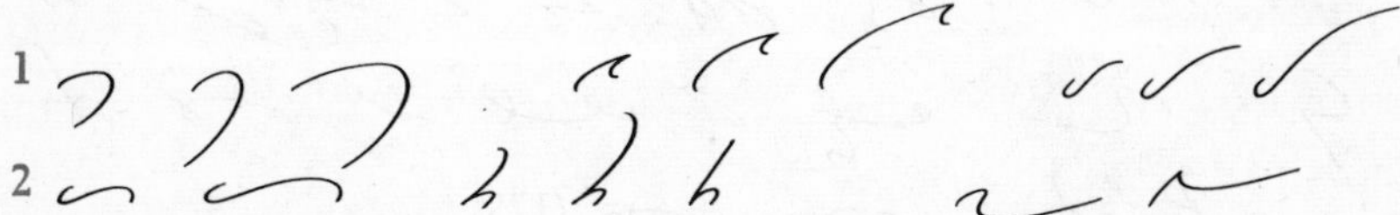

1. Confident-confidence, cover, govern; those, tense, times; of the, ordinary, of time.
2. Of course, organize; for you, have you, which you; you will, it will.

Reading and Writing Practice

570. Transcription Word Study

symptoms Signs.

semester One-half the school year, usually 18 weeks.

fracture A break in a bone.

571.

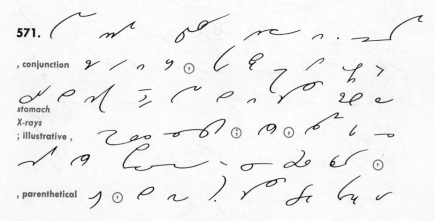

, conjunction

stomach

X-rays

; illustrative ,

, parenthetical

, introductory
symptoms

week's
relax

(125)

572.
patients
months'
, apposition

; because of comma
appreciate

suffered
nervous

24

sincerely
, *if clause*
(153)

573.
, introductory
minor
; no conjunction
, introductory
, *as clause*
, *and omitted*
painless
15
, parenthetical
scheduled
3
: enumeration
, series
advisable
, introductory
, introductory

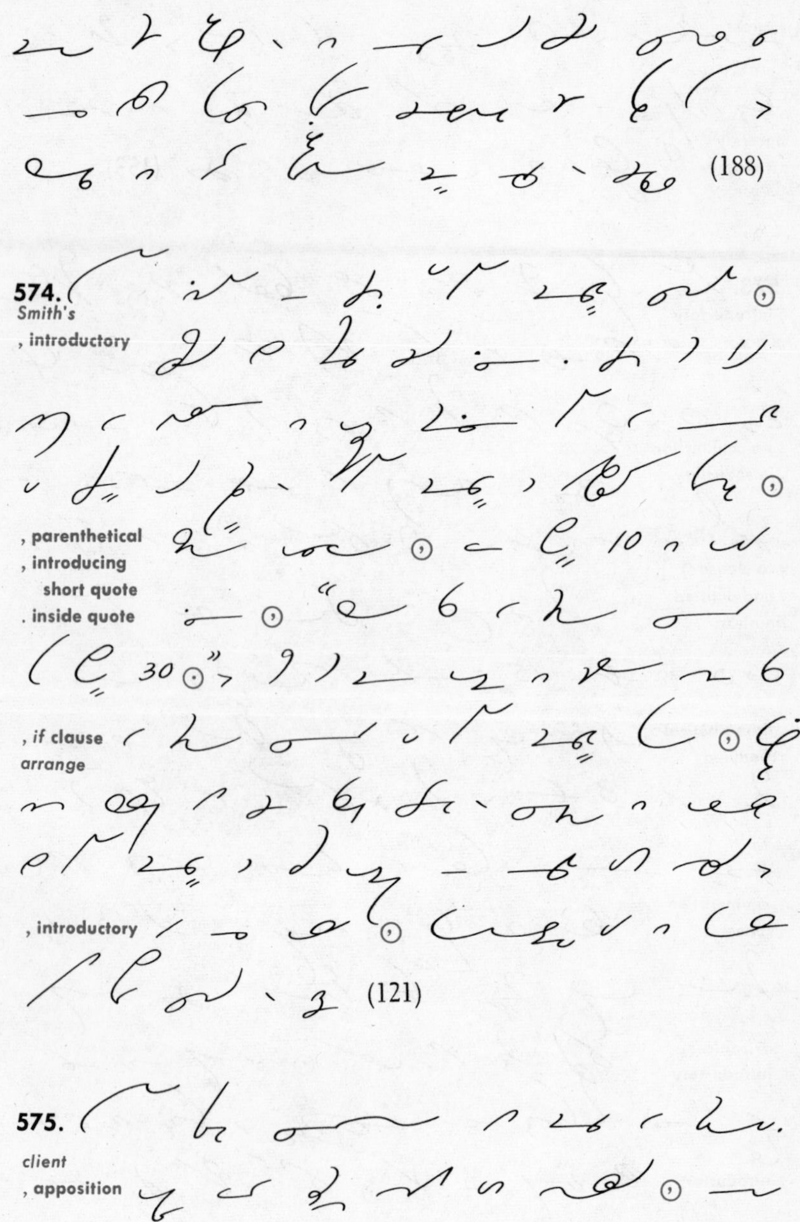

(188)

574.

Smith's

, introductory

, parenthetical

, introducing short quote

. inside quote

, *if* clause

arrange

, introductory

(121)

575.

client

, apposition

: enumeration

18 5:15

, when clause
shock
emergency

X-rays

, introductory
, nonrestrictive
bruises

, conjunction
, introductory

4

(153)

576.

doctor's
infection
, introductory

(57)

Lesson 78

577. Office-Style Dictation. Most dictators make only an occasional change in their dictation. Some, however, make so many changes that it is advisable to write in only one column of the notebook, using the second column for insertions or changes.

Illustration of Office-Style Dictation

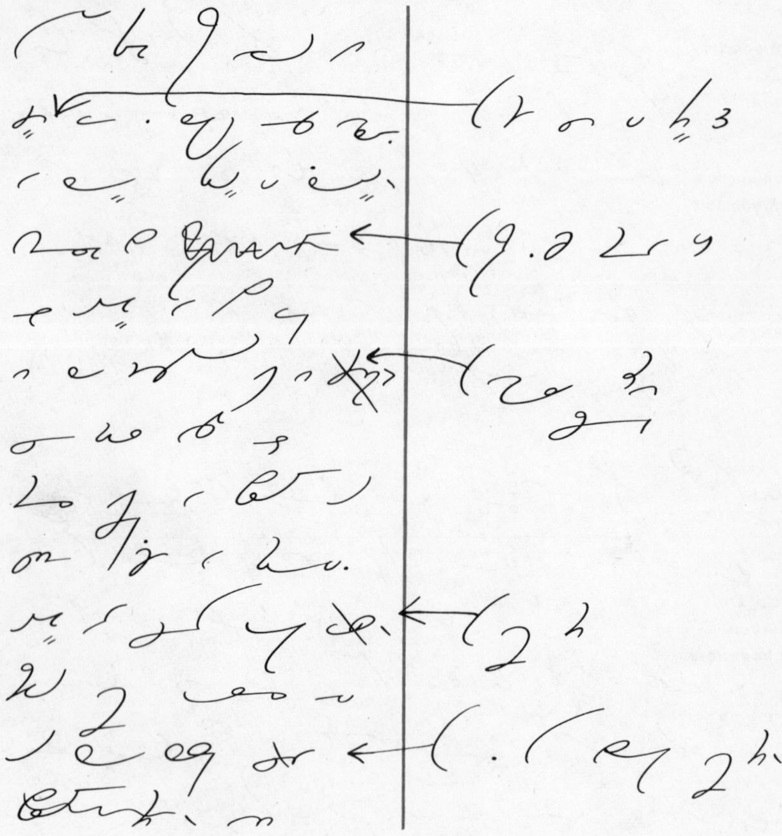

Reading and Writing Practice

578. Transcription Word Study

cast A rigid surgical dressing made of plaster, used to keep bones in place while fractures are healing.

blood pressure The pressure of the blood on the walls of the blood vessels.

579.

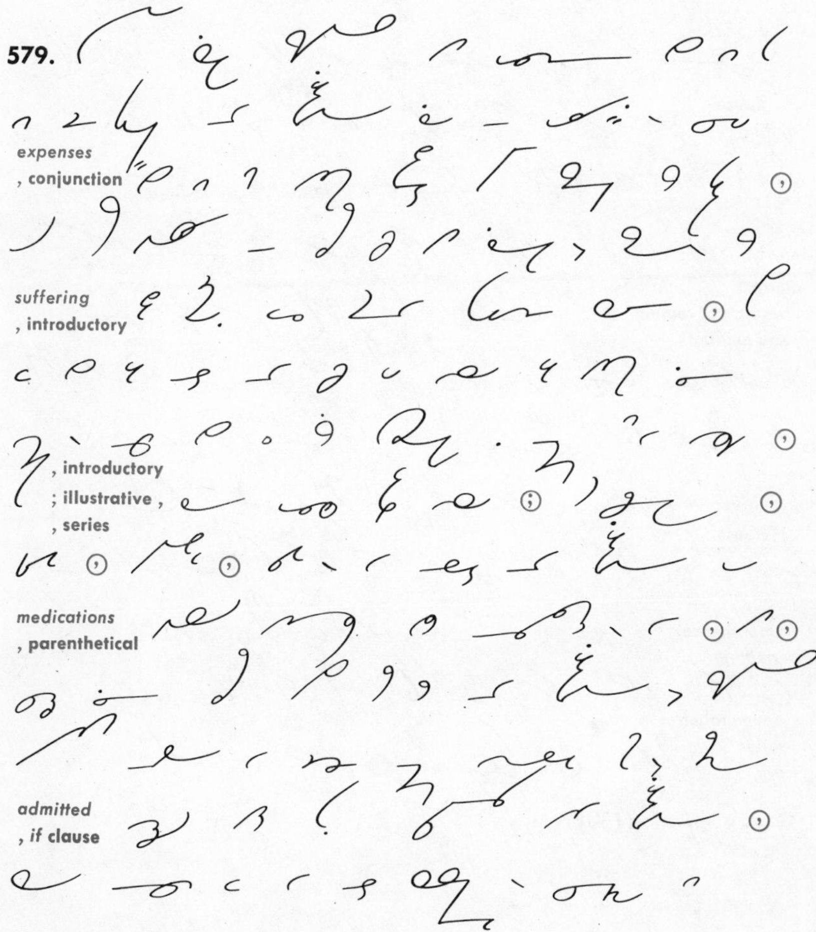

recommend
George's
(171)

580.
, parenthetical
physical

, as clause
fainting

all right
; because of comma
, and omitted

exercises
, if clause

, parenthetical
permitted

: enumeration
, series
track

(139)

581.

Women's
League
medicine

29

. inside quote

, introductory

50

12

, parenthetical
guest
, introducing
short quote
. inside quote

(151)

582.

, conjunction
pleasure

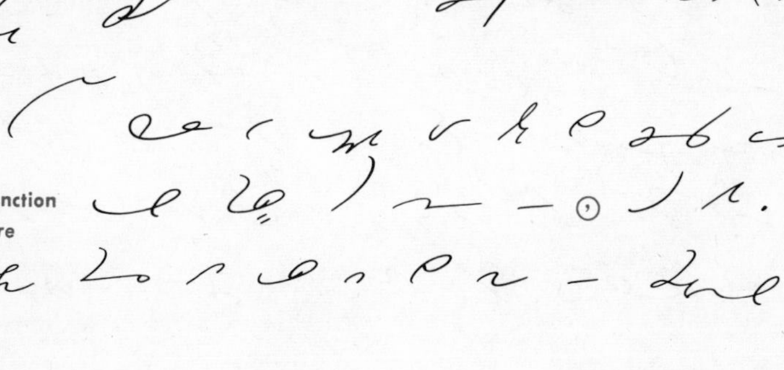

, nonrestrictive

, parenthetical
; because of comma
, nonrestrictive

180

(113)

583.

Philadelphia
, nonrestrictive
; no conjunction

, if clause

(120)

Lesson 79

584. Shorthand Spelling Drill

One-Syllable Words: *In one-syllable words that end with a consonant that is preceded by a single vowel, double the final consonant in adding terminations that begin with a vowel.*

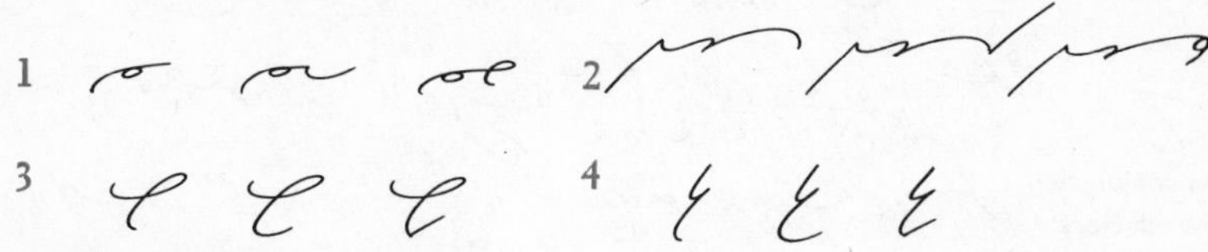

1. Thin, thinner, thinnest.
2. Drug, drugged, druggist.
3. Wrap, wrapper, wrapped.
4. Shop, shopper, shopped.

but

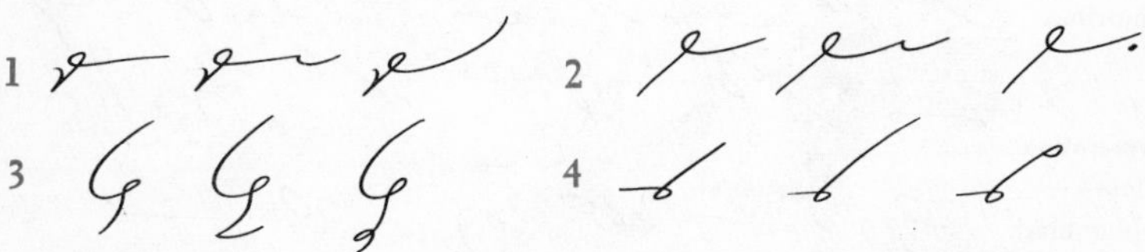

1. Steam, steamer, steamed.
2. Deal, dealer, dealing.
3. Brief, briefer, briefest.
4. Need, needed, needy.

Reading and Writing Practice

585. Transcription Word Study

ill effects Bad results.

temperature Degree of hotness or coldness of the human body. Normal temperature of the body is approximately 98.6 degrees.

cold shots Injections designed to protect a person from catching colds.

586. 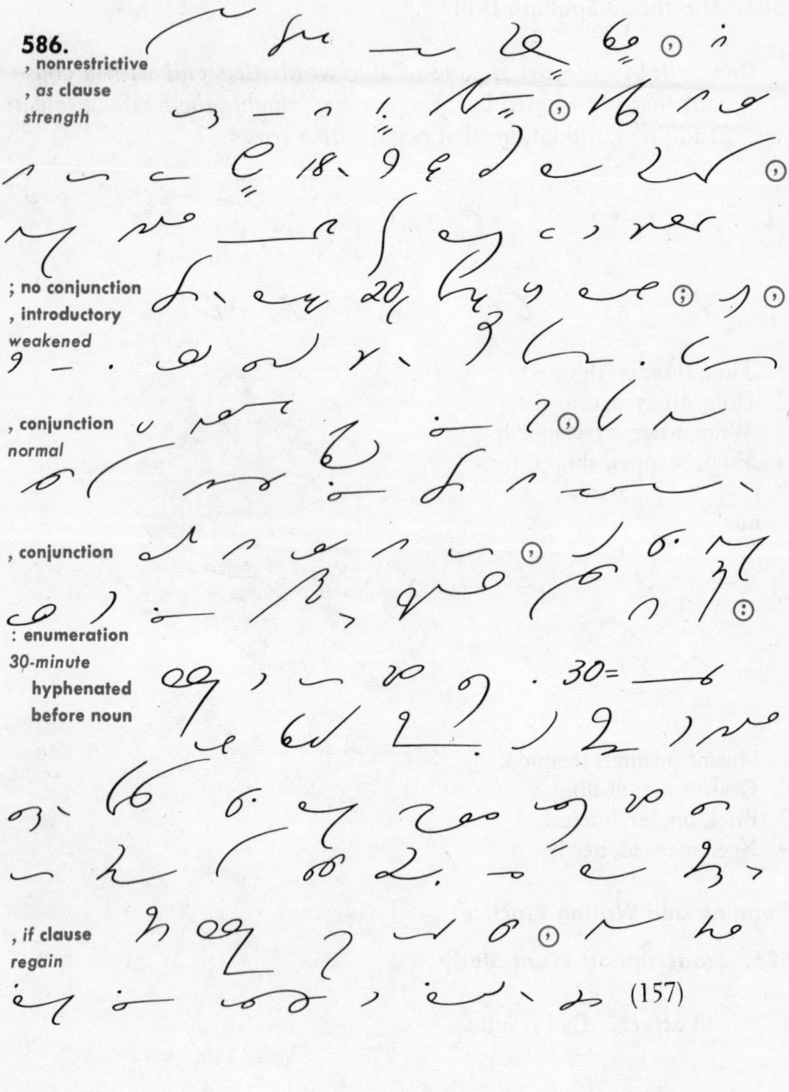
, nonrestrictive
, as clause
strength

; no conjunction
, introductory
weakened

, conjunction
normal

, conjunction

: enumeration
30-minute
hyphenated
before noun

, if clause
regain

(157)

587.

hay-fever
hyphenated before noun

, conjunction
Transcribe:
10 a.m.

10

development
, introductory

(128)

588.
Transcribe:
50 per cent

50,

received
permission
; illustrative ,

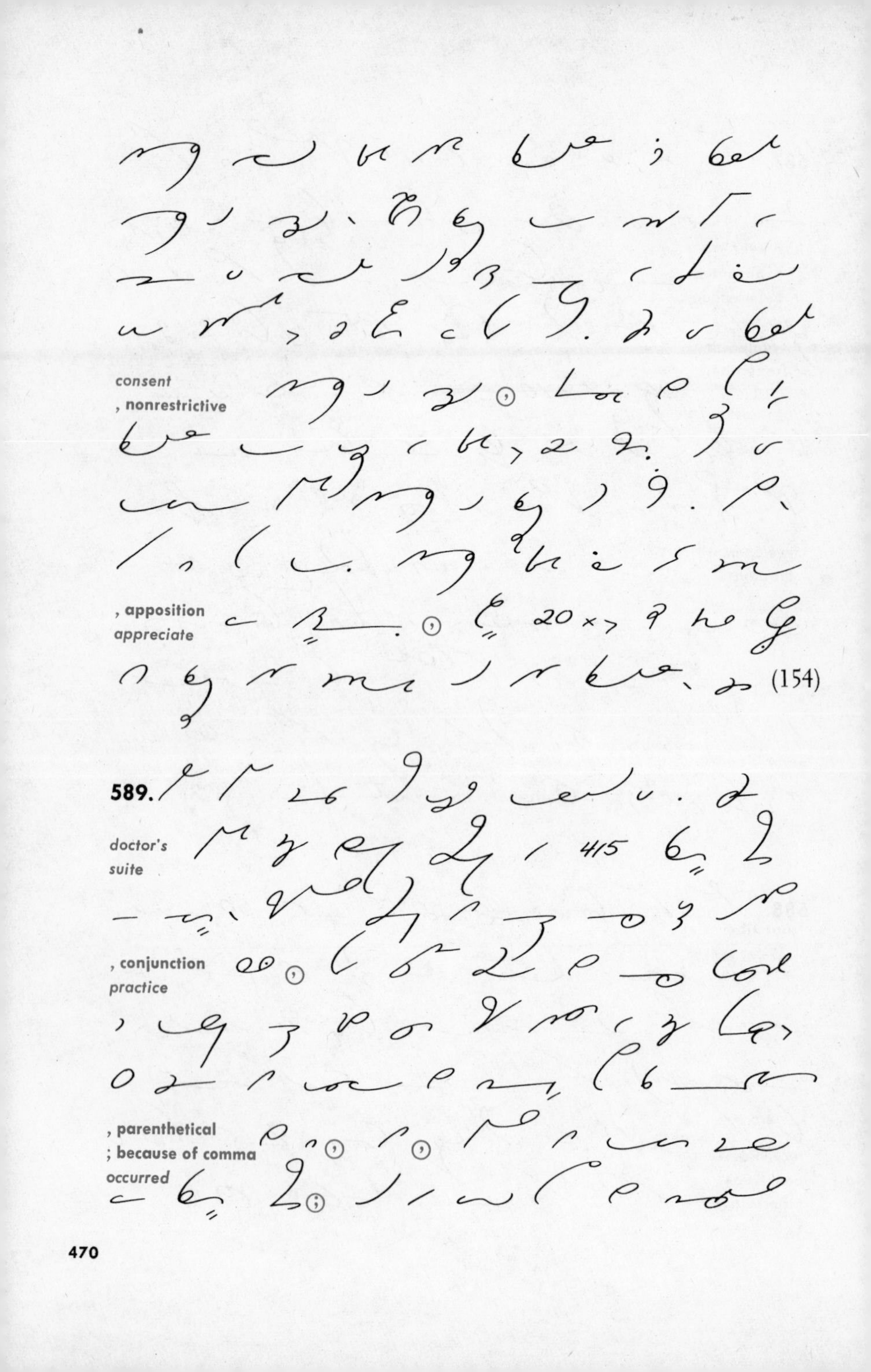

consent
, nonrestrictive

, apposition
appreciate

20

(154)

589.

doctor's
suite

415

, conjunction
practice

, parenthetical
; because of comma
occurred

appeals

, if clause

(124)

Transcription Quiz. Supply the necessary punctuation and the words missing from the shorthand. Also, correct the error in grammar in the second paragraph.

590.

17 23

19 ×

(104)

Lesson 80

591. Brief Forms and Derivatives

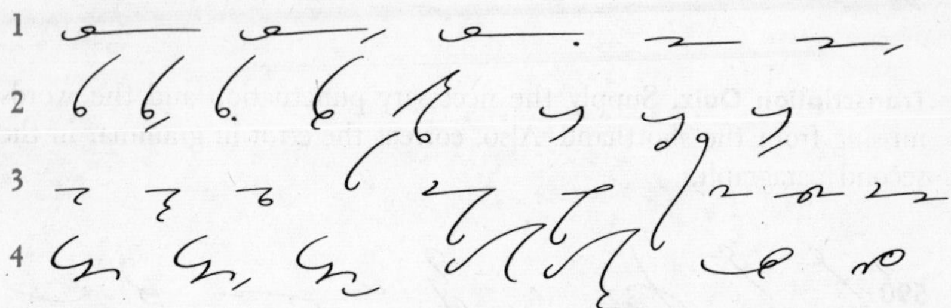

1. Remember, remembered, remembering; number, numbered.
2. Believe-belief, believed, believing, believes, disbelieve; refer-reference, referee, referred.
3. Instance-instant, instances-instants, instantly; body, somebody, anybody, everybody; one, anyone, someone.
4. Prosecute, prosecuted, prosecutor; automobile, automobiles; likewise; otherwise.

Reading and Writing Practice

592. Transcription Word Study

medical terminology The words and expressions used in medicine.

skin rash A breaking out of the skin.

diagnosis The art of recognizing a disease from its symptoms.

593.

months'

, conjunction
; illustrative ,
example

, conjunction
pressure

; because of comma
, if clause

, conjunction
accord

; no conjunction
courtesy
someday

(148)

594.

banquet
, when clause

, introducing
short quote
. inside quote

, conjunction

, nonrestrictive
; because of comma
accepted

recommended
; because of comma
, *if* clause

: enumeration
, series
telephone

(138)

595.
round-table
hyphenated
before noun
virus

, conjunction

, introductory
fairly
terminology

, if clause
, series

(130)

596.

, and omitted
courteous

ignored
, as clause

receive
, if clause

(124)

597.

assistant

, apposition

, introductory

; because of comma

resume

, parenthetical

physical

, introductory

(110)

598.

diagnosis

, introductory

(83)

Interoffice Memorandum

TO F. J. Marvin

LOCATION Personnel Department

SUBJECT Job Replacement

FROM A. R. Smith

LOCATION Foreign Department

DATE May 20, 19--

My secretary, Miss Helen A. Hicks, has just informed me that she is to be married on June 15. She plans to leave on June 1.

If it is possible, I should like to get someone to fill the vacancy immediately, so that Miss Hicks can help in the training of the new girl.

As you know, most of my correspondence is with customers in South and Central America. Consequently, it would be a great help to me if you could find a girl who has some degree of proficiency in Spanish.

I shall be in Cleveland on May 21 and 22, but I shall be back on the morning of May 23. I shall, therefore, be able to interview any girls you send me any time after May 22.

A. R. S.

ARS:HH

APPENDIX

RECALL DRILLS

List of Joined Word Endings

1. -ment

2. -less

3. -tion

4. -tial

5. -ly

6. -ily, -ally

7. -pose, -position

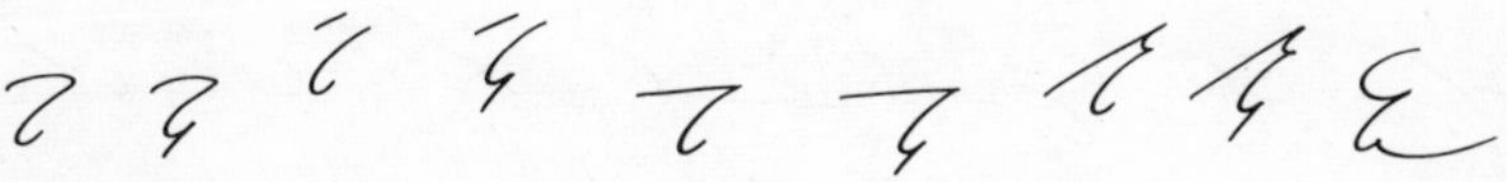

8. -ify

9. -ful

10. -sume, -sumption

11. -ble

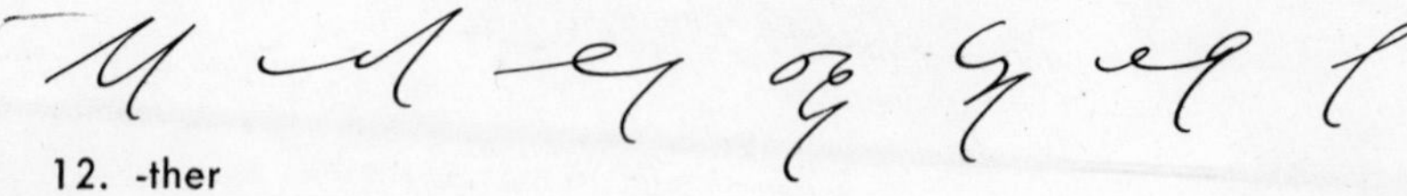

12. -ther

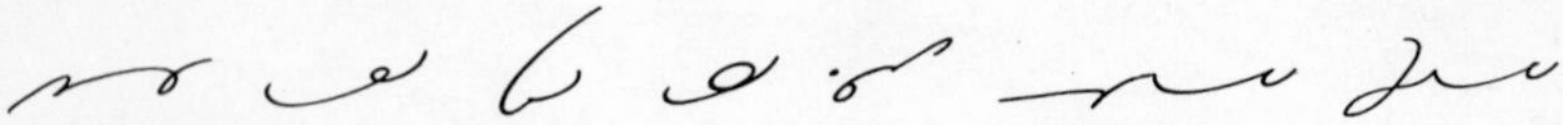

13. -ual, -tual

14. -ure, -ture

15. -self, -selves

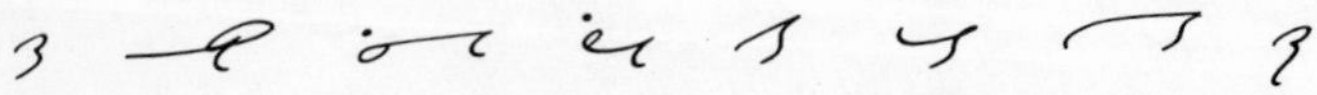

16. -ort

17. -tain

18. -cient, -ciency

List of Disjoined Word Endings

19. -hood

20. -ward

21. -ship

22. -cle, -cal

23. -ulate

24. -ingly

25. -ings

26. -gram

27. -ification

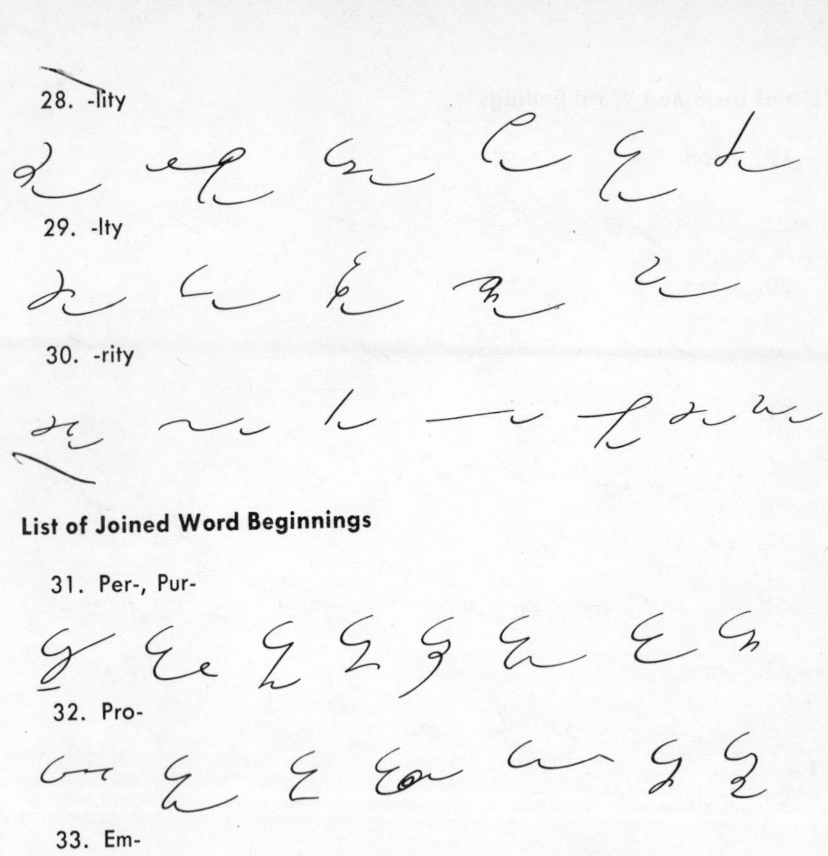

28. -lity

29. -lty

30. -rity

List of Joined Word Beginnings

31. Per-, Pur-

32. Pro-

33. Em-

34. Im-

35. In-

36. En-

37. Un-

38. Re-

39. Be-

40. De-

41. Dis-

42. Mis-

43. Ex-

44. Com-

45. Con-

46. Sub-

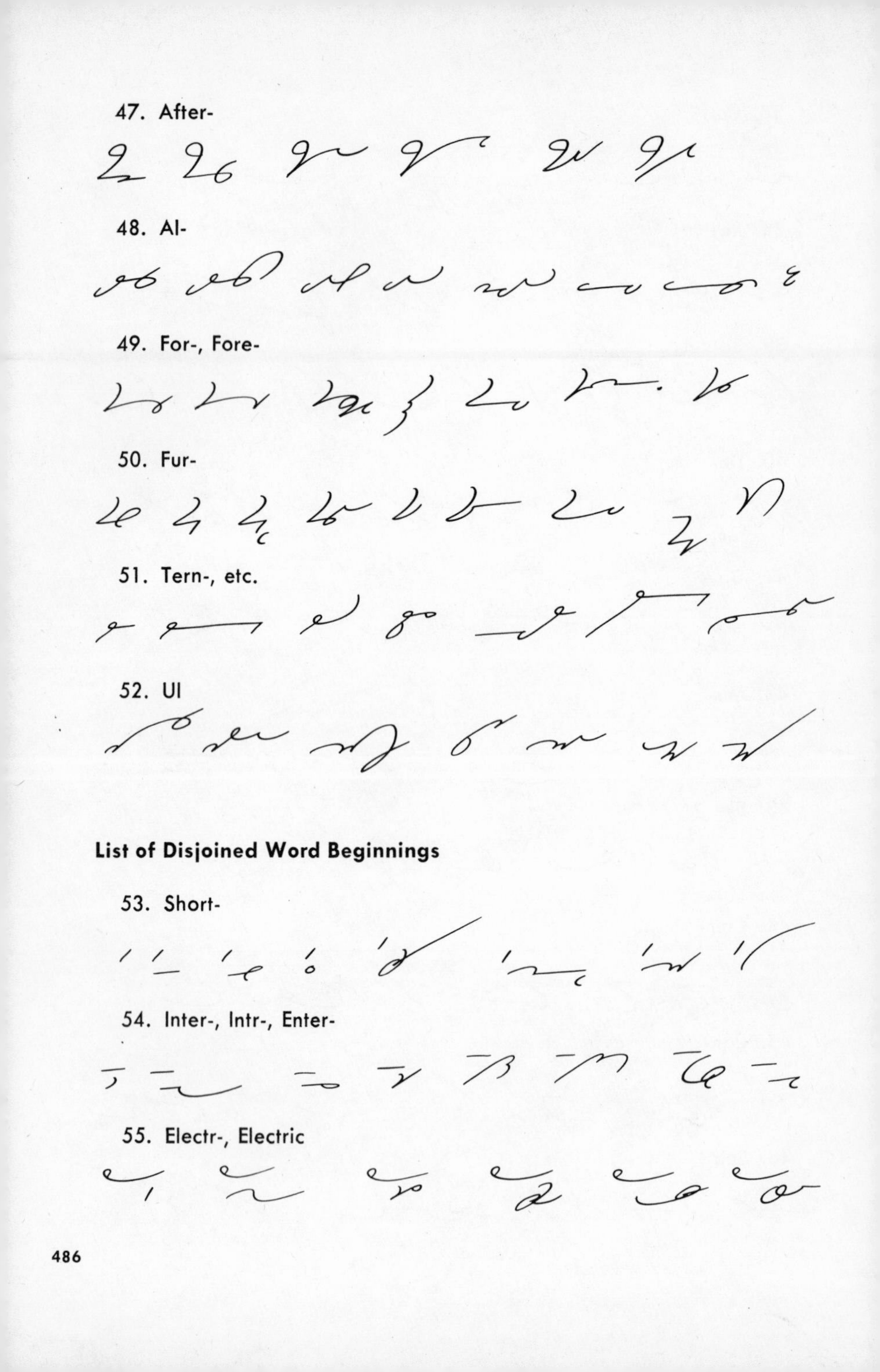

47. After-

48. Al-

49. For-, Fore-

50. Fur-

51. Tern-, etc.

52. Ul

List of Disjoined Word Beginnings

53. Short-

54. Inter-, Intr-, Enter-

55. Electr-, Electric

56. Post-

57. Super-, Supr-

58. Circum-

59. Self-

60. Trans-

61. Incl-

62. Ship-

63. Under-

64. Over-

List of Special Phrases

65. T For To in Phrases

66. Been Represented by B

67. Able Represented by A

68. Want Preceded by Pronoun

69. Ago Represented by G

70. Was Not, Is Not

71. Understand, Understood

72. To Omitted in Phrases

73. The Omitted in Phrases

74. Of Omitted in Phrases

75. And Omitted in Phrases

76. A Omitted in Phrases

77. Special Phrases

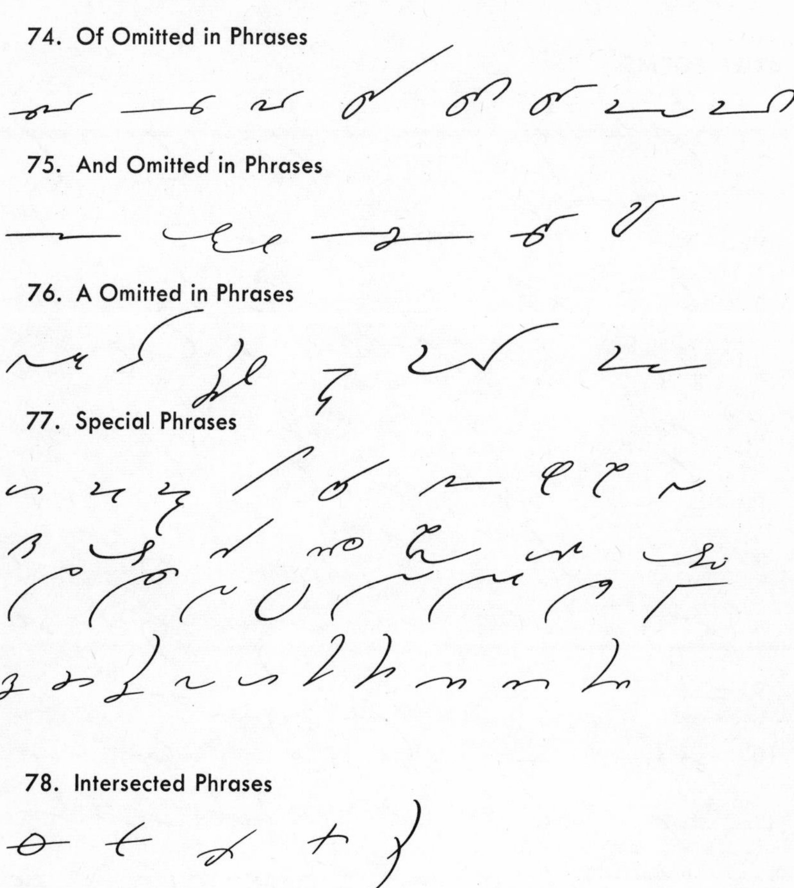

78. Intersected Phrases

BRIEF FORMS

	A	B	C	D	E	F
1						
2						
3						
4						
5						
6						
7						
8						
9						
10						
11						
12						
13						
14						
15						
16						
17						
18						

	A	B	C	D	E	F
19						
20						
21						
22						
23						
24						
25						
26						
27						
28						
29						
30						
31						

Addresses to be used for mailable transcripts

Chapter 1

1. Mr. Arnold Day, Electric Appliance Corp., 18 Franklin Square, Pittsburgh 6, Pennsylvania
2. Personnel Department, Carter & Delevan, 200 Spring Street, Euclid, Ohio
3. Mr. Hugh Casey, Casey Stores, Inc., 246 Downer Street, Dayton 2, Ohio
4. Mrs. Harold A. White, 14 Evergreen Circle, Dormont, Pennsylvania
5. Mrs. William Bass, Arcadia Gardens, South Hills, Pennsylvania
6. Mr. Arthur James, Scanlon & James, County Trust Building, Bismarck, North Dakota
7. Mr. Joseph Hayes, Jones Stationery Supplies, Fargo, North Dakota
8. Mr. Kevin Kelly, Credit Department, High-Fashion Styles, Lyric Building, Chicago 3, Illinois
9. Marcus & Lerner, Stationers, 2840 Leonard Avenue, Ann Arbor, Michigan
10. Mr. Herman Green, 222 Greenlawn Drive, Moline, Illinois
11. Sport Togs, Inc., Empire State Building, Room 2397, New York 1, New York
12. Mr. David Simms, Sales Promotion Manager, Kitchen Appliance Company, 2400 State Street, Trenton 10, New Jersey
13. Mr. John O. Macy, Office Equipment & Supply Company, 28 Journal Square, Jersey City 6, New Jersey
14. Mrs. Horace Brown, Smithfield Apartments, Verona, New Jersey
15. Mrs. John Joseph Casey, 47 Mortimer Parkway, Orange, New Jersey
16. Miss Marcia Stevens, 2011 Causeway, Montclair, New Jersey
17. Modern Home Furnishings, 50 Herkimer Street, Albany 2, New York
18. Mr. Truman Bates, Stamford Retail Credit Bureau, 20 Court Street, Stamford, Connecticut
19. Quality Furniture Store, 100 Barnum Square, Bridgeport 5, Connecticut
20. Dr. Clarence Baker, Medical Arts Building, 16 West 56 Street, New York 38, New York
21. Mr. Lawrence Jones, General Publishing Company, 1214 Fourth Avenue, New York 16, New York
22. Mr. Charles Treat, 214 Gateway Road, Ridgewood, New Jersey
23. Creighton's Citrus Cannery, R.F.D. 10, Inverness, Florida

24. Mr. Cabot Palmer, Palmer's Tea Garden, 20 Cypress Road, Macon, Georgia
25. Mrs. Brian Bates, Belmont Apartments, 28 Quaker Avenue, Philadelphia 6, Pennsylvania
26. Mrs. F. L. West, 93-12 168 Street, Jamaica 9, New York
27. Mr. Paul Cooper, R.F.D. 6, Simsbury, Connecticut
28. Miss Sara Jo Lee, 47 Concord Road, Sunnyside, L. I., New York

Chapter 2

29. Mr. Gerald May, Marketing Specialists, 210 Commonwealth Avenue, Boston 4, Massachusetts
30. Conway Construction Company, 380 Penn Avenue, Bethlehem, Pennsylvania
31. Mrs. Joshua Gray, 8 Farrier Street, Charleston 6, West Virginia
32. Mrs. Warren Irving, 364 Terrace Avenue, Richmond, Virginia
33. Mr. Alan Mead, 8 Lowell Street, Providence 11, Rhode Island
34. Mr. Albert Klein, 20 Fennimore Street, New Rochelle, New York
35. Mr. Truman Lee, 92 Cooper Lane, Silver Spring, Maryland
36. Mr. Jasper Pace, 2810 North Park Avenue, Tacoma 10, Washington
37. Mr. Carlton James, 329 Eagan Avenue, Walla Walla, Washington
38. Constant Oil Company, 1400 Beacon Street, Portland 10, Oregon
39. Mr. Everett West, 83 Nugget Lane, Oak Grove, Wisconsin
40. Mr. Warren Field, 219-B Salmon Avenue, Colfax, Washington
41. Mr. George Abbey, Abbey Enterprises, 1400 Price Street, Bremerton, Washington
42. Home Improvement & Remodeling Company, 2300 Glendale Boulevard, Los Angeles 35, California
43. Silver Electric Service, 162 Pacific Avenue, Whittier, California
44. Mr. Stephen Harper, Harper Remodeling Co., 434-436 West Market Street, San Francisco 16, California
45. Mr. Clarence Davis, 18-02 Citrus Lane, Lemon Grove, California
46. Mr. David Abbott, 24-A Capstan Road, Oceanside, California
47. Mrs. Andrew Smith, 23 Glenarm Circle, Palo Alto, California
48. Mr. Wesley James, Evergreen Nursery, Emerson Road, Madison, Connecticut
49. Mr. Gordon Green, Orchard Park Nurseries, Box 74, Heather Lane, Guilford, Connecticut
50. Mr. S. J. Gates, 146 Elm Avenue, Cheshire, Connecticut
51. Mrs. Alison Carr, Box 24, Park Lane, Bristol, Connecticut
52. Mr. Joseph Gray, 326 Barton Street, Jewett City, Connecticut
53. Mr. William F. Mason, Mason Lumber Company, Montpelier, Vermont
54. Mr. Spencer Ames, Ames & Stillwell Mfg. Co., 204 Cooper Street, Boston 20, Massachusetts
55. Mr. Charles E. Baker, 46 River Road, Cambridge 38, Massachusetts

56. Demarest Furniture Company, 30 North Concord Avenue, Lowell, Massachusetts
57. Mr. Conrad Nelson, 439 Mt. Hope Boulevard, Portsmouth, Rhode Island
58. Mr. Townsend Smith, 795 Green End Avenue, Middletown, Rhode Island
59. Mrs. Eric Olson, 322 Rogers Road, Kingston, Rhode Island

Chapter 3

60. Mr. David Ring, Florida Guaranty Trust Company, 1400 Crescent Boulevard, Miami 16, Florida
61. Mr. Thomas Shields, Southern Lumber Company, 288-94 Cypress Avenue, Miami 13, Florida
62. Orange Trust Company, Fifth Avenue at Twelfth Street, Jacksonville 8, Florida
63. Mrs. Milton Green, Everglades Apartments, 1800 Southern Cross Boulevard, Miami 7, Florida
64. Miss Charlene Baker, 23 Cotillion Drive, Columbus, Georgia
65. Mr. Herbert Nelson, Nelson, Wayne & Duff, 58 Davis Avenue, Macon, Georgia
66. Meredith, King & Company, Copper Trust Building, Phoenix 9, Arizona
67. Investment Counselors, 20 Kingman Avenue, Yuma, Arizona
68. Mr. Edward H. Pace, 184 Granite Boulevard, Boulder, Colorado
69. Mr. H. Stanley Brown, 26 Canyon Drive, Estes Park, Colorado
70. Mr. Clayton Baker, 410 Park Avenue, Kingman, Arizona
71. Mr. Elwood White, 11 McArthur Avenue, Chandler, Arizona
72. Mr. Robert N. Green, 46 Wilshire Road, Darien, Connecticut
73. Mr. Thomas E. Hunter, Hunter Packing Company, 640-650 West Bank Street, Moline, Illinois
74. Mr. Roger Lee, 448 Parker Avenue, Racine, Wisconsin
75. Mr. Anderson Smith, 63 Sunset Road, Winter Park, Florida
76. Mr. Francis Jones, Comstock Gardens, 397 Jessup Avenue, St. Petersburg, Florida
77. Mr. Leonard Day, 111 Lindley Avenue, Tenafly, New Jersey
78. Mr. Wilbur Jones, 40 Bradley Circle, Cresskill, New Jersey
79. Mr. Joseph Smith, Personal Loan Department, Fidelity Trust Company, 60 Esplanade, New Orleans, Louisiana
80. Mr. Douglas Jones, 28 Camellia Street, Opelousas, Louisiana
81. Mr. Everett Gray, Manager, Personnel Department, Woodward Trust Company, 1816 Columbus Avenue, Meridian, Mississippi
82. Mr. Joseph Mason, 93 West Main Road, Paris, Mississippi
83. Mr. Maurice A. Brown, 81 Seminole Street, Tampa 8, Florida
84. Mr. Samuel Green, 376 Blackstone Road, Tallahassee, Florida
85. Springfield National Bank, 200 South Third Avenue, Springfield, Ohio

86. Mrs. William E. Baker, 63 Quarrier Road, New Orleans 3, Louisiana
87. Mr. Albert Simms, Simms Furniture Company, 150 Main Street, Albany 7, New York
88. Republic Publishing Company, 104 Simons Avenue, Rochester 3, New York
89. Mr. George W. Chase, 333 Mountain Road, Windham, New York
90. Mr. Theodore Macey, 29 River Street, Hudson, New York

Chapter 4

91. Culver Magazine Agency, 873 Austin Avenue, Detroit 25, Michigan
92. Mr. Robert J. White, President, Ingham County Trust Company, 40 North Michigan Avenue, Lansing 9, Michigan
93. Mr. Thomas C. Walsh, Sheridan Chemical Corporation, 63-67 Columbus Avenue, Muskegon, Michigan
94. Mr. P. T. Samuels, 209 Adams Street, Menasha, Wisconsin
95. Mr. Francis Murphy, Ridge Road, Cliff Lake, Montana
96. Mr. Emerson Gray, Shelby Road, Evaro, Montana
97. Valcourt Publishing Company, 287-289 Sussex Street, Baltimore 40, Maryland
98. Mr. Frank Nelson, Nelson's Book Nook, 500 Calvert Avenue, Cumberland, Maryland
99. Mr. Everett Day, 365 Oak Street, Newbury, New Hampshire
100. Mr. L. E. Cole, Lytton's Bookcase, 40 Oak Street, Manchester 7, New Hampshire
101. Mr. Sidney Kramer, Kramer Personnel Agency, 3040 Chrysler Building, New York 18, New York
102. Mr. Chester Simms, 25 Seaview Road, Stapleton, Staten Island, New York
103. Mr. Albert Snow, The Book Shelf, 54 Nassau Street, New York 25, New York
104. Everett Publishing Company, Inc., 390 Essex Street, Greensboro, North Carolina
105. Mrs. Irene Gates, 144 West Street, Pittsburgh 16, Pennsylvania
106. Mr. Charles Rice, Gilroy Business College, 310 Jefferson Avenue, Spartanburg, South Carolina
107. Mrs. J. C. Strong, 86 Sentinel Street, Maplewood, Oregon
108. Mr. O. M. Jones, Jones Printing & Binding Company, 42-48 Walnut Street, Portland 16, Oregon
109. Duncan School of Business, 60 West Bryant Avenue, Pueblo, Colorado
110. Pyramid Book Company, 436 Fourth Avenue, New York 28, New York
111. Mr. Benjamin Brown, Brown & Bridewell, 100-130 Sunrise Boulevard, Garden City, Long Island, New York
112. Mr. Stanton Green, Green & Noble, Printers, 600 Mercer Street, Jersey City 5, New Jersey

113. Mr. Hobart Baker, Fleetwood Arms, 429 Harvard Street, East Orange, New Jersey
114. Mr. Martin Harvey, Adams High School, Third and Ocean Avenues, Asbury Park, New Jersey
115. Mr. Donald Morris, 119 Blackmer Street, Wilkes-Barre, Pennsylvania
116. Mr. John T. Roy, Roy, Talbott & Adams, 64 Anthracite Building, Harrisburg, Pennsylvania
117. Mr. Sherwood Burns, Essex Printers, Incorporated, Printers Lane, Essex, Connecticut
118. Mr. Andrew Drake, Drake Manufacturing Company, 260 North Street, Portland 6, Maine
119. Mr. Chester Miles, Green Bay Publishing Company, 670 West Superior Street, Green Bay, Wisconsin
120. Mr. Arnold Keith, Keith & Smith, Jewelers, 165 Lee Avenue, Falls Church, Virginia
121. Mr. Marvin Beck, Beck Printing Service, 1800 Salem Street, Providence 10, Rhode Island

Chapter 5

122. Mr. George E. May, 643 Randolph Street, Bridgeport, Indiana
123. Mr. Otto C. Simon, 615 West Main Street, Pittsburgh 16, Pennsylvania
124. Mr. Roger Gray, Gray & Chason, 80-84 Forrest Avenue, Indianapolis 8, Indiana
125. Mr. Charles James, 63 West Madison Street, Des Moines 7, Iowa
126. Mr. Albert Macy, 96 Evans Avenue, Evansville 8, Indiana
127. Mr. Edward H. Smith, Chelsea Arms Apartments, 2860 Lee Avenue, Mason City, Iowa
128. Winecoff & Kashin, Insurance Specialists, 620 Franklin Avenue, Kansas City 10, Kansas
129. Mr. Carlton Barry, 43 Osage Street, Denmark, Kansas
130. Osgood & Parkwell, 604 Tivoli Building, 900 Cherokee Avenue, Wichita 7, Kansas
131. Mr. Eugene M. Adams, 1818 Douglas Boulevard, Irvington, Nebraska
132. Mr. Harry E. Barnes, R.F.D. 3, Raymond, Nebraska
133. Mr. Stephen Crane, 94 South Marion Avenue, Hannibal, Missouri
134. Mr. Roger Jones, Jones Meat Market, 432 Alamo Avenue, Houston 8, Texas
135. Mr. Elwood Smith, Independence Insurance Company, 86 North Jackson Street, Independence, Missouri
136. Pratt & Dickinson, Incorporated, Johnson Building, 900-910 Greeley Avenue, Kansas City 7, Kansas
137. Mr. Theodore A. Jones, 63 Caldwell Street, Hannibal, Missouri
138. Mr. William Abbey, Box 103, Valley Road, Greenwood, Missouri
139. Mr. Sidney M. Travers, 362 Solomon Street, Gaylord, Kansas

140. Mr. Douglas P. Green, Green & Redmond, 47 Mills Street, Houston 11, Texas
141. Mr. Ordwell Macy, 540 North Central Avenue, Fort Worth 8, Texas
142. Mr. Clifford C. Clay, 960 Somerset Avenue, Baltimore 43, Maryland
143. Mr. Vernon A. Kelly, 37 Madison Street, Pine Bluff, Arkansas
144. Mr. Paul L. Donald, 66 Boone Road, Hensley, Arkansas
145. Mrs. J. J. Woods, Beauregard Gardens, 610 De Soto Boulevard, Lafayette, Louisiana
146. Mr. Edward G. Melvin, 418 Fulton Street, Covington, Kentucky
147. Chicago Insurance Company, 450 North Michigan Avenue, Chicago 46, Illinois
148. Mr. Franklin Pace, 23 Oneida Avenue, Lewiston, Idaho
149. Mr. Wilfred Stern, 1428 Canyon Drive, Nampa, Idaho
150. Mr. Charles Macy, 294 Valencia Street, Roswell, New Mexico
151. Mr. Andrew Smith, Silver Smith's Mining Company, 408 Grant, Silver City, New Mexico
152. Mr. Curtis N. Smith, 17 Sierra Glen, Crownpoint, New Mexico
153. Mr. Delbert Jones, El Rio Grande Apartments, 29 Bliss Road, El Paso, Texas

Chapter 6

154. Mr. Everett West, 480 Cascade Boulevard, Sherman, South Dakota
155. Quarry Bank & Trust Company, 150 North Sanborn Avenue, Sioux Falls, South Dakota
156. Mr. John J. May, 79 Perkins Street, Brookings, South Dakota
157. Miss Margaret E. Bailey, Iroquois Gardens, 946 West Park Avenue, Chicago 55, Illinois
158. Mr. Kenneth Nelson, 83 White Horse Pike, Laramie, Wyoming
159. Mr. Ferdinand Clay, Clay Repairs & Accessories, 206 Main Street, Fletcher Park, Wyoming
160. Mr. Keith F. Gates, 409 Palmer Building, Main Street and Edison Avenue, Detroit 33, Michigan
161. Mr. James O. Mills, Caine Motor Company, 600 West Superior Street, Detroit 29, Michigan
162. Mr. Henry Barnes, Barnes Trucking Service, 1428 Bonner Avenue, Missoula, Montana
163. Mr. Joseph E. Lowry, Bluestone Tire Company, 900 Fairlawn Avenue, Akron 5, Ohio
164. Mr. Arthur Simms, 690 Pine Bluff, Hillsdale, Wyoming
165. Mr. Geoffrey Ramsey, Ramsey Motors, Inc., 320 Commerce Street, Sioux Falls, South Dakota
166. Mr. John Andrews, 47 Gold Stone Hill, Havre, Montana
167. Mr. F. Herbert Morris, Kimball Road, De Witt, Nebraska
168. Mrs. George F. Harper, 98 Laurel Lane, Newark, Delaware
169. Mr. Albert Simons, 720 County Road, Milton, Delaware

170. Mr. Robert G. Holt, Holt, Arthur & Heather, 1540 Kent Avenue, Wilmington, Delaware
171. Mr. Duane Wade, 1810 Continental Avenue, S. W., Washington 34, D. C.
172. Mr. Christopher Davis, 273 Cherry Lane, Tacoma Park, South Dakota
173. Mr. Ashley Brown, 312 Talbot Avenue, Cumberland, Maryland
174. Mr. Howard G. Bates, 96 Magnolia Lane, Bethel, Delaware
175. Clinton Motor Service Company, 1470 Fisher Avenue, Dallas 20, Texas
176. Mr. John A. Walsh, Manager, Wilson Brothers, 555 Chestnut Street, Chicago 36, Illinois
177. Mr. John T. Murphy, Jack's Motor Freight, 420 Fulton Street, Cicero, Illinois
178. Mr. Alexander Grace, 368 Marshall Street, Clarksville, Tennessee
179. Mr. Arthur S. Mills, 740 West Clark Street, Chicago 92, Illinois
180. Mr. Chester E. Brown, Brown & Leeds Motor Service, 620 Whitman Avenue, Terre Haute, Indiana
181. Mr. Harry T. Walsh, 216 Carroll Street, Alton Park, Tennessee
182. Comstock De Luxe Car Interiors, 337 Anderson Avenue, Chattanooga 2, Tennessee
183. Drivers Monthly, 46 Clinton Street, Hamtramck, Michigan
184. Mr. Harvey Green, American Baking Company, 1550-1560 Girard Avenue, Philadelphia 25, Pennsylvania
185. Mr. Seymour Karp, Express Trucking Service, 473 Franklin Avenue, Minneapolis 5, Minnesota
186. Mr. Paul M. Lee, Lee Construction Company, 1800 Washington Avenue, Saint Paul 10, Minnesota
187. Mr. Michael Perry, Perry's Motor Service, 720 Pioneer Avenue, Salt Lake City 11, Utah
188. Mr. Samuel D. Jacobs, Motor Express Service, 910 Weber Street, Ogden, Utah

Chapter 7

189. Mr. Conrad L. Simms, Simms Business Institute, 546 Park Avenue, New York 22, New York
190. Sales Efficiency Corporation, 324 Lexington Avenue, New York 19, New York
191. Mr. Ferdinand Day, Harris Trust & Title Company, 300 Lincoln Avenue, Harrisburg, Pennsylvania
192. Mr. Andrew C. Jones, 819 Concord Street, Quincy 68, Massachusetts
193. Mr. John A. Chester, Treadway's Department Store, 98 North Front Street, Sunbury, Pennsylvania
194. Bedford Manufacturing Company, 80 North Clinton Street, Medina, Ohio
195. Mrs. Genevieve Reilly, Manager, Training Specialists, 1800 West Clark Street, Chicago 46, Illinois

196. Mrs. Edward Gates, 23 Freeman Street, Springfield, Illinois
197. Miss Dorothy W. White, Central High School, 900-910 State Street, Chicago 32, Illinois
198. Mr. Thomas Mason, Mason Motors, 620 Jackson Avenue, Waukegan, Illinois
199. Miss Mary C. Allen, 14 Brookdale Road, Brattleboro, Vermont
200. Mrs. Leonard Clay, Bristol Arms Apartments, 64 Bristol Street, Newton 58, Massachusetts
201. Mr. Thomas E. Davis, Davis Toy Company, 17 North Columbia Avenue, Salem, Oregon
202. Mr. T. J. Hoffman, Principal, North High School, 800 Jacinto Street, San Antonio 14, Texas
203. Mrs. Elwell Drake, Manager, Meredith Business Schools, 630 North Plymouth Street, Boston 15, Massachusetts
204. Mr. Charles Abbey, 29 Surrey Road, Morehead City, North Carolina
205. Mr. Harry Blackmore, 87 Florence Street, Lancaster, South Carolina
206. Miss Valerie Jones, Decatur Apartments, 444 Fanning Street, Moultrie, Georgia
207. Mr. Geoffrey Brown, 851 Arlington Boulevard, Alexandria, Virginia
208. Bannister Finance Company, Barnum Building, 40 Trumbull Avenue, Bridgeport 6, Connecticut
209. Mr. Raymond Warner, 680 Roosevelt Street, Freeport, Long Island, New York
210. Mrs. Everett Green, 142 Saxon Lane, Bay Shore, Long Island, New York
211. Miss Madeline Johnson, 30 Garden Circle, Summit, New Jersey
212. Mr. Albert Bailey, 61 Redwood Lane, Elk Grove, California
213. Home Arts Institute, 400-402 Butler Avenue, Cleveland 12, Ohio
214. Miss Bertha Sacks, 792 Warren Street, Belleville, New Jersey
215. Mrs. F. E. Leslie, Principal, Southside High School, Church Street at Blackwood Avenue, Camden 8, New Jersey
216. Miss Alice A. Chase, Riverview Apartments, 1890 Palisade Avenue, Cliffside Park, New Jersey
217. Mr. R. M. Ross, Clark High School, 750 Pershing Avenue, Las Vegas, Nevada
218. Mr. Philip S. Brown, Sheridan High School, Park Avenue at Cass, Freemont, Nebraska
219. Mr. Edmund Klein, Principal, Roosevelt High School, 14 Street at Dawes Avenue, Chadron, Nebraska
220. Mr. Martin Stacy, Principal, Clinton Avenue School, Clinton and Park Avenues, Flushing 31, New York

Chapter 8

221. Business Surveys, Inc., Golden Gate Building, 460 State Street, San Francisco 42, California

222. Air Travel Bureau, Chadwick Building, 320 South Wabash Avenue, Chicago 28, Illinois
223. Mr. Stanton Day, 1448 Parker Avenue, Maywood, New Jersey
224. Mr. Joseph B. Simms, Simms Manufacturing Company, 1200 Warwick Street, Lexington, Virginia
225. Mr. George Palmer, Palmer & Sons, Inc., 100 West Jackson Avenue, Clarksburg, West Virginia
226. Mr. Charles Macy, Jefferson Real Estate Company, 68 North Main Street, New Rochelle, New York
227. Mr. Andrew Smith, Hamilton Court Apartments, 96 Hamilton Avenue, Baltimore 99, Maryland
228. Mr. Anthony Jones, Manager, Smithdeal Department Store, 650 Penobscot Street, Bangor, Maine
229. Mr. Walter Pace, Presbrey & Clarkson Company, 98 Federal Street, Portland 8, Maine
230. Martindales' Hotel Guide, 74 North Erie Street, Albany 6, New York
231. Mr. Clarence Stern, Stern, Stern & Edwards, 402 Humboldt Building, Hawthorne, Nevada
232. Mr. Godfrey Banks, Stadler Publishing Company, 412 Brigham Avenue, Tooele, Utah
233. Mr. J. A. Allen, Allen Ranch, Great Falls, Montana
234. Mr. Everett N. Ray, Elroy Communications, Banks and Marshall Streets, Fond du Lac, Wisconsin
235. Caster Travel Agency, Lucas Building, 900 Railroad Avenue, Toledo 8, Ohio
236. Baker Transportation Company, 46 Comanche Lane, Denver 4, Colorado
237. Dallas Trade Exchange, Pecos and Clay, Dallas 14, Texas
238. Mrs. David C. Glass, Glass Enterprises, 84 Montcalm Street, River Rouge, Michigan
239. Mr. Jonathan Mead, Star Box Company, 46 Oneida Street, Menasha, Wisconsin
240. Mr. Robert M. Simms, Whitehall Apartments, 986 Franklin Avenue, Columbus 14, Ohio
241. Mr. Charles Brooks, Golden Arrow Railway Company, 300 Oakland Street, Topeka, Kansas
242. Mr. Arthur Trees, 42 Ellery Lane, Scarsdale, New York
243. Dr. Thomas L. Green, Medical Arts Building, Hamilton at Arbor Avenues, Hamden, Connecticut
244. Mr. Harold James, James Travel Agency, Iron City Building, Pittsburgh 16, Pennsylvania
245. President Steamship Company, Pier 98, North River, New York 14, New York
246. Mr. John J. Parks, 29 Mountainview Road, Concord, New Hampshire
247. Mr. William Billings, Billings Hardware Store, 40 East 183 Street, Bronx 42, New York

248. Mr. Thomas Kelly, 16 Simons Avenue, Athens, Ohio
249. Mr. Stephen D. Jones, Jones Appliance Company, 75 Morrison Avenue, Mankato, Minnesota
250. Mr. Donald R. Gates, Gates Printing & Publishing Company, 42 Alger Street, Grand Rapids 6, Michigan
251. Mr. Leonard Jones, Sr., 561 Peach Street, Decatur, Georgia
252. Mr. Wilson C. Smith, Smith Chemical Company, Elkhart Street, Valparaiso, Indiana
253. Mr. Edwin C. Jones, 39 Clay Avenue, Paris, Kentucky
254. Mr. Harold G. Brown, 47 Sierra Street, Clovis, New Mexico
255. Mr. Arthur Kramer, 602 Randolph Street, Montgomery, West Virginia

Chapter 9

256. Mr. Philip E. Casey, Retail Merchants of Chicago Association, 46 South Adams Street, Chicago 29, Illinois
257. Mrs. Durand L. Gates, 14-22 Brookdale Circle, Hicksville, Long Island, New York
258. The Connecticut Yankee Shop, 92 Market Street, Hartford 9, Connecticut
259. Mr. Herbert M. Taylor, Euclid Avenue Apartments, 635 Euclid Avenue, Springfield, Ohio
260. Mr. Jason Gates, 411 Campbell Street, Austin, Texas
261. Mrs. Oscar Green, 1818 Seneca Boulevard, Rochester 9, New York
262. Mrs. J. C. Leslie, 23 Lafayette Court, Fall River, Massachusetts
263. Mrs. Victor Kelly, Manager, The Mannequin Shop, 38 Main Street, Chatham, New Jersey
264. Needham's Department Store, 400 Osage Street, Oklahoma City 14, Oklahoma
265. Sara Jo Dress Shop, 87 Palmer Avenue, Fleetwood, New York
266. Mr. Clifford West, 47 Hamilton Avenue, Sherman, South Dakota
267. Mrs. Bradley Park, 863 Morrison Park Avenue, Minneapolis 17, Minnesota
268. Mr. Henry F. Brill, 61 Hennepin Street, Pipestone, Minnesota
269. Mr. Douglas Fox, 290 Knox Avenue, Bennington, Nebraska
270. Mr. Alfred M. Green, Green Clothing Store, 400-410 Decatur Avenue, Memphis 7, Tennessee
271. Mr. Lloyd Johnson, President, Beau Brummel Apparel, 750 Stewart Street, Chattanooga 18, Tennessee
272. Memo to Mr. Johnson from Mr. Jackson
273. Mr. Malcolm Lake, 241 Davis Avenue, South Bend 6, Indiana
274. Mr. Delbert Gray, 96 Cedar Lane, Boone, Iowa
275. Mr. Wilson Smith, 830 Gage Boulevard, Hastings, Nebraska
276. Mrs. C. G. Henry, 629 Hancock Street, Caribou, Maine
277. Mr. Merritt Herman, Hansel & Gretel Shoes, 468-470 Frederick Avenue, Hagerstown, Maryland

278. Little Princess Dress Shoppe, 53 Bedford Street, Falls Church, Virginia
279. The Children's Shop, 81 Simpson Street, Laurel, Mississippi
280. Mrs. Alan E. Craig, 153 Bayou Boulevard, St. Petersburg 4, Florida
281. Mr. George Sanders, 96 Clinton Avenue, Sandusky, Ohio
282. Mr. Albert O. Hodges, Lenoir Avenue Apartments, 117 Lenoir Avenue, Gastonia, North Carolina
283. Mr. Harvey Jones, 55 North Grant Street, Richland, Washington
284. Mr. Richard Baker, 931 Colfax Circle, Los Alamos, New Mexico
285. Freeborn Department Store, 416 West 33 Street, St. Paul 18, Minnesota
286. Mr. Maxwell Tracy, 354 Cliff Street, Trinity Heights, Texas
287. Austin's Department Store, 90 West Market Street, Rapid City, South Dakota
288. Mr. Frederick L. Jones, 67 Lycoming Street, Palmerton, Pennsylvania
289. Mrs. Thomas J. Lee, Garden State Apartments, Plainfield, New Jersey
290. Mr. J. Louis Day, 862 Rockleigh Road, Laconia, New Hampshire

Chapter 10

291. Mr. Chester Williams, County Telephone Service, 98 West Fourth Street, New York 22, New York
292. Mr. Samuel S. Jones, Webster Branch Exchange, 50 West Central Avenue, Allentown, Pennsylvania
293. Mr. Albert Sears, Vernon Telephone Branch, 70 West 14 Street, Los Angeles 65, California
294. Mr. John E. Samuels, 416 Monterey Road, Mount Wilson, California
295. Mr. Daniel James, 504 Wheeler Street, Astoria, Oregon
296. Mr. Roland Dix, 673 Butler Road, Selma, Ohio
297. Mr. Richard Harris, 52 Harding Avenue, Plattsburg, Ohio
298. Mr. A. J. Green, Little River Power & Light Company, 40 Wilcox Street, Little River, Alabama
299. Mr. M. C. Jones, Jones Electrical Service, 71 Graham Street, Bisbee, Arizona
300. Mr. Matthew Ames, Home Appliance Company, 48 North Jackson Street, Trinidad, Colorado
301. Fremont Gas & Electric Company, 370 Cedar Street, Scottsbluff, Nebraska
302. Medway Utilities Company, 64 North Davis Street, Springfield 9, Illinois
303. Mr. E. S. Banker, Mid-State Electric Company, 41 Smith Street, Morristown, New Jersey
304. Mr. Milton Young, 380 Hillside Avenue, Hudson, New York
305. Miss Mary Jane Day, Washington High School, Hopkinsville, Kentucky.
306. Mr. Joseph C. Kelly, Central Gas & Electric Company, 110 Seward Avenue, Chadron, Nebraska

307. Mrs. Stephen Martin, 680 Clark Street, Helena, Montana
308. Miss Marcia Mills, 47-A Lewis Street, Missoula, Montana
309. Galway Construction Company, 20 Broadway, Deming, New Mexico
310. Mr. Louis Nelson, 47 Wills Avenue, Artesia, New Mexico
311. Mr. George Travis, Wheatridge Products Company, 500 Washburn Avenue, Topeka, Kansas
312. Trenton Clarion, 240 South State Street, Trenton 3, New Jersey
313. Mr. William Nelson, Nelson, Graves & Conway, 380 Monroe Street, Jackson 20, Mississippi
314. Dallas Chamber of Commerce, 100 Main Street, Dallas, South Dakota
315. Mrs. Harvey Green, 215 Mercer Street, Halifax, Pennsylvania
316. Mrs. Adam Farley, Modiste Dress Salon, 28 North Bellevue Avenue, Newport, Rhode Island
317. Mr. Edward Paul, 1812 Wilson Avenue, Lexington, North Carolina
318. Mrs. Douglas C. Nelson, 512-A Carteret Street, Linwood, North Carolina
319. Memo to Eric Larson from James Miller
320. Mr. Frank W. Stone, Stone Manufacturing Company, Incorporated, 200 Scott Street, Clinton, Iowa
321. Mr. John G. Bass, Electric Power Company, 310 Lucas Avenue, Davenport, Iowa
322. Mrs. Leroy A. Parks, Louise Court Apartments, 98 Louise Street, Baton Rouge, Louisiana
323. Mr. Clifford White, President, White Tool & Die Works, 1860 New Haven Street, Waterbury 15, Connecticut
324. Mr. Joseph Mann, Mann & Keating, 450 Harris Avenue, Reading, Pennsylvania

Chapter 11

325. Mr. Anthony Ames, Ames Advertising Specialties, 110 Market Street, Newark 3, New Jersey
326. Mr. Frederick A. Thomas, Thomas Furniture Salon, 333 Palm Street, Sarasota, Florida
327. Mr. George Franklin, Franklin Office Furniture, Incorporated, 457 De Kalb Street, Brunswick, Georgia
328. Mr. Conrad Gray, Gray Metal Finishing Company, Jackson & Clark Streets, Wyandotte, Michigan
329. Mr. Herbert Crane, Crane Plumbing Company, 84 Calhoun Street, Fairmont, West Virginia
330. Mr. G. D. Moore, Moore Paper Products, 37 North Marquette Avenue, Green Bay, Wisconsin
331. Mr. Nicholas West, West & Durand, 420 Dodge Street, Madison 5, Wisconsin
332. Mr. Elliott E. Ramsey, Office Specialists, Incorporated, 64 Monroe Street, Green Bay, Wisconsin

333. Mr. Clark Johnson, Tele-Sales Company, 830 LaSalle Street, Chicago 89, Illinois
334. Mr. Otis Brown, Stellar Elevator Company, 1200 Edison Avenue, Lansing 6, Michigan
335. Mr. Garrett Carey, Carey Artists Supplies, 268 Harper Avenue, Detroit 42, Michigan
336. Miss Dorothea Tracy, Tracy Stenographic Service, 340 Custer Avenue, Tulsa 1, Oklahoma
337. Mr. Jeremiah Smith, Household Magazines, Incorporated, 51 Hamilton Street, Macomb, Illinois
338. Mr. Harvey James, James Furniture Company, 211 Newton Street, Fayetteville, Arkansas
339. Memo to Branch Managers from Harry J. Green
340. Mr. George Masters, Conway Book Company, 20 Lee Avenue, Decatur, Georgia
341. National Safe Company, 96 Dodge Street, Fort Madison, Iowa
342. Mr. Robin E. Lee, White Office Building, 28 Fulton Street, Searcy, Arkansas
343. Mr. Hubert Brown, Brown Insurance Underwriters, 600 Pulaski Street, Little Rock, Arkansas
344. Mr. Marvin Brown, Brown Realty Company, Burgess Building, South Norwalk, Connecticut
345. Mr. Walter Jones, President, Ellsworth Department Store, 400 Charles Street, Port Deposit, Maryland
346. Miss Mildred E. Stone, West End High School, West School Street, Wilkes-Barre, Pennsylvania
347. Jayson File Equipment Company, 1800 North Central Avenue, Poughkeepsie, New York
348. Mr. Thomas S. Green, Cane Department Store, 80 North Front Street, Covington, Kentucky
349. Mr. Redmond L. Jones, Jones Motors, Garrett Building, Hancock, Maryland
350. Mr. Robert G. Brown, Brown Confections, 710 Praline Street, Lake Charles, Louisiana
351. Mr. Thomas L. Gray, Kennebec Insurance Company, 400 West Hancock Street, Augusta, Maine
352. Mr. Edward Clay, Moderne Motors, Inc., 607 Ottawa Avenue, Ironwood, Michigan
353. Ridge & Randall, Inc., File Equipment Specialists, Ridge Road, Ridgefield, Connecticut
354. Mr. Carl Lyman, Lyman & Crosswell, 816 Dudley Avenue, Dorchester 72, Massachusetts
355. Mr. William Martin, De Luxe Cleaners & Dyers, 270 North Park Place, Houston 8, Texas
356. Hartwell & Meighan, Chandler Building, Bisbee, Arizona

357. Heirloom Clock Company, 412 South State Street, Hamden, Connecticut
358. Mr. Wilcox Miller, 1612 Brewer Avenue, Bangor, Maine
359. Mr. Harlan Z. Bell, Bell Nationwide Truck Service, 2600 Broad Street, Fairview, New Jersey

Chapter 12

360. Mr. Cecil Andrews, Andrews Advertising Agency, 900 Jewett Street, Muskegon, Michigan
361. Memo to Harry J. Barnes from A. B. Green
362. Mr. Kenneth E. Thomas, Hearthside Publishers, 450 North Hartwell Avenue, Cincinnati 31, Ohio
363. Mr. Alfred M. Foster, Memorial High School, Greenfield, Missouri
364. Mr. Henry Scott, Scott Canneries, Kitsap Avenue, Port Orchard, Washington
365. Mr. Edward Mason, 44 Laketown Drive, Randolph, Utah
366. Mr. David E. Kline, Acme Printing Company, 190 Howard Avenue, Hyattsville, Maryland
367. Mr. Dennis L. Wall, Wall Accounting Service, 67 Washington Avenue, Lewiston, Maine
368. Miss Evelyn C. Miller, Traverse County Consolidated High School, Dumont, Minnesota
369. Mr. Michael Crane, Crane Scientific Research Company, 60 Morris Avenue, New Brunswick, New Jersey
370. Mr. Donald Taylor, Cosmopolitan Drug Company, 200 Montgomery Avenue, Norristown, Pennsylvania
371. Mr. Raymond Davis, Davis & Wentworth, Attorneys, 98 Elizabeth Street, Hampton, Virginia
372. Mr. Everett Rice, Rice Insurance Company, 48 North Adams Street, Portsmouth, New Hampshire
373. Mr. Charles E. Lamb, Lamb Nuts & Bolts Company, 37 Kingman Street, Adams, Kansas
374. Mrs. J. C. Barrett, Duke Plastics, 160 Essex Street, Gloucester, Massachusetts
375. Mrs. James A. Smith, 75 Grove Street, Ann Arbor, Michigan
376. Mr. Charles Kelly, Manager, Miller's Shopper Service, 375 Boulder Avenue, Colorado Springs, Colorado
377. Mr. Matthew E. Jones, Jones Linen Service, 640 Fremont Street, Fort Madison, Iowa
378. Mr. Conrad Lewis, Community Bus Transit Company, 36 West Carroll Avenue, Westminster, Maryland
379. Moore Envelope Company, 1200 Plymouth Street, Dorchester 69, Massachusetts
380. Mr. Edward G. Brooks, Brooks Flower Mart, 391 Fulton Street, East Point, Georgia

381. Miss Clara Harris, Harris Antique Shop, 28 Bristol Street, Attleboro, Massachusetts
382. Mr. George Davis, President, Davis Business Institute, 56 Niagara Square, Buffalo 12, New York
383. Mr. Robert Douglas, Manager, National Equipment Company, 111-86 Parsons Boulevard, Flushing 69, Long Island, New York
384. Mr. George C. Lang, Quality Paper Products Company, 80 Lincoln Street, Livermore, Maine
385. Mr. Walter Ramsey, Ramsey Manufacturing Company, 41 Central Avenue, Sherman, Texas
386. Mr. Henry Walsh, Walsh Stationery & Office Supplies, 320 Harris Avenue, Gainesville, Texas
387. Green Bay Publishers, 404 Taylor Street, Green Bay, Wisconsin
388. Puritan Pencil Company, 512 Worcester Street, Shrewsbury, Massachusetts
389. Mr. Godfrey Fields, 87 Tuxedo Square, Averill Park, New York
390. Mr. Stephen A. Gates, Office Equipment and Supplies, 316 South Main Street, Spartanburg, South Carolina
391. Miss Virginia L. Harris, 63 Jefferson Street, Cullman, Alabama
392. Mr. Rovell A. Meyers, Meyers Jewelry Store, 74 Worth Street, Grand River, Iowa
393. Mr. Louis Johnson, Johnson Envelope & Stationery Company, 622 Erlanger Avenue, Covington, Kentucky
394. Mrs. Arthur Stockton, Stockton's Hosiery, 461 Bristol Street, Framingham, Massachusetts

Chapter 13

395. Mr. E. J. Blair, General Manager, Conway Chain Stores, Conway Building, Lexington, Kentucky
396. Mr. Stanley Hughes, Trade Wind Condiments Company, 1680 South Market Street, San Francisco 4, California
397. Mr. Charles J. Wagner, Wagner & Ewald Market, 490 Blackrock Turnpike, Fairfield, Connecticut
398. Mrs. Harvey Foster, 98 Colonial Drive, Mount Vernon, Iowa
399. Mr. Alex Conroy, West End Supermarket, 400-410 West Monroe Avenue, Johnstown, Pennsylvania
400. Mrs. Catharine Barnes, Cathy's Candy Kitchen, 153 Sumter Avenue, Hartsville, South Carolina
401. Ed & Bill's Sweet Shop, 419 Plymouth Court, Beverly, Massachusetts
402. The Corner Grocery, Main Street at Central Avenue, Dover, New Jersey
403. Mr. Harry Smith, 788 Palm Boulevard, Lake Worth, Florida
404. Mr. Raymond Jones, Steak House, 21 Main Street, Stratford, Connecticut
405. Mrs. Arthur L. Cook, 977 Spring Street, Ossining, New York

406. Mr. Perry Long, Ambrosia Extract Company, Incorporated, 640 Collier Street, Malabar, Florida
407. Mr. Roland Sharp, Sharp Department Store, 3033 Tyler Avenue, Lubbock, Texas
408. Mr. Gary Sands, 940 Lake Drive, Marquette, Wisconsin
409. Mr. Kermit A. Smith, Smith's Market, 1270 Amherst Street, Staunton, Virginia
410. Chicken Heaven, Route 37, Junction 10-A, Springfield, Ohio
411. Mr. Oscar Black, Golden Fruit Orchards, 1980 Valencia Road, Westminster, California
412. Mr. Malcolm Kelly, Manager, Gourmet Delicatessens, Incorporated, 560 Marion Avenue, Oregon City, Oregon
413. Memo to Charles Murray from Edward Smith
414. Miss Josephine E. Allen, Hunter High School, 600 Friendship Street, Huntington, Indiana
415. Mrs. Marion A. Green, 980 Decatur Street, Grand River, Iowa
416. Mrs. Harold Farley, 63 Serpentine Road, Chester Heights, Pennsylvania
417. Mr. Ralph Cooper, Garden Food Products Company, 510 Shawnee Avenue, Pittsburg, Kansas
418. Mrs. Emil T. Lincoln, 46 Windham Road, Colchester, Vermont
419. Mrs. Clarence E. May, 98 Bluestone Lane, Grimms, Wisconsin
420. Mrs. George W. West, Cherokee Gardens, 910 Wilson Avenue, Fort Worth 16, Texas
421. Mrs. Carroll Graham, 20 Spanish Moss Drive, Center Point, Louisiana
422. Mrs. Stephen D. Weeks, 68 Talbot Circle, Royal Oak, Maryland
423. Johnson's Citrus Products Company, Box 545, Crystal River, Florida
424. Mr. Russell Harper, Gold Label Supermarket, 424 Oxford Street, Eastport, Maine
425. Mrs. A. B. Long, 60 Sutter Street, Sacramento 11, California
426. Mrs. Martin G. O'Brien, 47 Scotts Bluff, Lincoln 4, Nebraska
427. Mrs. Francis X. Harris, 248 Polk Street, West Allis, Wisconsin
428. Mrs. Chester R. Jones, Grant Apartments, 430 Grant Avenue, Milwaukee 14, Wisconsin
429. Mr. Irving L. Gray, 38 South Ward Street, Wichita Falls, Texas

Chapter 14

430. Mr. Daniel F. Sullivan, 218 Clayton Avenue, Lancaster, Pennsylvania
431. Mr. A. J. Parks, Sorrento Pastry Shop, 329 Broadway, Seattle 7, Washington
432. Mr. Thomas R. Jones, Morgan & Johnson Real Estate Company, Putnam Avenue at Vine Street, Chattanooga 18, Tennessee
433. Mr. John E. Edwards, 446 Adams Street, New Bern, North Carolina
434. Mr. Randolph Davis, 14 Windsor Towers, 360 Parkside Avenue, Manchester, New Hampshire

435. Chalmers Realty Company, 580 Main Street, Dover, New Jersey
436. Mr. Emory L. Ames, 62 Culpeper Avenue, Greenfield, Virginia
437. Mr. James Thomas, 714 Pine Street, Granby, Connecticut
438. Mr. Andrew Wolf, The Highwood Agency, 20 Grant Street, Ann Arbor, Michigan
439. Mr. Henry Masters, R.F.D. 6, Mooresburg, Tennessee
440. Mr. Gordon L. Ward, 32 Clay Street, Robbins, Illinois
441. Mr. Charles Riggs, 512 Main Street, Florence, Alabama
442. Mr. E. John Hunter, 720 Meadow Lane, Craftsbury, Vermont
443. Mr. Murray Young, 396 Montgomery Street, Fort Worth 17, Texas
444. Mr. Raymond Childress, 42 Baker Street, Westport, Connecticut
445. Industrial Real Estate Company, 410 Buchanan Street, Buffalo 4, New York
446. Mr. David Kelly, Fillmore Apartments, 60 West Douglas Avenue, Omaha 14, Nebraska
447. Mr. C. D. Blair, Blair Real Estate Agency, 320 Archer Street, Dallas 14, Texas
448. Mr. Clayton Payne, 28 Pelham Drive, Westerly, Rhode Island
449. Mr. Edward H. Dale, 123 Burnham Road, Worcester 24, Massachusetts
450. Mr. Louis M. Myers, 26 Carroll Street, Laurel, Maryland
451. Mr. Peter G. Cox, 42 Cumberland Road, Martin City, Missouri
452. Mr. Charles E. James, Woodworth Realty Company, 420 Ocean Boulevard, Deal, New Jersey
453. Mr. Porter Harris, Harris & Mortimer, 648 White Plains Avenue, Pelham, New York
454. Mrs. D. G. Fine, Fine Property Management Company, Inc., 76 Howard Avenue, Clarksville, Maryland
455. Mr. Anderson White, 390 Gila Road, Palo Verde, Arizona
456. Memo to Arthur S. Henry from Edward Johnstone
457. Mr. Elmer P. Strong, 636 Shelby Street, Somerset, Indiana
458. Mr. John H. Allen, 14 Pendleton Street, Crockett, Texas
459. New Deal Realty Company, 161-18 Sunnyside Avenue, Long Island City 4, New York
460. Davidson Publishing Company, Davidson Building, 1700 North Central Avenue, Easton, Pennsylvania
461. Mr. Conrad L. Smith, 75 Lucas Street, Maple Plain, Minnesota
462. Mr. Louis N. Baker, R.F.D. 8, Macon, Illinois
463. Mr. Harold R. Jones, 51 Ridgway Street, Elkins Park, Pennsylvania
464. Mr. David O'Brien, 47 Merriwell Lane, Brentwood, Long Island, New York

Chapter 15

465. Mr. William Smith, Moore, Brown & Smith, 98 North Sussex Street, Jamestown, Virginia

466. Mr. Clayton A. Brown, Professional Building, 430 West End Avenue, Portland 3, Maine
467. Miss Sonya Phillips, 69 Marion Avenue, Dallas, Iowa
468. Mr. S. M. Morris, Morris, Clinton & George, 400 North Huron Boulevard, Pontiac, Michigan
469. Mr. Andrew Gale, 93 Caldwell Road, Carthage, Missouri
470. Mr. John F. Small, 78 Belmont Road, West Warren, Oklahoma
471. Mr. Arthur E. Peters, 35 Oneida Avenue, Elmira Heights, New York
472. Mr. Francis Bates, Curran & Bates, 81 First Street, New Canaan, Connecticut
473. Mrs. Anthony E. Lewis, 750 Mojave Boulevard, Kingman, Arizona
474. Mr. Peter Manning, Manning & Chadwick, 8900 Rhode Island Avenue, S.W., Washington 34, D. C.
475. Mr. Elwood E. Jones, 490 Davis Avenue, Highland Park, Iowa
476. Mr. Matthew Simms, 69 University Gardens, 624 Fountain Drive, Knoxville 7, Tennessee.
477. Mr. Charles E. Palmer, 39 Park Square, Suffolk, Virginia
478. Mr. Fred G. Adams, 697 – 45 Street, Union City, New Jersey
479. Mr. David L. Black, South High School, 900 South Ogden Avenue, Vancouver, Washington
480. Mr. Stephen C. Bates, Bates & Johnson, 40 West Union Avenue, Clovis, New Mexico
481. Nelson Company, 250 Market Street, Sedalia, Ohio
482. Miss Marcia Grace, 76 Magnolia Lane, Bogalusa, Louisiana
483. Mr. Peter Banks, Lapham & Banks, 64 Front Street, Richmond, California
484. Mr. Alvin Hodges, 391 Kent Street, Milton, Delaware
485. Peckham & Muller, 155 Central Avenue, Lenox, Massachusetts
486. Miss Mary Allen, 719 Webster Avenue, Decatur, Mississippi
487. Mr. George Stone, Stone & Brown, 79 North Seventh Avenue, Madison 19, Wisconsin
488. Mr. George Thompson, Thompson & Thompson, 640 West Harris Avenue, Harrisburg, Pennsylvania
489. Mr. Clyde R. Ralph, Ralph Reporting Service, 40 South Mallory Street, Memphis 6, Tennessee
490. Mr. Douglas C. Gates, Cardiff, Gates & Elwell, 690 Fairfield Avenue, Bridgeport 10, Connecticut
491. Mr. Philip M. Webb, Webb, Kendall & Redmond, 510 Battle Street, Concord, New Hampshire
492. Mr. Stanley C. Davis, 37 Belmont Avenue, Williston, North Dakota
493. Dr. Patterson Brown, Oklahoma State College, University Heights, Oklahoma City 18, Oklahoma
494. Mr. Edwin A. Rose, Rose & Martin, 750 Signal Hill, Long Beach 4, California
495. Mr. Clifford Gold, Gold, Tallman & Carroll, 98 Aurora Avenue, Roscoe, South Dakota

496. Mr. Edgar Miller, 436 Clay Street, Elkins, West Virginia
497. Mr. Carter Jones, Jones, Matthews & Jones, 600 North 14 Street, Kalamazoo 10, Michigan
498. Mr. Daniel M. Baker, Baker Motor Express, 49 North Market Street, San Francisco 29, California
499. Mrs. Clifford Evans, 1614 Elmwood Avenue, Syracuse 14, New York

Chapter 16

500. Dr. Amos L. Taylor, 503 Madison Avenue, Billings, Montana
501. Mr. Louis C. Temple, 24 Valley Road, Laurel, Montana
502. Miss Caroline Young, 110 Polk Street, Marianna, Arkansas
503. Mr. Robert L. Davis, 820 Saxon Avenue, Bay Shore, Long Island, New York
504. Mr. Fred Wells, 94 Crescent Way, White Plains, New York
505. Mr. Martin E. Davis, 46 Franklin Street, New Castle, Pennsylvania
506. Mrs. Adam O. Sloan, 71 Becker Street, Osage, Minnesota
507. Dr. O. D. Collins, 146 Ridgewood Circle, Glen Rock, New Jersey
508. Miss Janet D. Miller, 53 Maple Avenue, Westwood, New Jersey
509. Mr. R. S. Brown, 276 Exeter Street, Pittston, Pennsylvania
510. Memo to the Staff from John Barnes, Office Manager
511. Miss Julia Bennett, 320 Clinton Avenue, Richmond Hill, Georgia
512. Mrs. David Mason, Pulaski Gardens, 15 Henry Street, Somerset, Kentucky
513. Dr. Clifford A. Green, 224 Martin Avenue, Madisonville, Kentucky
514. Mr. Archibald Smith, 91 Potter Place, Temple, Pennsylvania
515. Mrs. Joseph D. Mills, 43 Mill Run, Albany, Pennsylvania
516. Mrs. Elmer E. Harvey, Merrick Gardens, 94-26 Merrick Road, Babylon, Long Island, New York
517. Quality Drug Store, 406 Main Street, Rochelle, Illinois
518. Dr. LeRoy A. Lewis, Medical Arts Center, 60 North Central Avenue, Peoria 4, Illinois
519. Dr. Samuel E. Reed, 159 Shawnee Avenue, La Crosse, Wisconsin
520. Mr. Edward C. Peters, 611 Wheeler Street, San Angelo, Texas
521. Mr. Edward C. Perry, 473 Raleigh Street, Burlington, West Virginia
522. Mrs. Sherman P. Brown, 26 Smith Street, Torrington, Connecticut
523. Mr. Charles G. Woods, Principal, Central High School, Lake City, Florida
524. Miss Genevieve Turner, 31 Grove Street, Homestead, Florida
525. Mr. James L. French, French's Machine Shop, 600 Cedar Street, Davenport, Iowa
526. Dr. Kendall Smith, Physicians & Surgeons Building, 406 South State Street, Boston 4, Massachusetts
527. Mr. David O. Harper, 75 Cecil Street, Hancock, Maryland
528. Dr. Milton Farmer, 1650 Lakewood Drive, Dallas 14, Texas
529. Dr. Dennis Collins, Medical Arts Center, 800-810 Tarrant Avenue, Birmingham 10, Alabama

530. Dr. Leo P. Day, 40 Perry Square, Erie, Pennsylvania
531. Dr. Morton Jones, 696 West 14 Street, Chicago 1, Illinois
532. Mr. Henry Smith, Forrest Building, 30 South Fourth Avenue, Pittsburgh 3, Pennsylvania
533. Medical Journal, 604 Norman Street, Rochester 3, Minnesota
534. Mr. Donald R. Smith, 731 Scott Street, Manhattan, Kansas